A NATION IN CONFLICT:
CANADA AND THE TWO WORLD WARS

The First and Second World Wars were two of the most momentous events of the twentieth century. In Canada, they claimed 110,000 lives and altered both the country's domestic life and its international position. *A Nation in Conflict* is a concise, comparative overview of the Canadian national experience in the two world wars that transformed the nation and its people.

With each chapter, military historians Jeffrey A. Keshen and Andrew Iarocci address Canada's contribution to the war and its consequences. Integrating the latest research in military, social, political, and gender history, they examine everything from the front lines to the home front. Was conscription necessary? Did the conflicts change the status of Canadian women? Was Canada's commitment worth the cost?

Written both for classroom use and for the general reader, *A Nation in Conflict* is an accessible introduction to the complexities of Canada's involvement in the twentieth century's most important conflicts.

(Themes in Canadian History)

JEFFREY A. KESHEN is the dean of Arts at Mount Royal University.

ANDREW IAROCCI is an assistant professor in the Department of History at Western University and a former collections manager for transportation and artillery at the Canadian War Museum.

THEMES IN CANADIAN HISTORY

Editor: Colin Coates

ANDREW IAROCCI AND
JEFFREY A. KESHEN

A Nation in Conflict: Canada and the Two World Wars

UNIVERSITY OF TORONTO PRESS
Toronto Buffalo London

© University of Toronto Press 2015
Toronto Buffalo London
www.utppublishing.com
Printed in the U.S.A.

ISBN 978-0-8020-9852-8 (cloth)   ISBN 978-0-8020-9570-1 (paper)

∞ Printed on acid-free, 100% post-consumer recycled paper with
vegetable-based inks

Library and Archives Canada Cataloguing in Publication

Iarocci, Andrew, 1976–, author
A nation in conflict : Canada and the two world wars / Andrew Iarocci
and Jeffrey A. Keshen.

(Themes in Canadian history)
Includes bibliographical references and index.
ISBN 978-0-8020-9852-8 (bound)   ISBN 978-0-8020-9570-1 (paperback)

1. World War, 1914–1918 – Canada.   2. World War, 1939–1945 –
Canada.   3. Canada. Canadian Army – History – World War, 1914–
1918.   4. Canada – Armed Forces – History – World War, 1939–1945.
5. Canada – History – 1914–1918.   6. Canada – History – 1939–1945.
I. Keshen, Jeff, 1962–, author   II. Title.   III. Series: Themes in
Canadian history

FC543.I27 2015   940.3'71   C2015-905451-6

University of Toronto Press acknowledges the financial assistance to its
publishing program of the Canada Council for the Arts and the Ontario
Arts Council, an agency of the Government of Ontario.

Canada Council   Conseil des Arts
for the Arts   du Canada

ONTARIO ARTS COUNCIL
CONSEIL DES ARTS DE L'ONTARIO
an Ontario government agency
un organisme du gouvernement de l'Ontario

Funded by the   Financé par le
Government   gouvernement
of Canada   du Canada

Canadä

Contents

Illustrations and Maps

Illustrations

Maps

A NATION IN CONFLICT:
CANADA AND THE TWO WORLD WARS

Introduction

The two world wars were arguably the most transformative events in the history of modern Canada. In each conflict, the country mobilized substantial military forces virtually from scratch, putting in uniform about 8 per cent of the population of the day. The wars generated tremendous patriotic expression but also profound national division. They accelerated Canada's transformation into an urban industrialized country; raised its international profile; changed its relations with Britain and the United States; enhanced federal powers; fostered government bureaucracy; sparked the creation of a social welfare system; brought new rights and roles for women; undermined civil liberties; and redefined social values. And not least, the two wars visited immeasurable personal loss on Canadians from all walks of life, claiming some 110,000 lives and leaving nearly 300,000 wounded. Virtually every Canadian knew someone who suffered the death of a loved one. Around the globe, Canada's war dead are buried in neatly manicured Commonwealth War Graves cemeteries. Many of the grave markers bear personal statements or epitaphs:

We, who lie here, were young; we too loved life and home, remember us.

Just another good soldier and son. Mom and Dad

I thought it was the right thing to do.

Canada's experiences in the world wars have generated a rich body of scholarly and popular historical writing, as well as plays, films, and television programs. Every bookstore, it seems, has at least one shelf dedicated to famous battles, personal war narratives, and studies of military leaders. Most universities offer at least one course in Canadian military history – and the seats are easily filled. Almost every community has its centrally placed war memorial. Across the land, public buildings are named in honour of war heroes, battles, and commanders; schools are named for Vimy Ridge in Edmonton, Alberta, and Ajax, Ontario.

As Canadians approached the centenary of the First World War's outbreak and the seventieth anniversary of victory in the Second World War, both conflicts attracted renewed interest. A new national war museum was unveiled in Ottawa in 2005. During the past two decades, increasing numbers of Canadians of all ages and backgrounds have travelled far and wide to the former battlefields of the world wars to see first-hand where their fathers, uncles, or grandparents fought, or perhaps to visit the grave of a relative who never came home. One of the authors of this book will never forget the day he accompanied a colleague to a quiet cemetery in Normandy where the man visited, for the first time, the grave of the father he had never met.

Canada's World Wars offers a comparative overview of the national experience in the First and Second World Wars, drawing on older and newer historical studies as frames of reference. It explores the fighting on land, at sea, and in the skies, as well as the impact of the two conflicts at home – in social, political, economic, and cultural terms. The book introduces readers to enduring debates and controversies. Was conscription necessary in each war? Did the conflicts change the status of Canadian women? Was Canada's role in the strategic bombing campaign against Germany during the Second World War worth the cost? The authors also assess the degree to which the First World War's legacy shaped important Canadian decisions in the Second World War.

The first chapter considers the related themes of politics and recruitment, underscoring essential differences between Prime Minister Robert Laird Borden's approach to recruitment during the First World War and Prime Minister William Lyon Mackenzie King's during the Second. The next chapter compares national mobilization for total war in each conflict. A "total" conflict is one that marshals broad segments of society at home in support of a major military effort at the fighting fronts. In each conflict, Canada's investment arguably went very far along the spectrum of totality, but there are distinctions to be made in the relative allocation of specific resources in each case. The third chapter examines the fighting on land. In both world wars, Canada committed sizeable ground forces, but the manner in which these two armies joined the fighting was quite different. Canadian soldiers of the Second World War, for example, served in a greater range of geographical settings than their predecessors had during 1914–18. The fourth chapter identifies key contrasts in the Canadian naval experience in the two world wars. Canada's navy played a rather minor role in the First World War; it was much more comprehensively involved in the vital struggle for control of the Atlantic shipping lanes throughout much of the Second World War. The next chapter considers the view from above, looking at Canadian participation in air operations. While thousands of Canadians flew in the First World War, a national air force was not created until 1924. In the Second World War, a significantly greater portion of Canada's military personnel participated in a much more intense air war. Finally, the sixth chapter traces the evolution of Canadian morality and society during a tumultuous half-century. While the world wars did not necessarily *cause* social transformation, they encouraged and even accelerated important changes in the lives of Canadians.

It must be noted that not everyone who wore a Canadian uniform during 1914–18 or 1939–45 was in fact Canadian.

In both conflicts, many who served had come very recently or even directly from other countries, especially the United States. At the same time, an untold number of Canadians served outside of the Canadian forces, including the thousands of young men who joined the Royal Flying Corps or Royal Naval Air Service in the First World War. The authors have done their best to account for these complexities of national identity. Above all, however, *Canada's World Wars* introduces readers to ordinary people who lived – and died – in extraordinary times.

1

Politics and Recruitment

"It was glorious weather. With our canoes and boats, with our swimming and tennis, our campfires and sing-alongs our life was full of rest and happy peace."[1] So remarked author Charles Gordon, better known as Ralph Connor, of the summer of 1914 by the Lake of the Woods, Ontario. On 2 August, two days before the outbreak of war, the young Ottawa socialite, Ethel Chadwick, returning from a day of swimming and picnicking in the Gatineau Hills, Quebec, remarked in her diary that it had been a golden summer. That afternoon, arriving back in Ottawa, she encountered tremendous commotion. Germany had invaded Belgium. Britain had issued an ultimatum: withdraw or face war with the British Empire.

In communities across Canada and the separate Dominion of Newfoundland, crowds converged on newspaper offices. Those in Montreal were as large as in Toronto, and newspapers made a point of saying that "La Marseillaise" was sung as robustly as "God Save the King." Outside the *Winnipeg Free Press*, an employee stood on a platform with a megaphone announcing the latest developments. On 4 August, with the crowds especially large, for it was a bank holiday, the news everyone waited for came: Britain and France had declared war against Germany and its allies.

Charles Gordon was packing his bags. An ordained minister and ardent imperialist, he would serve overseas as a military chaplain. Ethel Chadwick's days would soon be consumed by volunteer work on behalf of numerous war causes. William Lyon Mackenzie King, who was to lead Canada as prime minister in the Second World War, found his political mentor, opposition leader Wilfrid Laurier, sitting in an empty room at Ottawa's Rideau Club. As prime minister (1896–1911), Laurier had struggled with the Anglo-French division over Canada's participation at Britain's side in the Boer War (1899–1902). Although military experts were predicting that the new conflict would last only to Christmas 1914, the fact that it pitted the Triple Entente (Britain, France, and Russia) against the Triple Alliance (Germany, Austria-Hungary, and Italy) foreshadowed unprecedented death and destruction overseas. Laurier and Mackenzie King went for a walk, during which Laurier asked with exasperation: "Is it conceivable that men can want war? Is it conceivable that they can work for it, and against peace?"[2]

A quarter-century later, on 10 September 1939, Canada again went to war against Germany. Canadians had endured 60,000 dead and 173,000 wounded in the First World War, so in 1939 there were no cheering crowds. Until just months before the outbreak of the Second World War, Canada had resisted rearming and backed Britain's attempts to appease the Nazi leader, Adolf Hitler. Ultimately, however, Canada entered what it considered an essential fight to halt Nazi expansion. Only James Shaver Woodsworth, the leader of the Co-operative Commonwealth Federation, and a handful of Quebec MPs argued against involvement. All other MPs joined Prime Minister Mackenzie King in voting for the first time that Canada declare war in its own right. Canada's only other official declarations of war occurred in the same conflict, against Italy in June 1940 and then Japan in December 1941.

Although tensions had been brewing across Europe for some time, the First World War came as a surprise to many. Throughout the summer of 1914, newspapers had given more coverage to baseball scores than to international affairs. When war came, many feared what lay ahead. Irene Evans, the wife of former Winnipeg mayor Sanford Evans, who had several children approaching military age, expressed a sense of dread. However, such concerns were drowned out by outpourings of enthusiasm.

The causes for the war were complex. Historians still debate the relative importance of factors such as rival alliances and colonial ambitions, secret deals between governments that committed them to support each other militarily, an arms race between major powers, and general war fever that cascaded across Europe. Canada was still technically a colony of Britain when it came to foreign policy, so when Britain was at war, so was Canada. However, the scope of this country's participation was for Canadians to decide.

Throughout English Canada, enthusiasm for the fight was palpable. Like Britain, Canada viewed the war as one to preserve freedom from German militarism. Canadian imperialists, whose influence had peaked by the outbreak of the war, proclaimed that in this struggle, the country's gallant sons would demonstrate the courage and loyalty to secure for Canada a strong voice in shaping imperial affairs. Countless young men saw the war as an once-in-a-lifetime opportunity for travel and adventure; though with a steep economic downturn lasting into 1915, military life was also a chance for a job.

The Dominion of Canada entered the war with a small permanent military force of about 3,000. The federal government was modest in scale, with relatively little involvement in the daily lives of Canadians. The civil service was tiny, with nearly all major departments employing fewer than one hundred full-time workers, and professional standards were still in their infancy. Initially, the Canadian government committed $50 million to the war (slightly over $1 billion in 2015 dollars) – an unprecedented sum. By 1916 that would not be enough to pay for even two months of war-making.

Soon an unprecedented mobilization of men, material, and collective will was under way. In the opening weeks of the war, Justice Minister Charles Doherty presented legislation providing the government with extraordinary powers. Known as the War Measures Act, it permitted Ottawa to suspend *habeas corpus* (i.e., the right to a trial within a reasonable time), to intern those that government authorities deemed suspect, to censor and ban publications, and to stamp out free speech and association. Although passed by Parliament on 22 August, the act was made retroactive to 4 August. In other words, it would be possible to prosecute someone for an action that had been legal at the time it was performed.

The War Measures Act was one example of how the government interpreted the wartime context and moved quickly towards full mobilization. That meant, first and foremost, recruiting and training an overseas contingent. Sam Hughes, the Minister of Militia and Defence and one of Canada's most polarizing and eccentric political figures ever, took charge of these initiatives. Hughes had been a railway promoter, newspaper publisher, and schoolteacher before being elected to the House of Commons in an 1892 by-election in the constituency of Victoria, near Peterborough, Ontario. He was of Huguenot background – a trait he believed should appeal to Catholic French Canadians (it didn't) – and his family had strong and deep ties to the ultra-Protestant and viciously anti-Catholic Orange Order. He was a star athlete and "muscular Christian" who followed a strict regimen of physical fitness, temperance, and clean living.

Hughes commanded the 45th Victoria Battalion, a militia unit he had been associated with since childhood. He revered the part-time militia, contending that it produced far more adaptable and resourceful soldiers than the permanent army, whose members he cast as "barroom loafers" preoccupied with "parade-square regimen."[3] The prejudice was personal: Hughes saw permanent force commanders as rivals. Early in the war, he dispatched the Royal Canadian Regiment, one of the country's few permanent force units, to Bermuda for garrison duty, thus depriving Canada's army of experienced trainers, who were badly needed.

Hughes saw war as a manly sport and had sought desperately to command Canadian troops in the Boer War. He went to South Africa as a staff officer, secured a position as an intelligence officer, and performed bravely. At the Battle of Faber's Pat at the end of May 1900, he played a key role in saving a British contingent, and insisted later that his actions merited a Victoria Cross, the Empire's highest award for gallantry. Two months later the insufferably arrogant Hughes was sent back to Canada, where he boasted of deserving two Victoria Crosses.

For Robert Laird Borden, who led the Conservative opposition in the House of Commons at the time, Hughes was an effective attack dog against the Liberal majority government. Also, he had done much to deliver Ontario to Borden in the 1911 federal election, which had been key to the Conservative victory. Hughes lobbied hard for his dream cabinet portfolio, Militia and Defence. Many colleagues cautioned Borden that Hughes was too unpredictable, emotional, and egomaniacal. Borden, too, doubted Hughes's suitability, but he finally relented given his many connections, influence in Tory ranks, and apparently deep knowledge of military affairs.

Two days after the First World War was declared, Hughes bypassed the existing mobilization scheme and dispatched 226 telegrams to militia commanders across Canada, instructing them to send volunteers to a new military camp he was building from scratch on a sandy plain at Valcartier, north of Quebec City. Hughes could have used the existing camp at Petawawa, Ontario, as a concentration area, but Val-cartier was closer to a port of embarkation (Quebec City).

Construction proceeded at a frenetic pace. At sixty-one years of age, the single-minded Hughes seemed to be every-where, barking out orders and sometimes openly weeping under the strain, which led some to think he was coming unhinged. Allegations of mismanagement, waste, and graft abounded. Still, somehow, it all came together. In October 1914, the Canadian Expeditionary Force (CEF) ventured overseas, 36,267 in all, the largest military force ever to depart Canada.

In the early part of the war, young men's enthusiasm for fighting seemed pervasive. Prior to September 1915, sixty-nine of seventy-one infantry battalions easily attained full strength. It was almost as if men were trying to join an exclusive club. For the first year of the war, married men had to produce a letter of permission from their wives in order to enlist. Still, there were signs of trouble ahead. Two-thirds of the volunteers in Canada's 1st Division had been born in Britain; these men had a stronger attachment to the Mother Country. Canada had many recent British immigrants, and a significant number of them had joined Canada's expeditionary force as a means of getting overseas to switch to the British Army.

Local military authorities enjoyed tremendous autonomy. The government set no geographic recruiting boundaries and made no plans to send existing militia units overseas. Instead, it permitted the creation of all manner of new overseas battalions, generally with local or regional affiliations. Because the Department of Militia and Defence provided little money for recruitment publicity, those costs were often covered by regimental funds or a wealthy command-ing officer. Appeals often emphasized ethnic heritage. For example, a poster for the 236th Kilties, a New Brunswick bat-talion, depicted a soldier in tartan who asked "if you possess the fighting spirit of your forefathers."[4] Chums' battalions were established among men who knew one another from work or local communities. The 205th Battalion, known as the Tigers, billed its soldiers as friends and fans of the Hamilton Tigers football club.

High school senior classes and universities became more female. Most universities gave students who volunteered for military service credit for the full academic year, a practice that later came under criticism for producing ill-qualified graduates. Dr George Cutten, the president of Acadia University in Nova Scotia, made it a practice to address graduating classes in khaki. In early 1916 the universities of British Columbia, Alberta, Saskatchewan, and Manitoba formed a Western Universities Battalion.

Local recruitment drives intensified. Community leaders lent their support, directing harsh language against those seen as avoiding service. After heavy Canadian losses at the Second Battle of Ypres in April 1915, Winnipeg mayor Richard Waugh declared: "I would ten times rather have my son lying dead on the field of battle than have him a coward and turn his back on danger"[5] – a belief that was tested when one of his sons was killed at Cambrai in 1917. Recruiters scoured cities, making their pitches at street rallies, theatres, worksites, and other public venues. Church sermons became recruiting rallies.

However, such pressures had little impact on francophone Quebeckers or on other French-speaking groups like Acadians and Franco-Ontarians, who tended to view the war as a British imperial venture. Hughes compounded these problems. In the 1st Division, there were enough French-speaking volunteers to start an all-French battalion, but Hughes had these men scattered among English-language units. Hughes spoke of creating a pan-Canadian military, but many French Canadians perceived his decision as just another example of anglophone dominance in the armed forces; indeed, at the war's outbreak, only 3 per cent of Canadian officers were francophone.

In the autumn of 1914, prominent Quebeckers, led by the wealthy Montreal physician Arthur Mignault, provided $50,000 to help raise a French Canadian battalion. On 22 October, recruiting began for the 22nd Regiment, a unit that came to be known as the Vandoos. Despite a national recruitment effort, the battalion did not reach its full complement of 1,100 men until March 1915. By late 1915, as Canada's forces reached 300,000 men, the number of French Canadians stood at only 14,000.

Ontario's Regulation 17, dating back to 1912, which had banned state-supported French and bilingual education past grade two, fanned the flames of French Canadian anger. In 1916, at Ottawa's Guigues School in the largely French district of Lower Town, the dismissal of the school board and of several teachers who had challenged Regulation 17 prompted parents to occupy the building. Quebec nationalist leader Henri Bourassa rhetorically asked why francophones should volunteer for a war billed as a fight to defend democracy when their children were denied the use of their language in Canada. Thus initial recruitment drives had produced large numbers of volunteers, but they had also revealed – and exacerbated – French–English divisions and portended growing discord along linguistic lines.

Wartime nationalism heightened intolerance towards several groups. The municipal governments in Toronto and Ottawa fired all their German Canadian employees. Some German Canadians sought protection by anglicizing their names. The citizens of Berlin, Ontario, voted in 1916 to change their town's name to Kitchener in honour of Britain's war minister, Lord Horatio Herbert Kitchener, who had been killed that spring when the HMS *Hampshire* struck a German mine west of the Orkneys.

The federal government initially declared that all Canadian residents would have their rights protected as long as they obeyed the laws of the land. However, in October 1914, retired General Sir William Otter, whose military career

stretched back to the Fenian Raids of 1866, was appointed
as Director of Internment Operations. Nearly 6,000 enemy
aliens, people who were not naturalized British subjects of
Canada, were interned. Most were of Galician background –
that is, Ukrainians from the Austro-Hungarian Empire, an
enemy state. Enemy aliens were transported to remote areas
such as Kapuskasing, Ontario, and Spirit Lake, Quebec,
or to national parks like Banff, Alberta, where they were
assigned hard labour, such as clearing timber and building roads. Many would recount that they were treated like
slaves, forced to live in unheated quarters, issued with insufficient clothing, and subject to abusive guards.

Censorship also focused on those of enemy background.
Canada's chief censor insisted that printed media serving
such ethnic groups be held to an especially high standard.
The Canadian government banned scores of enemy-
language publications printed in the neutral United States,
many of which denigrated Britain and its allies. In September 1918, a federal Order in Council compelled publications in Canada serving those of enemy alien background
to print in English, driving many into bankruptcy just as the
war was ending. Canadians saw themselves as engaged in a
noble struggle to preserve democracy, yet their fears and suspicions presented serious challenges to freedom at home.

As the war approached what was to be its halfway point, it
became harder to attract fresh recruits. By then, workers
in urban centres were enjoying higher wages. The growing
demand for Canadian foodstuffs meant that farm labour was
at a premium. Between 1911 and 1916, the acreage under
wheat cultivation in Canada's prairie provinces increased
from 57 to 72 million; between 1914 and 1918, monthly
farm wages, excluding room and board, nearly doubled
from $36 to $70. Although support for the war remained
strong in English Canada, daily casualty lists printed in
newspapers no doubt dampened some men's enthusiasm
to volunteer.

In July 1915, the military reduced the minimum height and chest measurement requirements in an effort to attract more recruits. New Citizen Recruiting Leagues provided speakers and funded printed material, pleading with "mothers, wives and sweethearts ... [to] think of your country by letting your sons go and fight."[6] At recruitment rallies, women tried to shame men into military service by placing white feathers on those in civilian clothes.

The growing demand for soldiers brought about only modest social change. Efforts were made to enlist African Canadians and Aboriginals, groups initially rejected for what many military leaders called a White Man's War. The recruitment of African Canadians began in mid-1915 with the No. 2 Construction Battalion, a Nova Scotia–based unit that was to perform heavy labour, such as digging trenches and building roads. Many African Canadians hoped that displays of loyalty would bring expanded rights at home. However, they remained segregated, not only by military unit but also in terms of training, transport to Europe, and access to recreational facilities.

Many Aboriginal people saw action, having been stereotyped as natural warriors. After the war, the Ontario-based Six Nations established a Pan-Canadian League of Indians. Its first leader, Mohawk Fred Loft, a former army sergeant, argued that having served in the war, Native people deserved a better deal. However, Aboriginal veterans would be disappointed – for example, unlike white veterans, they would be refused loans and financial grants, such as to start farms, because white authorities deemed them unable to manage debt.

In October 1915 the federal government raised the recruitment cap to 250,000. Then on New Year's Day of 1916, Borden declared that Canada would provide a 500,000-man volunteer army, a force representing about one-sixteenth of country's population at the time. Maj.-Gen. Willoughby Gwatkin, Chief of the Canadian General Staff, told Borden that the goal was unrealistic for a volunteer army and predicted the need for conscription.

Initially, the announcement of the target sparked excitement and a boost to recruitment, with more than 90,000 enlisting over the next three months. After that, the flow dried up. Indeed, in no month after June 1916 did more than 10,000 men volunteer for overseas service. Appeals in Quebec to assist France failed to resonate with the population. Borden, referring to the strong influence of the Catholic Church in Quebec and the anticlerical republican government in France, commented that the "Quebec peasant was sometimes told that the sufferings of the French people were just retribution for the unholy spoliation and humiliation of the Church in France."[7] Hughes's management did not help either, as surprisingly little effort was made to secure prominent French-speaking recruiters.

Over the course of 1916, Borden sought to wrest powers from Hughes. Early that year, Hughes travelled to Britain to receive a peerage from the king. Despite that honour, he was openly critical of British military leadership, portraying it as rigid. Overriding Borden's instructions, Hughes created a Sub-Militia Council in England to administer the overseas forces; the council was to answer directly to Hughes. Convinced that Hughes had gone too far, Borden established the Ministry of Overseas Military Forces under High Commissioner Sir George Perley. Hughes was enraged and let Borden know it in a blistering letter. Hughes believed, mistakenly, that Borden was weak-willed. The prime minister demonstrated his resolve by sacking Hughes on 9 November, replacing him with Sir Edward Kemp, a twenty-year parliamentary veteran, as Minister of Militia and Defence.

By now, pressure had mounted in Canada for conscription. Historians often cite the April 1916 declaration by Hamilton's Recruiting League calling for "equality of sacrifice" as the trigger for a conscription campaign. That declaration, known as the "Hamilton Memorial," was quickly adopted by recruiting associations in Saskatchewan, Manitoba, Ontario, New Brunswick, and Nova Scotia.

In September 1916, Ottawa created the National Service Board to set priority classifications for civilian jobs so that military recruiters could focus on occupational groups whose absence would minimally disrupt the Canadian economy. Under the ruthlessly ambitious Calgary Conservative MP, R.B. Bennett, the board launched an extensive advertising campaign in the last week of 1916 to have men over eighteen fill in cards that asked questions on matters such as citizenship, health, marital status, and dependents. Bennett insisted that the government would not use the information to impose conscription, a message he personally conveyed to Quebec Archbishop Paul Bruchési and Cardinal Louis-Nazaire Bégin. Over 80 per cent of the cards were returned nationwide, but 15 per cent of these were blank or incomplete.

Some sought to bridge the divisions between francophones and anglophones. One prominent initiative was the Bonne Entente Movement, launched in late 1916 by Toronto lawyer J.M. Godfrey and journalist Arthur Hawkes. Both men were concerned about the rising anger in French Canada, where calls were rising for a boycott of Ontario products. The Bonne Entente arranged well-attended public dialogues in Quebec City and Toronto, but it quickly became apparent that discussions never progressed beyond platitudes. Meanwhile, in Quebec, physical attacks on pro-war French Canadians, anglophones, and soldiers came to the attention of authorities. A Quebec City mob smashed the windows of the pro-government newspapers *L'Evénement* and the *Quebec Chronicle*, and dynamite was left outside the door of the pro-conscription mayor of Outremont, a Montreal suburb. Tensions were rising inexorably, threatening to tear the country apart along French–English lines.

While the war cut into the social fabric at home, Canada's sacrifices abroad generated nationalistic pride, particularly in English Canada, as well as growing demands for more international recognition. Borden was already on record as stating that because Canada was paying such a high price, it had to have input into Allied strategy, especially when it came to the use of Canadian forces.

The opportunity for change came at the end of 1916. British prime minister Herbert Asquith, under fire for the unsatisfactory course of the war, was abandoned by more than one hundred of his Liberal MPs, which led to his replacement by War Minister David Lloyd George. Convinced that greater sacrifice would be required from the British Dominions, Lloyd George invited their leaders to gather in London in March 1917 to participate in an Imperial War Conference. The delegates lacked formal powers but would meet twice weekly to consult on Allied strategy. The March 1917 conference produced Resolution 9, for which both Borden and South African General Jan Christiaan Smuts claimed authorship. Reflecting the growing stature of the Dominions, but also their continuing ties to the Empire, the resolution stated that the Imperial War Cabinet "place[d] on record their view that any ... readjustment [in imperial relations] ... be based upon a full recognition of the Dominions as autonomous nations of an Imperial Commonwealth."[8] These sentiments were buttressed by the Canadian Corps' April 1917 capture of Vimy Ridge during the Battle of Arras, an accomplishment that sparked outpourings of Canadian nationalism.

The war also strengthened ties between Canada and the United States. Defence-related cooperation expanded notably, starting in 1916, when German U-boats (submarines) showed that they could cross the Atlantic by paying calls on Rhode Island and Massachusetts. With the Americans joining the war in April 1917, the US Navy assumed responsibility for the defence of southern Nova Scotia and the Bay of Fundy. The same year, Canada's finance minister, Thomas White, brokered a deal with the United States that would allow Britain to use a portion of money loaned to it by the

Americans to purchase items from the Canadian-based Imperial Munitions Board so long as those items incorporated American raw materials and components. In February 1918, Canada established a War Mission in Washington to deal directly with US government agencies to coordinate the distribution of raw materials. Such decisions further integrated the economies of the two North American countries and contributed to the long-term decline of British influence in Canada.

While Canada was strengthening its autonomy in foreign relations, the Borden government faced mounting problems at home. Scandals had erupted over munitions contracts. Two of the country's three transcontinental railways were bankrupt, and the government found itself drawn into what many considered an overpriced buyout of two lines, which saddled Ottawa with crushing extra debt. Labour dissent was rising, fuelled by galloping inflation – estimated at 40 per cent over the last two years of the war – and the growing prospect of conscription. Many unions insisted that the government should conscript wealth, through taxation, *before* conscripting men. With a strong wartime employment market, workers were more willing to join unions, whose membership rose from 166,000 in 1914 to 249,000 in 1918. Although most labour leaders pledged patriotism, person-days lost to strikes increased from 500,000 in 1914 to 1.1 million in 1917.

Some historians have argued that Borden pushed conscription as a way to rebuild political support in English Canada by compelling French Canadians to fight. More convincing is that he acted out of a sincere belief in the absolute military necessity of compulsory service. By early 1917, the situation overseas seemed desperate. Russia's war effort was near collapse with the revolution against the Tsar; Italy, fighting on the side of the Allies, was faltering against Austria-Hungary; and plummeting morale among French troops sparked mutinies in the ranks that summer. America's declaration of war in April 1917 offered hope, but its mobilization would take months if not years. In January 1917, Canada's National Service Board conducted a nation-wide survey that indicated nearly 300,000 civilian men were eligible to fight. In April and May 1917, Canadian casualties from the Vimy-Arras offensive reached 24,000. Fewer than half this number of men volunteered for military service during the same period. For Borden, conscription seemed the only way to make up the difference.

In May 1917, Borden instructed Solicitor General Arthur Meighen to draft a Military Service Act. Declaring that military necessity must trump partisanship, Borden approached Wilfrid Laurier to form a coalition government whose cabinet would contain equal numbers of Liberals and Tories. He even offered to step down as prime minister to facilitate the merger, but members of his own party said they would not consider such a change. Laurier refused the offer, citing philosophical antipathy towards conscription and displeasure over Borden's introduction of the bill prior to offering the coalition, and expressing fear that such collaboration would hand Quebec over to the more extreme nationalist forces led by Henri Bourassa.

The Military Service Act, which was introduced to Parliament on 11 June, targeted men aged twenty-one to thirty-five who were unmarried or childless. Three days earlier, one of Borden's few Quebec cabinet ministers, E.N. Patenaude, had resigned. In each of the three readings of the bill, which received Royal Assent on 29 August, nearly all French Canadian MPs, including nine Conservatives on the final ballot, voted against the act, though overall it carried by a majority of fifty-eight, support that included twenty-two English-speaking Liberals who broke ranks with Laurier.

In September, two months before the scheduled federal election, which became necessary when the idea of a coalition collapsed, the government invoked closure (i.e., cut off parliamentary debate) to pass the Wartime Elections Act and the Military Voters Act. The first of these acts denied the franchise to conscientious objectors and to those of enemy background naturalized as British subjects of Canada after

Anti-conscription parade at Victoria square, Montreal, May 1917. McCord Museum, ANC-C68 59.

March 1902. The latter group, particularly Ukrainians in western Canada, had traditionally voted Liberal. The same act enfranchised the wives, daughters, and sisters, aged twenty-one or older, of men in uniform, who were assumed to be sympathetic to conscription. The second of these acts permitted the governing party to determine the provincial distribution of overseas soldier ballots in cases where a soldier did not specify his electoral riding. An estimated 92 per cent of Canadian soldiers voted for the government.

On 12 October, after wooing several pro-conscription Liberals, Borden formed the Union Government with a cabinet of thirteen Conservatives and ten Liberals. Borden presented the Union as holding forth the prospect of many reforms, including fairer taxation, agricultural cooperatives, and the weeding out of government patronage. However, conscription overshadowed everything else and generated a bitter and divisive election in late 1917. Union publicity declared: "If Laurier wins ... the French-Canadians who have shirked their duty in this war will be the dominating force in the government of the country."9 In Quebec, Union candidates required police protection; in Toronto, Liberal candidates and supporters were physically attacked.

The Union won a strong majority with 153 seats and 57 per cent of the popular vote compared to 82 seats and 40 per cent of the popular vote for the Liberals. However, the Liberals took 62 of 65 seats and 72 per cent of the vote in Quebec; the three ridings that went Union were English-speaking enclaves. Only 8 of 82 constituencies in Ontario and 2 of 57 in Western Canada voted Liberal. Laurier, writing to his former justice minister, Allan Aylesworth, lamented: "The racial chasm which is now open at our feet may not be overcome for generations."10 A month later, J.N. Francoeur, who represented the riding of Lotbinière just south of Quebec City, introduced the following resolution in the Quebec Assembly: "This house is of the opinion that the province of Quebec would be disposed to accept the breaking of the Confederation pact of 1867."11 It was seriously debated, though defeated.

Over strong opposition, conscription came into effect. Of the first 20,000 compelled to serve, only 1,500 were francophone. Most men sought exemptions, often claiming that their absence would cause severe family hardship. In Quebec, of the 115,602 called up under the Military Service Act, 113,291 sought an exemption, though the figure across Canada also exceeded 90 per cent. In all, some 99,600 conscripts were actually taken on strength with the Canadian Expeditionary Force (the target had been 100,000); about

47,500 of them reached the United Kingdom, and over 24,000 had made it to France by war's end. It is likely that if the war had lasted into 1919, many more conscripts would have reached the firing line.

In March 1918, the new Communist regime in Russia signed the Treaty of Brest-Litovsk with Germany. This nominally ended fighting in the east between Russia and the Central Powers, allowing the German Army to transfer more forces to the Western Front. The Germans now planned a massive offensive to turn back the Allied forces there. Using its remaining elite formations to spearhead the attack, Germany struck with all its might on 21 March, breaking through Britain's Fifth Army and threatening Paris.

Responding to the emergency, on 19 April the Union Government eliminated conscription exemptions and lowered the age of military compulsion from twenty-one to nineteen. Much of rural Canada spoke of betrayal, given that Borden had promised in the election campaign to protect farm labour from military service. Strong efforts to locate those evading conscription heightened tensions. A principal target was Quebec, where over 40 per cent of the men conscripted failed to report for duty. On 28 March 1918, two Dominion Police officers in the Quebec City working-class district of St-Roch arrested a young man in a bowling alley who did not have exemption papers. A mob estimated at 2,000 followed the three to the police station. The man was released, but the crowd attacked and damaged the station. The unrest continued for several days. On 1 April, troops moved in to stop protesters gathered on Place Jacques-Cartier. The rioters threw stones, snowballs, and chunks of ice. Soldiers, claiming they had been shot at, killed four civilians and wounded nearly seventy. Conscription had produced one of the largest and deadliest anti-government riots in Canadian history.

Pacifists also faced increasing hardships. Several Mennonites, as was the case with other groups legally exempt from military service, undertook alternative, non-combat service roles, such as in the Canadian Army Medical Corps or with labour battalions. However, conscription boards sometimes took a harsh approach, for example, by refusing to exempt Mennonites because baptism into the faith did not occur until the age of twenty-one. By the end of the war, 117 conscientious objectors had been jailed. In Winnipeg, two Jehovah's Witnesses and one Pentecostal were taken to the Minto Street Barracks, where, in frigid conditions, they were doused with cold water to convince them to drop their opposition to military service, a process that nearly killed one man.

Fears also grew over the spread of communism to Canada. Censorship authorities targeted the socialist press during the final year of the war. On 2 August 1918, Vancouver workers staged a one-day general strike over what they claimed was the murder of Albert "Ginger" Goodwin, the socialist and pacifist vice-president of the British Columbia Federation of Labour, by a Dominion Police officer who was pursuing Goodwin for evading conscription. Activists fuelled labour discontent in western Canada, arguing that the Trades and Labour Congress (TLC), which was dominated by moderate craft unions mostly from central Canada, had failed the working class. At the September 1918 TLC conference in Quebec City, motions from western Canadian delegates favouring militant industrial unionism and the use of general strikes were defeated.

Labour militancy continued to rise after the war ended in November 1918. Inspired by the Vancouver protest, the Winnipeg General Strike evolved from a walkout on 1 May 1919 by metal trade workers, a group that had been trying for more than a decade to win union recognition. The next day, building trade workers joined them, calling for wage increases. With no prospect for a settlement, both these groups came before the Winnipeg Trades and Labour Council to seek support. Over 90 per cent of the council members voted to start sympathy strikes.

Some 30,000 workers left their jobs at 11 a.m. on 15 May, and walkouts followed in more than thirty communities across the country. After six weeks, on 17 June, the authorities acted. A pre-dawn raid saw the arrest of twelve strike leaders. Four days later, strikers assembled for what authorities deemed an illegal gathering. When the protesters refused to disperse, the mayor read the Riot Act, and on cue, Royal North-West Mounted Police on horseback, with revolvers drawn, charged into the crowd, killing two, injuring one hundred, and arresting thirty. The following month, Section 98 was added to the Criminal Code to put the "iron heel" to radicalism. It set a maximum penalty of twenty years' imprisonment against anyone printing, publishing, writing, editing, issuing, or offering for sale "any book, newspaper, periodical, pamphlet, picture, paper, circular, card, letter, writing, print, publication, or document of any kind in which it is taught, advocated, advised or defended ... that the use of force, violence, terrorism or physical injury be used as a means of accomplishing any governmental, industrial or economic change."[12]

Many Canadians came out of the war with a stronger sense of pride and nationalism. Canada had made a difference in the war's outcome; its troops had proven the equals of those from across the Empire, including Britain; and Canadian forces had spearheaded the Allied offensive in the last months of the conflict. Across Canada, war memorials were constructed conveying the theme of noble sacrifice to save freedom. Yet, Laurier's concerns had also come to pass. The First World War had left deep and long-lasting divisions between French and English Canadians and between workers and capitalists, as well as strong discontent in large parts of rural Canada. Many soldiers who had given their lives ostensibly for British democracy would perhaps not have recognized the Canada that emerged shakily out of wartime.

A more independent Canada became a member of the new League of Nations after the First World War. But having just suffered a quarter-million casualties, including

60,000 dead, Canada also shied away from international commitments. Both Conservative and Liberal governments rejected Collective Security (an arrangement in which individual states committed themselves to respond with collective military action against unjustified armed aggression against any league member), believing it would get Canada involved in Europe's seeming propensity to fight wars. In the interwar years, Canada's army was reduced to a skeleton force, and Canada was a leading voice in the campaign to appease Adolf Hitler.

Yet there was no escaping Hitler's ambitions to dominate Europe. Germany remilitarized the Rhineland (Germany's western frontier) in 1936, annexed the German-speaking Sudeten region of Czechoslovakia in 1938, and absorbed the whole of Austria the same year. In March 1939, after Germany invaded the remainder of Czechoslovakia, Britain prepared for war and offered guarantees to protect Poland and Romania. Meanwhile, Prime Minister Mackenzie King searched desperately for a peaceful solution. Only weeks before the conflict started, he suggested that Britain's king and queen visit Germany to plead with Hitler to avoid war. Some historians criticize Mackenzie King for promoting appeasement and leaving Canada unprepared for war; others argue that by demonstrating that he had pursued every opportunity for peace, he was able to convince Canadians that there was no other option but war, thus bringing a united country into the conflict.

On 1 September, Germany invaded Poland. Two days later, Britain declared war. In Canada, there were no celebratory crowds like those of 1914. Newspapers described people as "tight-lipped," "solemn," and "grim-faced."[13] Canada waited a week before following Britain to declare war. Determined to show Canada's autonomy, Mackenzie King said that Parliament would decide, although the delay also enabled Canada as a non-belligerent to purchase military equipment from the United States, whose 1935 Neutrality Act prohibited arms sales to nations at war. However,

Canada's participation was a foregone conclusion. On 7 September, Mackenzie King spoke for three hours in Parliament, building a case for war by pointing to unrelenting Nazi expansion. Using words reminiscent of the First World War, he declared: "The forces of good and evil are locked in mortal combat."[14]

Despite the massive casualties of the First World War, many young men, believing they were invincible and moved by a sense of duty, clamoured to enlist in Canada's armed forces. But the carnival atmosphere of August 1914 and the antics of Sam Hughes had no place in the 1939 mobilization. This time, recruitment proceeded through existing militia regiments, not by creating new units for overseas service. In September, the opening month of the war, Canada's army grew from 5,000 to 61,000. Ultimately it would reach 700,000 personnel; the air force, 230,000; the navy, 100,000.

The federal government moved quickly to empower itself for what it realized could be a long struggle. On 1 September, the federal cabinet proposed passage of the War Measures Act, which was formalized soon after Parliament reconvened. It created a series of regulations known as the Defence of Canada Orders. Initially sixty-four in number, they included censorship of the press and radio as well as the power to detain "potential enemy aliens and suspected spies," to suspend trials and *habeas corpus*, and to prohibit "any statements that could hinder recruitment or prejudice the war effort."[15]

Again, anti-German prejudice spiked. In the autumn of 1939, the Canadian National Exhibition in Toronto prohibited pavilions where the German language was used. By the end of 1940, some 1,200 enemy aliens had been interned, about half of them German nationals. Many internees belonged to pro-fascist groups like the *Deutscher Bund Kanada* and the National Unity Party in Quebec, which was led by Canada's most famous fascist, Adrien Arcand.

In the conflict's early stages, Prime Minister Mackenzie King spoke of Canada fighting a war of "limited liability," meaning it would seek to emphasize the contribution of resources and technology over men in combat. The goal was to minimize human losses as well as the possibility of conscription for overseas service, something Mackenzie King promised would not be implemented, particularly in Quebec.

Up until the spring of 1940 (a phase known as the Phoney War), relatively little fighting occurred beyond the invasion of Poland. Still, for Mackenzie King, political challenges arose. Quebec's *Union nationale* Premier Maurice Duplessis warned, correctly as it turned out, that Ottawa would exploit the conflict to grab more power within the federation. This trend was already evident, he asserted, with the establishment in 1937 of the Royal Commission on Dominion–Provincial Relations – better known as the Rowell–Sirois Commission – which was charged with examining ways to restructure federalism to better deal with crises like the Great Depression. Although Duplessis had a majority government and did not have to call an election for another two years, on 25 September 1939 he decided to seek another mandate, framing the campaign as one of "provincial autonomy versus the Dominion government." Convinced that his re-election would compromise the war effort, King's key cabinet ministers from Quebec, Postmaster General Charles "Chubby" Power, Public Works Minister P.J.A. Caron, and Justice Minister Ernest Lapointe, let it be known that they would resign if Duplessis was re-elected. The message to Quebeckers was that this would leave the federal government fully under anglophone control, thus making conscription more likely. The *Union nationale* had won 76 seats to the provincial Liberals' 14 in 1936; this time, the results on 25 October 1939 saw the Liberals under Adélard Godbout win 70 seats and 54 per cent of the popular vote compared to 15 and 39 per cent for the *Union nationale*.

At the same time, in Ontario, provincial Conservative opposition leader George Drew attacked the Mackenzie

King government for not doing enough to help Britain. In this, Drew was supported by Liberal premier Mitchell Hepburn, who had a dreadful relationship with Mackenzie King, over issues such as the prime minister not backing him in his crusade against unionization in Ontario's auto sector. Consequently, on 20 January 1940, by a vote of 44 to 10, the Ontario legislature passed a resolution condemning Ottawa's war effort. Mackenzie King replied by calling an election for 26 March 1940.

Although Mackenzie King had been prime minister for nearly five years, the new federal Conservative leader Robert Manion said he would support the extension of Parliament to focus on the war, and he was led to believe that this was Mackenzie King's intention. Manion, who had won the Military Cross at the Battle of Vimy Ridge, appeared to agree with Mackenzie King's measured approach to the war, including his opposition to conscription. The election call caught Manion and the Tories off-guard. Manion proposed the creation of a non-partisan coalition government to best meet wartime challenges, and his candidates ran under the banner of the National Government. To most Canadians, a coalition seemed unnecessary, and in Quebec it conjured memories of Borden's Union Government and the Conscription Bill. Also, Manion had banked on Duplessis's support in Quebec, but Godbout's victory had strengthened the Liberals. The result was the greatest majority government to date, with the Liberals taking 184 of 245 seats. Manion lost his own seat in London, Ontario, and resigned as party leader. R.B. Hanson, whom historian J.L. Granatstein would describe as "slow and ponderous," became temporary leader.[16] In November 1941, former prime minister Arthur Meighen, a long-time archrival of Mackenzie King, was persuaded to take the job of opposition leader.

Within two weeks of the Liberals' electoral landslide, Germany launched a major offensive, quickly conquering Denmark and Norway. After this, the Nazis overran the European Low Countries, and invaded France, which fell in June 1940. The Canadian government responded on 14 June with the National Resources Mobilization Act (NRMA), which permitted conscription, initially for thirty days, but only for home service in the defence of Canada. Although most Canadians accepted this measure, including Quebeckers, it was not free from controversy. Montreal's mayor, Camillien Houde, was interned for four years for advising people to defy the registration order. In January 1941, the term for home service was extended to four months; in April, to the duration of the war. On assuming the Conservative leadership, Meighen had insisted that conscription for overseas service was essential. Canada again faced a difficult debate over the issue that had split the country in 1917–18.

To help secure acceptance of conscription for home defence from Quebec's powerful Catholic Church, the federal government used the Defence of Canada Regulations to ban activities of the Jehovah's Witnesses, who were both pacifist and strongly anti-Catholic. Cardinal Jean-Marie-Rodrigue Villeneuve and Justice Minister Ernest Lapointe, a devout Catholic, championed the measure. Other pacifists faced repression. In Alberta, Loyalist Leagues emerged, demanding the confiscation of Hutterite land. This hostility was partly rooted in the Hutterites' success as farmers, including the fact that they had managed to expand their holdings during the war while many family farms suffered from labour shortages because their men were fighting overseas. In 1944, Alberta's Social Credit government passed the Land Sales Prohibition Act, which prevented new sales or leases of property to Hutterites.

As in 1918–19, attention focused on the political left, on the premise that many leftists had earlier supported Germany as a consequence of the Nazi–Soviet non-aggression pact of August 1939. Soviet leader Joseph Stalin directed Communist parties worldwide to denounce the war as motivated by capitalist greed. Soon after the fall of France, the government outlawed the Communist Party of Canada and arrested over 130 of its members. However, after the Nazis invaded the USSR in June 1941, the Soviets joined the Allied side. Following directives from Moscow, Canadian communists now harnessed their energies to defeat fascism, and the Allies entered into a military alliance with the Soviets. In September 1942, Canadian authorities released Communists arrested under the Defence of Canada Regulations. Still, the ban remained on the Communist Party. In 1943, it was allowed to reappear as the Labour Progressive Party, and that year it won two seats in the Ontario provincial election as well as a federal by-election in Montreal.

The federal government banned publications produced by several ethnic groups viewed as sympathetic to the enemy, or to socialism. Also, as in the First World War, African Canadians were recruited only into labour battalions. Aboriginals saw action but again would later be excluded from numerous veterans' programs. At the same time, authorities sought to engage ethnic groups considered to be loyal. In October 1941, it established a Nationalities Branch. To promote attachment to Canada, the branch highlighted ethnic traditions, though in ways that made them seem quaint. Reflecting the view of Canada as a British nation, it also stressed the primacy of the English language and British culture, which it linked to "liberal democratic values, constitutional monarchy, and the capitalist economic system."[17]

While the federal government dealt with some ethnic groups in a nuanced manner, this was certainly not the case with Japanese Canadians, 90 per cent of whom lived in the Vancouver area. RCMP surveillance stretching back to the late 1930s had not detected any subversion. British Columbians, however, resented Japanese Canadians for their economic success, especially as fishers, and accused them of being overly aggressive in their business dealings. Japan's armed forces inspired widespread public fears during the 1930s as they ripped through China in a frighteningly brutal invasion. Rumours abounded that in places like Burma and Ceylon (Sri Lanka), the local Japanese were acting as fifth columnists to pave the way for invasion.

By 1940, in British Columbia, the public was boycotting Japanese-run stores and lawbreakers were vandalizing them. Demands for the internment or forced evacuation of Japanese Canadians rose to a fever pitch in December 1941 with Japan's attack on Hong Kong, which was garrisoned by Canadian troops, and on the American naval base at Pearl Harbor, Hawaii. Vancouver City Council spoke of the local Japanese population as a "potential reservoir of voluntary aid to our enemy."[18] The tide of prejudice became unstoppable when, on 20 February 1942, the United States ordered an evacuation of its Japanese population. Four days later, Canada did the same, barring some 23,000 Japanese – many of them naturalized British subjects of Canada, some of them Canadian First World War veterans – from living within 160 kilometres of the Pacific coast. Most evacuees were sent to rapidly constructed, overcrowded, and generally nasty government housing complexes in the BC Interior. Officials permitted each adult to bring just 70 kilograms of baggage, and 35 kilograms per child. Multiple families shared washrooms and bathing facilities, and oil lamps replaced electricity. Japanese-owned houses and farms were put up for sale, and fetched only a fraction of their value, even in Vancouver's red-hot wartime real estate market, where an influx of war workers created a severe housing shortage.

In August 1944, with the tide turning towards Allied victory, the government told Japanese Canadians to choose between settling east of the Rocky Mountains or moving to Japan. Initially, 10,397 Japanese Canadians opted to leave Canada. Soon after, 4,720 sought to rescind that decision, having realized just how much destruction Japan had suffered. In all, 3,964 returned to Japan, of whom 1,979 were Canadian-born. By contrast, after the First World War, though Germans and Austrians were denied entry into Canada until 1922, they were not deported. Race meant that some ethnic groups were regarded as far more Canadian than others.

The expanding scope of the war had profound implications for the balance of power between the state and individuals, and between the federal and provincial governments. Ottawa required unprecedented resources to prosecute the war. The costs of the First World War had peaked at around a million dollars a day; this more mechanized conflict was already costing nearly 80 per cent more in real dollars by the end of 1940.

The Rowell–Sirois Commission provided the basis for change. It had completed its report in early 1940, but Mackenzie King did not release its controversial recommendations until after that year's federal election. The results justified Duplessis's concerns about the expansion of federal powers, as well as similar ones expressed by Ontario premier Mitchell Hepburn and Alberta premier William Aberhart. The commission proposed that the federal government assume control over income, corporate, and inheritance taxes; in exchange, it would implement a national unemployment insurance scheme and rebate money to the provinces based on population. Although its recommendations related to empowering Ottawa to deal more effectively with calamities like the Great Depression, the need for money to finance the war lent urgency to the proposals.

The federal government pushed for implementation at a January 1941 Dominion–Provincial Conference. Aberhart and BC premier Duff Pattullo had doubts about the scheme; Hepburn was hostile; Quebec's Adélard Godbout was non-committal. Ottawa proceeded nevertheless to create an unemployment insurance program in 1941. Although a milestone in the development of Canada's social welfare system, the result was far less comprehensive than what organized labour had advocated. Employees had to contribute to the plan for a considerable amount of time before qualifying for benefits, and it excluded many workers, such as those in logging and fishing who faced seasonal unemployment.

Claiming that Mackenzie King was endangering Confederation, Hepburn even talked about creating a new Liberal Party. However, the Ontario premier miscalculated. Given wartime needs, Aberhart and Pattullo tempered their opposition, and other premiers, as well as the Ontario public, increasingly viewed Hepburn as obstructionist. Federal Finance Minister J.L. Ilsley played hardball, declaring that if necessary Ottawa would proceed unilaterally by imposing new taxes as an emergency measure. In May 1942, under the Dominion-Provincial Taxation Agreement Act, the provinces "rented" their control over income, corporate, and inheritance taxes to Ottawa for the remainder of the war in exchange for a federal subsidy linked to their populations. Four months later, Hepburn left office, though not before calling Mackenzie King a Nazi. The following year, federal expenditures ballooned to nearly $3 billion, a 56 per cent increase from the previous year, with taxes providing 49 per cent of the total.

Increased revenues were necessary not only for munitions production and the expansion of military forces but also to fund the massive expansion of the federal bureaucracy from 46,000 to 115,000 personnel. Among these were small numbers of high-ranking bureaucrats ("mandarins"), who planned and managed the war economy and powerfully shaped domestic and foreign policy.

The war pushed Canada ever closer to the United States. Mackenzie King believed he enjoyed a special relationship with President Franklin Roosevelt. The two often discussed world affairs, and Mackenzie King fancied himself a presidential confidant, especially since Roosevelt had told him to phone when he felt it was necessary.

Early in the war, Washington was concerned about the poor state of Canadian defences and how this could compromise North American security. The president spoke of the need for hemispheric defence cooperation. On 17 August 1940, Mackenzie King met Roosevelt at Ogdensburg, New York, just across the St Lawrence River from Prescott, Ontario, where the President had come to inspect troops. Mackenzie King arrived with a list of specific military items required by the Department of National Defence. Supposedly he expected nothing else, though his diary expressed no surprise when the president proposed a Permanent Joint Board on Defence, an idea that Mackenzie King supported. The board would have four representatives from each country; its task would be to plan for continental security.

Economics drove Canada and the United States still closer. Britain had difficulty paying for its growing Canadian war orders. Canada needed those British payments to settle its trade deficit with the United States. September 1940 brought the Lend-Lease agreement between Britain and the United States, under which, for example, Britain's hard-pressed Royal Navy would receive American destroyers in exchange for American leasing rights to British bases in the Western Hemisphere. Lend-Lease threatened Canadian economic interests because it encouraged Britain to go to America to obtain military equipment and munitions. On 16 April 1941, Mackenzie King made a personal appeal to Roosevelt, warning of dire economic consequences for Canada by the end of the year should present trends continue. Roosevelt was sympathetic. The result was the Hyde Park Agreement, the details of which were drawn up by US Treasury Secretary Harry Morgenthau and Canada's Deputy Finance Minister Clifford Clark. The United States agreed to increase purchases in Canada and for Britain to use a portion of its Lend-Lease money to buy Canadian goods. This solved Canada's liquidity crisis by the end of the year.

Even while drawing closer to the United States, just as it had in the First World War, Canada sought greater international recognition. To this end, Canadian representatives advanced the Functional Principle, often attributed to Hume Wrong of the Department of External Affairs. According to that principal, Canada in certain functions was a leading international power and thus deserved a significant role in making decisions. Overcoming resistance from the major powers, especially Britain, Canada successfully applied the Functional Principle to obtain membership on the Combined Allied Production Board in 1942, and on the more powerful Combined Food Board the following year. So in the Second World War just as in the First, Canada moved more quickly towards greater autonomy and a broader international presence.

Much like it had during the First World War, the question of conscription came to define domestic politics. Growing wartime commitments meant more pressure to increase military recruitment. Quebec posed the most formidable challenge. Ultimately, 19 per cent of eligible Quebeckers would serve in uniform during the Second World War, compared to 12 per cent during the First, but this was still less than half the rate among English Canadians.

With Parliament set to resume in January 1942, Mackenzie King realized that Tory leader Arthur Meighen was determined to push hard for conscription for overseas service. Some parts of the country supported his position strongly; for instance, a month earlier, Manitoba's legislature had passed a pro-conscription resolution. Meighen was set to pounce following the government's Throne Speech, which he expected would offer a series of self-congratulatory platitudes. But in a strategic masterstroke, Mackenzie King announced that the government would hold a non-binding plebiscite for April in which Canadians would be asked if they would release the government from its pledge not to implement conscription for overseas service.

Opposition in French Quebec was intense. The young *Le Devoir* journalist André Laurendeau launched *La Ligue pour la défence du Canada*. Thousands took out a $1 membership to join the league. The response was broad enough to fund the league's anti-conscription publicity and strong enough to spawn a nationalist political party, the *Bloc populaire canadien*. Nationwide, nearly 70 per cent voted to allow the government to proceed with conscription for overseas service. However, in Quebec, the result was 73 per cent *non*. Both sides claimed victory. Seeking to the bridge the divide, Mackenzie King responded with Bill 80, which revised the National Resources Mobilization Act by removing geographic restrictions on those called up to provide military service for home defence. However, the government insisted it still had no plans to send such men overseas. Mackenzie King famously described his approach as "not necessarily conscription but conscription if necessary." In Parliament, Bill 80 passed easily, 141 to 45, but only four French-speaking Liberals voted for the measure; the rest abstained or were absent for the vote. On the other side, Defence Minister J.L. Ralston offered his resignation over Bill 80, believing that partisan considerations – namely, Mackenzie King's fear of alienating Quebec – had trumped military needs. Convinced that the resignation would trigger a political crisis, Mackenzie King pleaded with the minister to stay on board, couching his request in terms of duty to the nation, a tactic that influenced Ralston, a First World War veteran and honorary militia colonel. However, Mackenzie King kept Ralston's resignation letter on file in case it proved useful at a later date. At least for the moment, Mackenzie King had adroitly calmed the clamour for and against conscription.

Besides conscription, Mackenzie King faced growing challenges from organized labour and rising concerns among Canadians that the end of the war would see a return to Depression-like conditions or the social turmoil that had followed the First World War. Wartime union membership climbed rapidly, from 358,967 in 1939 to 724,188 by 1944. People were working longer hours and earning

more money, but they were also facing higher taxes, shortages of consumer goods, and a wage freeze since October
1941. Another long-standing source of discontent was the
absence of collective bargaining legislation that would guar-
antee union recognition should a majority of workers vote
in favour of such representation.

The leaders of the Trades and Labour Congress and the
Canadian Congress of Labour (CCL) officially discouraged
strikes. A.R. Mosher, the CCL president, declared in 1942:
"It is more important ... to defeat Hitler and his gangsters
than to bring the most tyrannical and reactionary employer
in Canada to his knees."[19] Still, the TLC executive added,
workers "ha[d] a right ... to be assured that [their] patriotism would not be exploited."[20] Strikes did occur, and they
could be bitter. An example was the six-month walkout by
abysmally paid gold miners at Kirkland Lake, Ontario, starting in November 1941. In the end, that strike failed. In
1939, Canada experienced 120 strikes at a cost of 224,588
workdays, numbers that in 1943 reached 401 and 1,041,198
respectively.

Canadians fretted about the looming transition from
an intensified wartime economy to peacetime production,
especially with the absence of social programs or definitive
plans to cushion any downturn. Britain's Beveridge Report
of 1942, which laid out the framework for a modern social
welfare system, received extensive and positive press coverage in Canada. In February 1942, Arthur Meighen, running
in a parliamentary by-election in the Toronto riding of York
South, which had voted Tory since 1904, lost to the left-
wing Co-operative Commonwealth Federation (CCF) can-
didate Joseph Noseworthy. Meighen had run on the need
for conscription; Noseworthy had spoken of planning the
transition to a peacetime economy. Following Meighen's
defeat, some 160 Tories gathered in Port Hope, Ontario,
for a policy conference. While declaring capitalism the best
system, delegates also recommended national collective
bargaining legislation, a low-cost housing plan, improved

pensions for the elderly, and a national health insurance scheme. At its autumn 1942 convention in Winnipeg, the Tories chose former United Farmers of Manitoba Premier John Bracken as their leader. As a nod to Bracken's past, and to project a new image, the Conservatives changed the party's name to Progressive Conservative.

While pressure for improvements in labour and social policy continued to build on Ottawa, threats to political survival prompted quicker action at the provincial level. The Ontario Liberals tried to win working-class support for an approaching provincial election by passing an act guaranteeing collective bargaining rights. However, in the election of August 1943, both the Conservatives – running on the Port Hope policies – and the CCF supported similar legislation. In that contest, George Drew's Conservatives squeaked in with 37 seats, three more than the CCF. Five days after the Ontario vote, the federal Liberals lost four by-elections, two to the CCF and one each to the Tories and the Labour-Progressive Party. In September 1943, a national public opinion poll showed that the CCF had the support of 29 per cent of decided voters compared to 28 per cent each for the other two national parties. The Liberal Party's strength seeming to be wavering.

The gathering storm over conscription threatened Mackenzie King's hold on power. It was becoming more difficult to obtain adequate numbers of military volunteers. The booming war economy was providing attractive opportunities at home. Even with wage and price controls in effect, electricians, plumbers, and carpenters, for example, saw their hourly rates rise from 75 cents to about $1 an hour over the course of the war. The labour shortage also drove up farm workers' pay: the Great Depression had reduced their monthly salaries (excluding room and board) to $40 in 1939; by 1945, that figure had climbed to $97.

Young men still felt great pressure to enlist. One group that came under considerable criticism was the National

Hockey League. It was permitted to continue, but more than 100 players had enlisted. University students in good standing could obtain a deferment, but male students had to join the Canadian Officer Training Corps, which required 110 hours of military preparation during the academic year and two weeks during the summer. By 1943, due to labour shortages, certain jobs had been classified as essential, such as coal miners, meatpackers, and longshoremen. Workers were not to leave these positions for different civilian ones unless permission was obtained from an official with the Department of Labour. However, the rules were not strictly enforced, and military enlistment was permitted, though men with these jobs could rightfully claim they were performing crucial roles.

Mackenzie King continued to delay action on conscription, hoping that needs could be balanced and that Germany would be defeated by the end of 1944, as some military analysts were predicting. As of late August 1944, army officials estimated deficiencies in front-line Canadian infantry units at 4,500. That same month, Maurice Duplessis, who had warned against conscription, was re-elected as Quebec premier. Nationwide, just over 60 per cent of Canadians favoured conscription for overseas service. The most prominent advocate for it was the defence minister, Ralston. Overseas in late September, he met with Canadian military commanders and learned of an impending crisis: many units were under-strength and exhausted. Convinced that Ralston was leading a pro-conscription conspiracy against him, Mackenzie King pulled out the defence minister's 1942 resignation letter before a stunned Liberal cabinet and fired him.

Mackenzie King replaced Ralston with General Andrew McNaughton, who believed the voluntary system could still work. But after three weeks at his new post, only three hundred NRMA men had opted for active (overseas) service, and he admitted that voluntarism was not going to produce the numbers needed. Facing a possible cabinet revolt,

Mackenzie King finally relented on conscription. But he remained cautious to the end. The government authorized the conscription of 16,000 NRMA men for overseas service, the bare minimum called for by the army. Ultimately, 12,098 men were sent overseas; 2,463 of these saw action, 313 became casualties, and 69 were killed. Mackenzie King feared resignations by French Canadian members of his government, but to his relief, he found them "exceedingly friendly."[21] On 7 December, parliament passed Mackenzie King's conscription plan, 168 to 43, but it was openly supported by fewer than half of French Canadian Liberals. The response on the streets in Quebec was less violent than the reaction to conscription had been during the First World War. Still, 2,000 rallied against the measure in Montreal, and smaller protests broke out in Quebec City and Chicoutimi. On this issue, Mackenzie King's delaying tactics had averted the violence over conscription that had broken out during the First World War.

Conscription remained a political powder keg, but Mackenzie King's ministers were busily preparing for peace. In 1944, Clarence Decatur (C.D.) Howe was shifted from the Munitions and Supply portfolio to head up a new Department of Reconstruction. Under the National Emergency Transitional Powers Act, Howe assumed ongoing controls over resources and, if necessary, other areas of the economy, to facilitate civilian production. He introduced accelerated depreciation tax write-offs for new equipment; this cost the government revenue but also saved industry over $250 million between November 1944 and January 1946 and hastened reconversion to peacetime production.

Plans for new social policies built on recommendations made by the Advisory Committee on Reconstruction that Mackenzie King had appointed in 1941. Key to this committee's impact was its research director, Leonard Marsh. In 1943, he was tasked with producing a Report on Social

Security. Marsh viewed social programs as a moral impera-
tive to ensure a minimum standard of living; as a proponent
of Keynesian economic theory, he also saw them as a means
for maintaining a spending stream to offset economic
downturns, like the one anticipated following the war.
Marsh's report recommended a "cradle to grave" approach
to social policy that included family allowances, health and
sickness benefits, improved old age pensions, and death
benefits. For Mackenzie King, this was too much too fast.
He focused on the Family Allowance, which would become
known as the Baby Bonus. This was Canada's first universal social program, in the sense that it did not include an
income test. Scheduled to take effect in July 1945, just after
a federal election, it would pay parents $5 to $8 monthly
for each child, depending on their age, up to sixteen years
old. In February 1944, the government introduced Order
in Council PC 1003, which guaranteed union recognition
for workers under federal jurisdiction when more than half
the workers indicated support for such representation. Its
impact was indisputable: between February 1944 and April
1945, 133 new union locals were certified; only 28 were
rejected under the provision.

By the end of 1944, the Liberals stood at 36 per cent of
popular support, compared to 28 per cent for the Tories, 23
per cent for the CCF, and 5 per cent for the *Bloc populaire.*
Still, Mackenzie King was worried about an election. Military analysts warned that heavy fighting lay ahead now that
the Nazis were defending their homeland. Mackenzie King
delayed the election call until 16 April 1945, hoping that
the war in Europe would end before Canadians went to the
polls on 11 June. In April, Mackenzie King's government
introduced a White Paper on Income and Employment.
Written by Queen's University economist W.A. Mackin-
tosh, it recommended that the federal government use its
new taxing and spending powers acquired in wartime to
ensure continuing high levels of employment. The Liberals
appeared to accept this recommendation.

Mackenzie King and the Liberals had negotiated through very turbulent times, though good fortune also played a part. Germany's surrender on 7 May mooted the conscription debate. The Liberals' main campaign theme was a "New Social Order for Canada." Technically, Mackenzie King won a minority government, with 118 seats out of 245, though he could count on the support of eight independent Liberals, who soon rejoined his caucus. He expressed satisfaction with the results, but also personal hurt over losing his own seat in Prince Albert, Saskatchewan, by fewer than two hundred votes, due largely to weak support among veterans. He later returned to the House of Commons in a by-election for Glengarry, Ontario. Alone among Allied war leaders, Mackenzie King continued to hold power during the period of reconstruction.

As the Second World War drew to its devastating close with the release of atomic bombs over Hiroshima and Nagasaki in August 1945, delegates to a Dominion–Provincial Conference in Ottawa were wrapping up their sessions. Amidst euphoria across the land, politicians were once again bickering. The federal Liberals had introduced the Green Book, which proposed that the federal government retain its wartime taxing powers to pay for new social programs and other policies to retain high levels of employment. Leading the opposition were the provincial governments in Ontario and Quebec. The result was extended tax rental arrangements, along with ongoing provincial demands that federal powers be curtailed. At the time, however, public opinion supported Ottawa. Canadians feared the return of the Great Depression that many associated with laissez-faire policies.

Mackenzie King was a student of history. Throughout the Second World War, he sought to avoid the pitfalls that had beset and at times threatened to overwhelm the Borden government during the First World War. Determined to preserve unity, he saw conscription as driving a dangerous, nation-destroying wedge between English and French Canada. Although organized labour came out of the Second World War with strong demands – such as for hefty raises (following the wartime wage freeze) – that contributed to a record 4.6 million strike days in 1946, there was still much to be happy about – namely, new collective bargaining legislation and wide-ranging and popular social policies.

Did Mackenzie King really provide bold wartime leadership? When it came to protecting minority rights, his government's record was hardly better than Borden's. What of the troops overseas who desperately needed reinforcements? Did Mackenzie King support them? Were critics fair to characterize his obsession with national unity as a thinly veiled preoccupation with Liberal fortunes, especially in Quebec? Borden had lost Quebec as a result of conscription, even though he held off until mid-1917, and in the history books he has not fared as well as Mackenzie King. But Borden arguably governed with greater conviction. As historian Tim Cook wrote in his study of these two wartime leaders: "Canada had never faced as grim a year as 1917, when its own total of men killed in action surpassed 30,000, and the Allies faltered on all fronts, and when there was a very real likelihood that the war could be lost."[22] Borden was more decisive, but while conscription reinforced the Canadian Corps at a crucial moment in the war, it did not significantly influence the war's outcome, and it left French—English relations in tatters. Borden's successor, Arthur Meighen, an architect of conscription, lost to the Liberals under Mackenzie King in the 1921 election, in large part because Quebec's 65 sixty-five seats all went Liberal. By contrast, Mackenzie King won re-election in 1945, and his Liberal Party remained in power until 1957, making it the most successful in the Western world. Borden was bolder, but Mackenzie King was the better politician.

2

Mobilizing for Total War

When it came to business organization, many people considered Joseph Flavelle a genius. As president of the William Davies Company, a meat-processing plant in Toronto, he had organized the shipment of millions of kilograms of bacon to wartime Britain. With Canada delivering defective artillery shells, hopelessly behind in meeting munitions production targets, and facing widespread charges of profiteering and corruption, Flavelle was seconded by the British government to serve as head of a new Canadian-based Imperial Munitions Board (IMB). The board was technically an arm of the British government, but it was run in Canada. It demanded deliverables on time and at modest profit margins. Flavelle would receive a peerage for his service with the IMB. In late 1916, after returning from England, he spoke to a group of contractors in Toronto. Several complained about inadequate profit margins. "Profits?" shouted an incredulous Flavelle. "I have come straight from the seat of a nation where they are sweating blood to win this war ... Profits! Send profits to hell where they belong."[1]

Around the same time, Prime Minister Robert Borden appointed a Cost of Living Commissioner to address rising inflation. The food processing industry was one of the first sectors investigated. The commissioner revealed that William Davies, with which Flavelle had retained close ties, had earned an 85 per cent profit on its capital over the past year. Suddenly, one of Canada's most revered men found himself denounced in the press as the "Baron of Bacon."

A quarter-century after the establishment of the IMB, Prime Minister Mackenzie King appointed C.D. Howe as Minister of Munitions and Supply. Howe had trained as an engineer and succeeded in construction, becoming a leader in building grain elevators across the Canadian prairies. Elected as part of the Liberal majority government in 1935, Howe was appointed to cabinet, initially in the dual post of Minister of Railways and Canals *and* Marine and Fisheries. Not reticent about using government to pursue national development, in 1937, as Minister of Transport, he created the government-owned Trans-Canada Air Lines.

Demand for munitions during the Second World War was unprecedented. Howe relished the challenge, driving Canada to create the Allies' fourth-largest air force and third-largest navy. He focused on results and was unwilling to tolerate bungling. In late 1942, when the giant National Steel Car company failed to produce Lancaster bombers as promised, Howe fired its directors and established the government-owned, and highly successful, Victory Aircraft, in Milton, just outside Toronto.

In both wars, total mobilization involved far more than getting men, and eventually women, into uniform, or optimizing munitions production. It included efforts to convince Canadians to give their time and money to war-related causes. Public information campaigns mobilized Canadian minds and spirits by both filtering and infusing content.

Over time, Canadian leaders and policy makers adopted increasingly sophisticated and successful approaches to total mobilization. In each war, state involvement greatly expanded. The policies and approaches followed during the Second World War, and their outcomes, demonstrated that government, military, and social leaders had learned valuable lessons from missteps made during the First.

Grassroots voluntarism spread quickly throughout Canada and Newfoundland with the onset of the First World War. The volunteer movement reflected robust patriotism and a jingoistic spirit and provided many with a greater sense of purpose and respect. It was also exciting and fun. One newspaper cartoon from 1916 depicted a weary but immaculately dressed couple, with the man remarking: "Terrible war, isn't it?" To which the woman replies: "Frightful: seventh Red Cross dance I've had to go to this week."[2]

Wealthy individuals made large and well-publicized contributions. For example, Andrew Hamilton Gault in the opening weeks of the war donated $100,000 (over $2 million in 2015 figures) to raise Princess Patricia's Canadian Light Infantry, the first battalion of Canadian troops to reach the front. Myriad local campaigns emerged, like that of the Ottawa Kennel Club, which donated the proceeds from the sale of prize-winning dogs to supply comforts for men in uniform. Volunteers fanned out across communities, selling tags for war-related causes that people were to wear to prove they had contributed.

Across Canada, communities rallied behind the Commission for Relief in Belgium ("Belgian Relief") to assist civilians in Belgium and northern France who had suffered under German occupation. Such campaigns were led by prominent local figures, mainly from politics, business, the churches, and women's groups. Newspapers promoted Belgian Relief and many other campaigns with eye-catching visual and rousing written appeals, as well as by printing the names of those who had contributed, thus putting pressure on those who had not.

The same approach characterized the annual nationwide drives for the Salvation Army, the YMCA, the Red Cross, and the Knights of Columbus to furnish sporting equipment, recreational centres, and canteens for servicemen in Canada and overseas. The Red Cross also provided prisoner-of-war relief: some 3,800 Canadian soldiers were in enemy hands by mid-1917. Canadians were urged to give two dollars monthly to cover the costs of sending, via the Red Cross in neutral Switzerland, packages to prisoners containing non-perishable food, cigarettes, and other items to ease the burdens of captivity.

Volunteers organized four nationwide grassroots drives for the Canadian Patriotic Fund. Established by Parliament two weeks after the war began, the fund was to provide financial assistance to the wives and dependents of men who had enlisted. It paid from $12 to $20 monthly and was supplemented by a government separation allowance worth a maximum of $20 monthly, as well as money garnisheed from soldiers' pay (amounting to a sum roughly equivalent to an unskilled labourer's annual salary of $500). The campaign results were overwhelmingly positive – for instance, only a couple of weeks into the first drive, the City of Ottawa had exceeded its target of $350,000 by 10 per cent. Yet the fund ultimately proved inadequate as growing numbers of servicemen translated into more claimants. Local volunteer boards determined the specific level of support. For example, while the monthly average award in Hamilton stood at $20, it was $16.63 in Ottawa. Boards often judged applicants harshly. Some women were denied assistance because they were considered frivolous or immoral. Many also suffered because support levels from the fund remained static in the face of rising prices. Not until December 1917, just before the first federal election in which Canadian women could vote, did the government raise the monthly separation allowance from a maximum of $20 to $25. Although patriotic volunteerism engaged millions and produced very impressive results, it also had its limits in terms of meeting wartime needs.

Propaganda encouraged support for the war. For much of the conflict, state involvement in this area was minimal, while a cultural tendency towards jingoism and voluntarism went a long way. Press reports from overseas served as powerful engines of mobilization. The most prominent figure in transmitting news about Canadian troops from the battlefront was William Maxwell Aitken. A wealthy expatriate Canadian financier who owned the *Daily Express* in London (UK), before the war Aitken had been elected to Britain's Parliament. In 1917 he was named Britain's first Minister of Information. In 1915, Hughes named him Canada's "official eye-witness" at the front, though in fact he spent nearly all of the war in London.

In 1916, Aitken established the London-based Canadian War Records Office (CWRO), a repository of documentation on Canada's military contributions. Under his direction, the CWRO began to generate material for home consumption, much of which Aitken wrote. His stories sought to inspire more than to inform. For instance, in the April 1916 battle for the St-Eloi craters in Belgium, Canada's failure to achieve operational objectives, and many of its nearly 1,400 casualties, were attributable to poor intelligence and questionable leadership. For public consumption, however, Aitken wrote only of the "endurance, courage, and cheerfulness" of Canadian troops, whose "attacks were delivered with an unabated fury."[3]

By mid-1916, the CWRO had official photographers in the field. Standard fare for public consumption included, as described in captions, photos of "enemy guns seized, Germans quite happy to be prisoners, and decimated churches to prove the wanton destruction of the Hun."[4] The CWRO also provided newsreel footage, which was sent to Canada by Britain's Cinematograph Committee. One camera operator recalled that 90 per cent of the footage he took of dead bodies hit the cutting room floor.

Canadian civilians understood, and patriotically endured, the high costs of war. They read long casualty lists in newspapers. They received letters providing brutal descriptions, such as one from a lieutenant who told his father: "Just fancy, the dead are piled in heaps and the groans of the wounded and dying will never leave me."[5] Many servicemen feared running afoul of military censors or self-censored their letters to avoid upsetting or frightening loved ones. Wanting to appear manly, they also exuded bravado, like one serviceman who reported to his parents that though he had "been in the trenches" for over a year, he was "not yet tired of the sport."[6]

In Canada, the War Measures Act provided the basis for official censorship. The leakage of sensitive information by the press during the opening months of the war, such as the timing of troopship departures, convinced the federal government to establish a Chief Press Censor's office in June 1915. Lt.-Col. Ernest J. Chambers was selected to run it. A journalist, an ardent imperialist, and a former militia officer, Chambers proved untiring and unyielding in his efforts to shelter civilians from anything that might compromise their commitment to the war. He banned many publications, especially from the neutral United States, for being written in enemy languages, for expressing pacifist or anti-British views, or for promoting socialism. Many sources took the precaution of having Chambers vet material before going to press. After dealing with Chambers, the *Monetary Times* excised the line "the man who said war was hell did not know anything about it, for it [was] far worse," before reprinting a letter from the front.[7]

Not until relatively late into the conflict did Canada's government become actively involved in generating propaganda. This shift reflected growing challenges on the home front and the need for greater sacrifice. By 1917, besides conscription, Canada was facing fuel and food shortages as well as more difficulty financing the war.

In June 1917, C.A. Magrath, the founder of the Northwest Coal and Navigation Company and an Alberta Tory well known to and respected by Borden, was appointed Fuel Controller. New regulations limited Canadian households to a two-month stockpile of coal. In most Ontario urban communities, street lighting was stopped between 5 and 8 p.m., and for the remainder of the night every second light was shut off. Communiqués and press advertisements from the Fuel Controller urged Canadians to keep house temperatures down. As well, in February and March 1918, when shortages became most acute, heatless Mondays were implemented.

Also in June 1917, Ottawa appointed a Food Controller with the power to manage pricing, distribution, and consumption. In early 1918, this office became the Canada Food Board, which soon expanded its operations, including with respect to propaganda. The latter half of the war saw a sharply rising overseas demand for food; for instance, by 1917, Britain, France, Italy, and Belgium were achieving only 60 per cent of their pre-war wheat output. In Canada, farm labour shortages due to military recruitment and rural migration to better-paying urban jobs also adversely affected food production.

Canadians did not face coupon food rationing. However, laws prohibited hoarding and prevented restaurants from distributing large quantities of free bread, butter, and sugar. Meat could be served on designated days but never in quantities exceeding eight ounces (227 grams) per person. More than a million pledge cards were distributed for display in households where people had signed a promise "to carry out conscientiously the advice and directions"[8] of food control officials. Posters, flyers, and cookbooks advised on how to use readily available foods more effectively. The *Canadian Food Bulletin*, a newspaper that reported on food control efforts, was distributed to some 45,000 opinion makers such as clergy, politicians, and business leaders. Publicity campaigns also promoted government farm labour programs. For example, Soldiers of the Soil brought out over 20,000 high school youth to work on farms for up to four months at 50 per cent the normal pay, so long as participants were in good academic standing.

Financing the war required more government action to mobilize Canadians. For Canada, the daily costs of the conflict doubled to $1 million between 1915 and 1917. Under the War Finance Act of 1914, Canada went off the gold standard (which had limited the money supply to the equivalent gold stocks the country held) to print more money, though initially just $50 million (enough to fund about one hundred days of war for Canada's armed forces), with only 25 per cent being backed by precious metal. Small increases on custom duties followed, as well as new fees on banknotes issued by private banks (which those banks continued printing until 1944), telegraph messages, railway and steamship tickets, postage stamps, patent medicines, and wine. In July 1915, Ottawa borrowed for the first time on New York's money markets, initially $25 million; within a year, however, this had increased tenfold despite the relatively high interest rate of 5 per cent.

The most obvious other means of securing funds was to borrow from Canadians. Before the war, the federal government had raised only a maximum of $5 million through this means. Typically, Ottawa had turned to British investors, for the Canadian capital market was considered too modest, with too few millionaires and major financial institutions. This practice changed during the war. In November 1915, Ottawa offered for sale $50 million in war bonds at 5 per cent interest to mature in ten years. By that time, the Canadian economy was enjoying an upswing, and in just eight hours, $100 million in bonds were sold. In September 1916 and March 1917, the government asked Canadians to purchase a total of $250 million in war bonds, and attracted $460 million.

Government intervention to raise money also expanded in February 1916 when Ottawa introduced a tax on business profits. However, this was a cautious initiative that was meant to expire in three years, and because of low tax rates, it was capable of raising just $25 million annually. A year later, a tax on personal incomes followed, also intended to expire in three years. With a base tax rate of 4 per cent on income exceeding $1,500 (around $25,000 in 2015 figures), it raised about the same amount as the new corporate tax.

With record war expenditures planned for fiscal 1917–18, any remaining caution about war bond sales was abandoned. In November 1917, with the interest rate on bonds rising to 5.5 per cent, 820,035 people subscribed to securities worth $413.6 million. The following November, in 1918, some one million Canadians loaned Ottawa $660 million ($9.6 billion in 2015 dollars). A final loan in late 1919 to pay for leftover war costs and veterans' programs generated $680 million.

The government managed war bond campaigns more carefully over time. The Finance Department arranged for banks, stock and bond houses, and insurance companies to sell bonds on a commission basis. A Dominion Publicity Committee within the Department of Finance orchestrated a propaganda campaign that dwarfed all previous ones. No other cause could appeal for funds during the three-week-long Victory Bond campaigns, which kicked off in communities across Canada with parades, speeches, and the unveiling of giant displays – the thermometer being most popular – to record fund-raising progress. By agreement, the Canadian Press Association wrote stories on fund-raising successes. Posters and newspaper pages informed Canadians that it was their duty to buy bonds. In the more than four million letters delivered to households during the 1918 drive, Finance Minister Thomas White told Canadians that "money is urgently required ... to support our gallant soldiers in the field."[9] New technologies were used: White paid $15,000 to American filmmakers so that audiences could cheer the Canadian-born Hollywood star, Mary Pickford, as she bashed the German Kaiser on the head with a baseball bat labelled "Victory Loan."

Economic mobilization drove growing government intervention. Although long-standing attachment to the "limited state" influenced early policy making, this changed substantially as war-related spending tripled to 16 per cent of the GNP. Compared to the Second World War, the First demanded relatively little of Canadian industry. Air forces were still in their infancy. On the ground, even as late as 1918, the British forces employed about six horses for each motor vehicle. Even so, the war brought about strong industrial expansion. Iron and steel exports from Canada increased from $68.5 million in 1915 to $441.1 million in 1917. In 1913, less than 7 per cent of Canadian manufactured goods were exported; by 1918, that figure was 40 per cent, with the overwhelming majority relating to armaments.

The war's economic impact was linked mainly to the production of munitions. Canada entered the war with virtually no involvement in this area; its only enterprise was the Dominion Arsenal in Quebec City, which manufactured the Ross rifle. Charles Ross, Sam Hughes's good friend, promoted the weapon, but it had been in production since 1903, well before Hughes became Minister of Militia and Defence.

Cronyism characterized early munitions production in Canada. Within weeks of the war's outbreak, the federal government established the Shell Committee to distribute war contracts. It answered to Hughes, who had played a key part in selecting its members, many of whom were friends, including the committee's chair, Alex Bertram, the owner of a steel company in Dundas, Ontario. The committee's procedures utterly lacked accountability. Its members awarded contracts to friends, business associates, and companies in which they had personal financial interests, and the committee was haphazard about enforcing standards or controlling profits. One blatant case of abuse involved committee member J. Wesley Allison, a personal friend of Hughes and a well-known Tory supporter from Morrisburg, Ontario, who accepted kickbacks for arranging contracts with American firms. Many companies that received contracts were incapable of delivering as promised, and they provided a high proportion of defective products, including shells that maimed or killed the soldiers who fired them by exploding in the gun. By the end of May 1915, the Shell Committee had delivered only $5.5 million worth of shells out of $170 million in orders.

The British, frustrated with Canadian products, redirected munitions orders to the United States and demanded a reorganization of Canadian arms production. Borden heard complaints personally while visiting London in June 1915. In November, he dissolved the Shell Committee and agreed to replace it with an Imperial Munitions Board, answerable to Britain's Ministry of Munitions but directed in Canada by Joseph Flavelle.

Flavelle focused on filling some $250 million in back orders. When contracting with firms, he insisted that the prices charged not be higher than in other Allied countries and that production flow just as quickly. The IMB was not without its problems. In many parts of the country, Flavelle was criticized for apparently directing war contracts to central Canada. For example, Winnipeg had about one-third the population of Toronto but received only 0.3 per cent of the money spent by the government on the war effort compared to 8 per cent for Toronto. But for Flavelle, what mattered most was selecting the firms best able to carry out the tasks, and in his view those firms were the larger and more capital-intensive ones in urban, central Canada. Organized labour criticized Flavelle for refusing to implement a fair wage policy that would have guaranteed pay rates considered normal for the sector. For Flavelle, however, such a measure would have unnecessarily increased costs. When responding to strikes by munitions workers in Hamilton, Ontario, he directed censors to quash any news of them.

Under Flavelle, companies faced penalties for late deliveries, and product quality improved in large part because of the hiring of 8,000 inspectors. By the end of 1915, the IMB was associated with 400 factories and 175,000 workers; two years later the latter figure peaked at 350,000 workers, making it the largest enterprise in Canada. The IMB established a purchasing department to help industry acquire raw materials and machinery. A transportation department worked with carriers to ensure efficient product delivery. Shipments of Canadian-manufactured shells rose from 5,377,000 in 1915 to 23,782,000 in 1917.

When private companies failed to perform, the IMB formed government-owned enterprises. Among the largest of these was British Chemical in Trenton, Ontario. With 204 buildings and covering 100 hectares, it produced millions of kilograms of sulphuric acid, nitric acid, pyro-cotton, nitrocellulose powder, and TNT. Near Ashbridges Bay in Toronto, the IMB built the National Steel Factory, which housed the world's largest electric furnace. The IMB led in establishing an aviation sector, creating Canadian Aeroplanes Limited, which produced some 2,600 JN-4 trainers and 30 F-5 flying boats. The latter was one of the largest airplanes at the time, with a wingspan of approximately 30 metres. The IMB also became involved in shipbuilding (by 1917, German U-boats were destroying vessels off North America's Atlantic coast). New IMB shipbuilding facilities were rapidly set up in Toronto, Welland, and Midland, Ontario. The IMB also contracted with fourteen private shipyards in the Maritimes, Ontario, and Quebec, including Canadian Vickers in Montreal, the country's only covered shipyard, which could operate year round and even produced submarines.

The IMB also established an Innovations Division, which solicited ideas from the public, nearly all of which resulted in "polite rejections" as they included suggestions for "perpetual-motion machines, electric-arc rays, and the use of cayenne pepper to make the enemy sneeze."[10] Canada at the time had relatively little scientific expertise. No government department existed to advance research, and in 1918, only thirty-seven Canadian firms had their own research facilities. Although McGill University and the University of Toronto had made notable strides before the war in scientific research, overall results remained modest. Most Canadian universities were small, and many were church-affiliated. At the time of the First World War, there were fewer than 10,000 university students in Canada, and in 1918, total university revenues stood at just under $12 million (or $175 million in 2015 dollars, compared with over $37 billion in 2008), certainly not enough to support major scientific research. A

Ribs of a ship being constructed for the war effort at Ashbridges Bay, Toronto, 1917. Archives of Ontario, I0003569.jpg.

1917 survey identified only fifty scientists at Canadian universities undertaking pure research.

The war, by demonstrating the destructive potential of technology, was drawing greater attention to scientific applications, and with government assistance, it precipitated notable developments. In June 1916, a federal Order in Council established a Cabinet Subcommittee on Scientific and Industrial Research, chaired by Trade and Commerce Minister Sir George Foster. This led six months later to the founding of the Honorary Advisory Council for Scientific and Industrial Research, soon to become known as the National Research Council (NRC), which hired, funded, or consulted with many of Canada's most prominent scientists and engineers.

It would grossly overstate matters to suggest that the First World War transformed the place of science in Canada. In Foster's view, most cabinet ministers were "indifferent or antagonistic" to the Advisory Council and Borden seemed "oblivious." Still, as historian James Hull writes, "wartime research provided a few more rhetorical arrows to the quivers of research boosters" and generated an "evolution of Canadian attitudes towards science."[11] This trend became much more pronounced during the far more heavily mechanized Second World War.

Canada started the First World War with no experience in the mass mobilization of resources and little government involvement in economic affairs. Before the war's halfway point, however, major change had become essential. The federal government took a far more active role in managing the economy, and under the direction of Flavelle, Canada became an important player in munitions production, eventually supplying one-third of British shells. It was a lesson not lost on the federal government in the Second World War, which saw far more intervention and substantial results that would play a major role in transforming Canada into a truly industrialized nation.

In the opening months of the Second World War, Canadians again threw themselves into all types of patriotic campaigns. In early 1940, for example, many of the 2,500 citizens of Red Deer, Alberta, participated in a drive that raised $2,000 to purchase a military ambulance. Over the course of the conflict, the 50,000-strong Imperial Order Daughters of the Empire sent Canadian servicemen over 13 million magazines and newspapers and nearly 7 million cigarettes. Once again, Canadians were mobilized to buy Victory Bonds in highly organized and extensively advertised campaigns. Nine nationwide drives between 1942 and 1946 attracted over $11 billion ($157 billion in 2015 figures) from a population of some 11.5 million.

Although grassroots responses remained fundamental to the success of nearly all war-related volunteer-driven campaigns, in the Second World War the federal government became involved early and to a far greater extent than had been the case in 1914–18. All campaigns had to register with and receive approval under the War Charities Act by supplying documentation showing the procedures followed in establishing the fund, the total expected to be raised, the estimated costs of collecting the money, a list of directors, and the principal objects on which expenditures were to be made. Administrative costs were not to exceed 25 per cent of the money raised. The government disallowed some prospective campaigns because they unnecessarily duplicated other efforts, as in the case of Montrealers who sought to raise $45,000 for a third naval canteen when the city's two existing facilities were not being used to capacity.

In mid-1940, the Department of National War Services started promoting local efforts to form – and to register with the federal government – "citizen committees" to better coordinate and optimize the efforts of volunteers. National War Services also determined when, where, and for how long appeals could occur to prevent donor fatigue, to reduce overlap, and to maximize results. Based on experiences during the First World War, the government discontinued the Patriotic Fund and replaced it with a state-financed Dependents Allowance that provided financial support to servicemen's wives and up to four children per family to the age of sixteen. In November 1939, Ottawa named the YMCA, the Salvation Army, the Knights of Columbus, and the Canadian Legion as official auxiliaries, meaning that they received government funding – ranging from $2 million to $5 million annually – to ensure adequate recreational and educational services for military personnel.

State management of volunteerism extended to new areas, one of which was air raid protection (ARP). As early as 1931, the *Canadian Defence Quarterly* pointed out that "aircraft carriers ... could sail to within a few miles of the

Canadian coast, then send off attacking forces to bomb major cities."[12] Within a month of the war's outbreak, Ottawa began coordinating with provincial governments in the Maritimes, Quebec, and Ontario to form ARP committees to prepare for the possibility of aerial attacks and to manage blackout drills. Thousands of volunteers took courses paid for by the federal government and taught principally by the St John's Ambulance Association in which they learned first aid and how to conduct themselves during blackout drills.

Individual contributions extended to households. In the spring of 1942, the federal government established a National Salvage Committee with a healthy advertising budget that ran appeals in more than one thousand publications. Canadians were told that old pots and pans made guns and tanks, that tattered rags could be transformed into uniforms, and that in a broken refrigerator there was enough steel for three machine guns. By war's end, nearly 1,700 local salvage committees had collected over 300 million kilograms of reusable material. It was transported by municipal sanitation trucks, vehicles donated by private businesses, and groups like the Salvation Army, as well as in wagons, boxes, or large baskets by young volunteers, with the Boy Scouts playing a major role. As in the First World War, volunteer activities engaged millions of Canadians, but in the Second, government more closely managed these efforts.

Information management, which was more extensive and nuanced than during the First World War, helped persuade citizens to make even greater economic sacrifices. The earlier conflict had demonstrated the importance of propaganda; in the 1930s, the Nazis had used it expertly to consolidate their power. The interwar years had also seen the rise of advertising firms and public relations experts.

Canada's federal government established the Bureau of Public Information (BPI) on 5 December 1939 to release communiqués and to conduct weekly news conferences. Its senior managers were mostly public relations executives and journalists. Staff reporters wrote about activities at military installations and war factories, and a Photographic Branch provided images to accompany those articles. A Poster Division hired freelance graphic designers and artists and used the services of advertising firms.

The BPI suffered from administrative problems as well as what many viewed as rudderless leadership. Prime Minister Mackenzie King believed that the bureau had not adequately explained controversial Liberal policies, as demonstrated by the pummelling the Liberals had received from organized labour and agricultural interests over its October 1941 wage and price freeze. The BPI had also failed badly at convincing Quebec to back the federal government in the April 1942 plebiscite to release it from its pledge of "no conscription for overseas service."

In May 1942, a new Wartime Information Board (WIB) replaced the BPI. It hired more journalists to produce engaging material, and it commissioned nationwide surveys from the Canadian Institute of Public Opinion (CIPO) to identify the most effective propaganda. Copying the Gallup polling organization in the United States (founded in 1935), the CIPO was established in 1941 and used extensively by the Mackenzie King government to gauge support for its war policies. The WIB also cooperated closely with the National Film Board (NFB). Founded in May 1939 with just five permanent employees, by the end of the war the NFB had a staff of nearly eight hundred and had produced more than five hundred films, mostly on Canada's war effort. The WIB also coordinated its activities with the CBC, as radio had become a fixture in most households by 1939. The CBC became involved in several war-related campaigns; for example, it produced the serial *La Fiancée du Commando* to promote Victory Bond purchases.

Censors screened broadcasts from overseas, just as they did newspaper copy. The transmissions reflected the mood of a Canadian population that viewed the Second World War with less starry eyes than it had the First. The legendary CBC correspondent Matthew Halton, who covered Canadian operations in Italy and Northwest Europe, tried to inject drama into his reports, even practising his lines like an actor. Of the December 1943 battle at Ortona, Italy, he told listeners that "against an enemy fighting ... like the devil to hold us, the Canadians attack, attack, attack." Halton also noted that "the fighting in the streets resembled the antechamber of Hell."[13]

Halton's prose was not censored, but the censorship service established in September 1939 scrutinized many other communications. It did not tolerate publications deemed to be fascist, pacifist, or communist. In all, 325 printed sources were declared illegal, about 20 per cent more than during the First World War. Nearly half of these banned publications originated in enemy countries and found their way into Canada through the neutral United States. A few mainstream Canadian publications received small fines as warnings. For example, the Ottawa newspaper *Le Droit* was fined in early 1942 when it reported that Allied bombing raids against occupied France had killed many women and children.

Most Canadian-based censors were former journalists and believed it was misguided to try to shelter Canadians the way that Ernest Chambers had done during the First World War. On several occasions, Canada's censors resisted calls from the military for tighter controls, such as to obscure the very real German U-boat threat in the St Lawrence during the summer and autumn of 1942. Wilfrid Eggleston, who managed the day-to-day operations of the Censorship Branch, persuaded Mackenzie King that if the public came to equate censorship with bogus reporting, the result would be greater public anxiety and a loss of morale on the home front. The authorities considered it essential to excise certain information for military security reasons, but they also understood that the milieu had changed since Chambers's day to one where people had a more realistic understanding of combat. So they adopted a more sophisticated approach, one that managed news in a way that maintained its legitimacy in the eyes of the public.

Much of the public mobilization campaign focused on motivating Canadians to achieve extraordinary industrial output and to preserve scarce resources. The Second World War ultimately claimed over half of federal government expenditures. In the 1938–39 federal budget, only $36 million had been earmarked for defence; that figure would increase more than fivefold during the first, and least intensive, year of the war.

At first, the federal government proceeded cautiously with rearmament to show that it was not eager for war and to avoid controversies of the sort that had been associated with the Shell Committee during the First World War. One of its few prewar initiatives to rearm, a 1938 contract to produce 5,000 Bren light machine guns for Canada and Britain, ran into problems because the firm chosen, John Inglis (formerly British Engineering Limited), did not have to go through an open and competitive tendering process. Ottawa insisted that no other company had expressed interest or was as capable as Inglis of producing the weapon – a position later borne out by the delivery of high-quality machine guns on schedule. Still, to provide cover from allegations of wrongdoing, the Liberals struck a royal commission whose January 1939 report exonerated the government. Ottawa also responded by establishing a new War Supply Board to manage a tendering process for military contracts worth over $5,000. That board, however, was so cumbersome that it became difficult to obtain bidders.

Caution also characterized Canada's early contribution to the air war. Since 1936, Britain had been pressuring Canada for an agreement to train Commonwealth air crews because Canada had plenty of flat, treeless terrain ideal for this purpose. King resisted, not wanting to give the impression that Canada was preparing for war, and prodded the British to fund a greater percentage of the costs. Not until November 1939 was a deal finally reached for what became known as the British Commonwealth Air Training Plan (BCATP), under which Canada paid $313 million, Britain $218 million, Australia $97.4 million, and New Zealand $21.6 million.

When the war began, Canada had only five aerodromes; the BCATP called for the construction of sixty-four. Some of the required land belonged to Aboriginal communities, including the Mohawk of Tyendinaga Plains, Ontario, where work on an air facility started before a deal acceptable to the Native people had been reached. Before the war, Canada had been graduating about 125 new pilots annually; under the BCATP, that number rose to 1,500 aircrew per *month*.

Over time, the 1939 deal was hugely expanded until its total cost reached $1.76 billion, of which Canada paid $1.59 billion. To build facilities, Ottawa created a new directorate under R.R. Collard, the manager of a prominent Winnipeg construction company. In many cases, contractors and labourers were brought in to sparsely populated areas. For example, at Yorkton, Saskatchewan, an $800,000 aerodrome was constructed by companies and crew from Winnipeg and Saskatoon.

Northern Albertans complained that most BCATP bases were located in the south of the province. But of great significance to Edmonton and points farther north was the building of the Northwest Staging Route in late 1941, which supplied the Soviet Union with military hardware, including aircraft. The Americans, who directed the staging route, spent $60 million to build a line of thirteen small airports, eleven of which were in Canada. Between 1941 and 1944, the route accommodated some 9,000 flights by fighter and bomber aircraft.

Even greater in scope was the Alaska Highway. Managed by the US Army Corps of Engineers, it was constructed between February and November 1942 against the possibility of a

Japanese attack from the northwest. The road stretched just over 2,500 kilometres from Dawson Creek, British Columbia (already connected by road to Edmonton), to Fairbanks, Alaska, with all but 400 kilometres running through Canada. The project involved 14,000 American military personnel, 77 civilian contractors, and 6,000 civilian employees, and cost some $130 million ($1.9 billion in 2015 dollars). Most heavy equipment came from American sources, but Canadians were very much involved. Toronto's R. Melville Smith Company served as one of four civilian project managers, and thousands of Canadians were hired as construction workers. The impact on many isolated communities was profound. The US Army built water mains, sewage facilities, telephone lines, and recreational centres. The influx of newcomers spread contagious diseases among local Aboriginal populations, sometimes with deadly results. Facilities along the route, such as houses, shops, and restaurants, were often overwhelmed. Dawson Creek had been a town of 728 residents before the highway came; during construction, the population ballooned to more than 9,000. Across the country, citizens experienced first-hand the results of mobilization, which were diverse and sometimes contradictory.

The greatest economic impact came from the mobilization of resources to feed war industries. In 1940, with the end of the Phoney War, the Department of Munitions and Supply was created with C.D. Howe in charge. Howe ordered industries to shift to war production; those that refused found themselves denied resources to produce civilian goods. To speed the transformation, the department arranged for discounted loans and grants, permitted companies to write off depreciation against taxes at double the normal rate for renovations and machinery acquisition, acquired assistance from British and American technical experts, and through its War Industries Control Board secured raw materials for firms engaged in war production.

With the sweeping powers conferred on him under the Munitions and Supply Act and the War Measures Act, Howe cut through red tape to meet the needs of the war. He often circumvented the lengthy tendering process by making oral agreements with firms and sending them letters of intent so that they could get moving on production; formal contracts would follow. "Dollar-a-year men" – sector experts typically drawn from private sector firms, which continued paying their salaries – joined Munitions and Supply. Some appointments generated concern over possible conflicts of interest, for example, when the BC lumber baron H.R. Macmillan was appointed Timber Controller. But Howe insisted that qualifications trumped all other considerations and that protection from abuse had been ensured by a 5 per cent cap on profits. He had little patience for inefficient management and was prepared to have Munitions and Supply assume control over firms that failed to meet demands.

Munitions and Supply, like the IMB, targeted its huge orders at larger companies based in urban Ontario and Quebec. In Montreal alone, the gross value of industrial and manufacturing production rose from $483 million in 1939 to $1.2 billion in 1944. As before, this trend generated regional discontent, and many smaller and medium-sized firms expressed displeasure at being left out, though several did benefit through subcontracting arranged by Munitions and Supply's Industry and Sub-Contract Coordination Branch.

Munitions and Supply grew to eighteen departments specializing in areas that included Aircraft, Automotive and Tank, and Engineering Design. Before the war, Canada's aircraft industry had consisted of eight modest plants that produced about forty small planes per year. By the early 1940s, this had grown to over 4,000 aircraft manufactured annually, including some of the most modern and sophisticated for the time, such as the Lancaster and the Mosquito. The value of Canadian war production would eventually top $11 billion. Though this paled in comparison to the nearly $300 billion spent on war production by the United States and the more than £20 billion (roughly 100 billion in

Canadian dollars) spent by Britain, for Canada, war expenditures were massive, accounting for over half of all federal spending.

Where private industry was unable to respond as required, Howe, to a far greater extent than Flavelle, had the government fill the void. Munitions and Supply created twenty-eight Crown corporations. These employed 55 per cent of Canada's 104,620 aircraft workers. The scope of these corporations extended to areas such as chemicals, explosives, shells, and small arms and ammunition. With Munitions and Supply as a driving force, research and development of newer technologies played a significant role in the Second World War. The Crown corporation Research Enterprises Limited, along with British and American scientists, developed radar, optical glasses, cathode tubes, and various electrical items.

Although Canadian universities and Canada's scientific community remained modest in size, notable growth and professionalization had occurred since the end of the First World War. The NRC had moved in 1932 into its own laboratories in Ottawa. Now it became heavily involved in developing military technology; in 1940, 80 per cent of its activities fell under this category. This was bolstered by an August 1940 visit to Canada and the United States by a British Scientific and Technical Mission that sought to establish a three-way relationship that would "integrat[e] defence research, development, and production."[14]

NRC scientists made important contributions. For example, they developed proximity fuses for artillery ammunition (which exploded near a target, thus obviating the need for a direct hit), a new super-explosive called RDX, and a device to throw off the acoustic homing torpedoes used by German submarines. By 1943, it was closely coordinating with and providing funding for nearly three hundred projects at universities and other research facilities. The NRC supported scientists at the Université de Montréal working on atomic research in coordination with British and

American counterparts involved in the Manhattan Project, which developed the atomic bomb. This association was made possible by the Department of Munitions and Supply purchasing the Eldorado uranium mines in the Northwest Territories. Although Canada's involvement in producing the atomic bomb was minimal, wartime advances in nuclear research led to the construction in 1949 of the prototype CANDU nuclear reactor at Chalk River, some 200 kilometres northwest of Ottawa. Canada also produced chemical and biological weapons, such as at Suffield, Alberta, where military personnel exposed to gas underwent psychological testing.

The effectiveness of scientific research was compromised by rivalries: Canada's army, air force, and navy insisted on running their own programs. Historian David Zimmerman argues that the navy thought the "NRC was too focused on establishing its international reputation ... and did not pay enough attention to the utilization of science in the most effective way by the RCN (Royal Canadian Navy)."[15] Poor cooperation led to operational deficiencies, such as when the RCN dragged its feet in transitioning from inferior asdic (sonar) to radar for anti-submarine warfare; the NRC was the Canadian leader in radar development. Still, the overall results with military production must be judged a great success. Building on the interventionist approach of the IMB, the quality, quantity, and breadth of activity for Canada in the Second World War was remarkable.

Mobilization in the Second World War required far more control over a considerable range of goods and services. Inadequate controls during the First World War had encouraged rampant inflation that contributed to growing social unrest. Determined to avoid the same scenario, the federal government established a Wartime Prices and Trade Board (WPTB) a week before Canada declared war on Nazi Germany. The board had the power to set prices and wages, license firms to sell consumer goods, prosecute hoarders, and manage supplies.

The war generated high employment but also limited the availability of consumer goods. As had been the case in the First World War, inflation was the result. Between August 1939 and the end of 1940, the wholesale price index (based on the total cost of a representative "basket" of goods and services) rose by 14 per cent. In October 1941, the government approved a comprehensive freeze on wages and prices. Organized labour expressed its discontent, saying that wages had not yet recovered from the Great Depression; farmers argued that commodity prices were still too low. However, public opinion polls showed that some three-quarters of Canadians supported the freeze, as they recalled or knew about the destabilizing impact of inflation during the First World War. The freeze continued to garner strong support, especially as officially recorded inflation remained below 3 per cent between late 1941 and the end of the conflict.

Some Canadians were reluctant to make personal sacrifices, or even worse, they exploited shortages to line their own pockets. The number of people fined for breaking WPTB rules rose from 1,201 in 1942 to 4,170 by 1944, though officials said these numbers represented only a small fraction of rule breakers. The migration of people to urban areas, mainly to take war jobs, reduced vacancy rates to alarmingly low levels, such as to 0.25 per cent in Vancouver. Countless homeowners generously opened their doors to newcomers; even so, many tenants endured scandalously high rents. In Vancouver, where rent guidelines classified a two-storey, seven-room home near the major shipyards at $44 per month, single rooms in the area fetched as much as $60 and small houses $90.

The WPTB imposed controls in many other areas to ensure a fair distribution of scarce resources among civilians. By the end of 1940, it had prohibited appliance companies from introducing new lines; the following year, it ordered output cut by as much as half. Accompanying this process were new rules that set maximum prices on used items based on condition and age. This became particularly essential in the case of automobiles. In 1940, 102,664 cars had rolled off Canadian assembly lines; two years later, only 11,966; in 1943 and 1944, the sale of new vehicles to civilians was prohibited. Many cases came to light of used car sales exceeding the price ceiling, as well as scams such as charging the legal price for the car but exorbitant fees for accessories like car rugs. In such instances, fines were levied and perpetrators' names were printed in newspapers, but this did not bring a halt to such lucrative larceny.

Starting in spring 1942, with rubber shortages caused by Japanese expansion throughout the Pacific, only people in designated essential services were permitted to purchase new or retreaded tires. At the same time, with growing demands from the armed forces and war industries, civilian motorists began receiving gasoline coupons that limited most to 545 litres per year, enough to travel about 3,500 kilometres. The vast majority of motorists followed the rules, but counterfeit coupon rings emerged, and checks by authorities resulted in gasoline stations having their pumps padlocked for allowing people to purchase gasoline, presumably at a premium, without surrendering their coupons.

Canadians settled for less variety in clothing in order to ensure that military needs were met. Among items cut from production by 1942 were lounging pyjamas, parkas, ski suits, evening dresses, skirts longer than 50 centimetres, cloth-on-cloth designs, double-breasted suits, tuxedos, full-length dinner jackets, suit vests, long top coats, pleats, pant cuffs, epaulets, and shoulder pads. To maximize output, clothing and footwear were standardized to fewer and simpler styles. Many Canadians complained that standardization should have, but did not, translate into lower prices. They further suggested that manufacturers and retailers were grabbing extra profits by offering shoddier goods. The WPTB responded in mid-1943 by establishing a Standards

Branch to license clothing and shoe lines and to periodically check quality, though it laid few charges.

Coupon rationing extended to several consumable goods as imports became more difficult to obtain, and also because of rising demand from overseas, as well as within Canada as more civilians had money to spare. On 1 July 1942, sugar was rationed at about 225 grams per person per week. As of 3 August, those twelve or older were permitted about 110 grams of coffee or 10 grams of tea per week. On 21 December 1942, butter was restricted at 225 grams per person per week, and dropped as low as 170 grams later on. May 1943 brought alcohol rationing – to forty ounces of spirits, four bottles of wine, and thirty bottles of beer per month – as the government conscripted distilleries and breweries once again into war-related production (alcohol was used for smokeless powder for shells, for synthetic rubber and plastics, and for de-icing chemicals for planes). Meat rationing started at the same time; depending on the type and cut, the weekly allowance per person ranged from 450 to 1,100 grams.

Most Canadians adapted, for example, by sweetening their food with juices and keeping butter out of the refrigerator so that thin amounts could be spread easily. Some broke the rules, however; some butchers took bribes to provide better or extra cuts of meat. Still, polls showed that three-quarters or more of Canadians supported rationing, viewing it as their patriotic duty to make small sacrifices and as the fairest method of managing scarce resources. Certainly these were small inconveniences compared to the suffering and hardship endured by soldiers and civilians overseas.

The end of the war did not mean the end of supply challenges. Canadians held some $6.5 billion in accumulated savings, and after years of doing without, first during the Great Depression and then in wartime, they were keen to spend. The federal government implored patience, reminding Canadians that the absence of price controls after the First World War had fuelled rapid inflation and social unrest.

Under the National Emergency Transitional Powers Act, the WPTB retained control over prices, distribution, and consumption levels. Canadians heard about the critical need for food in liberated countries. Besides drawing motivation from humanitarian impulses, governments feared that desperate people overseas might become radicalized and turn to communism. Butter rationing continued until early 1947, with individual allotments set at 170 grams per week. Between June 1945 and January 1946, the sugar ration was cut by 10 per cent to compensate for devastated crops in the Philippines and Java. Meat rationing, which had been suspended in March 1944 due to transportation bottlenecks and shortages of cold storage space, returned between September 1945 and early 1947. With pressure mounting from unions, whose memberships had more than doubled during the war, wage controls were phased out in 1946. Price controls were removed from items when their supply was judged adequate to meet consumer demand, a process that was more or less completed by the end of 1947. Despite some criticisms of the management of supplies, citizens largely accepted domestic deprivations in order to support the war effort and an orderly transition to peace. Never before or since has the Canadian government intervened so much in the family life of non-Aboriginal Canadians. Seldom has it been so successful in doing so.

Both world wars required the extraordinary mobilization of material and human resources. Grassroots organization remained a central feature of volunteer efforts but became more coordinated by government in the Second World War. Censorship and propaganda were keys to mobilizing Canadians, but not until relatively late in the First World War did the federal government become extensively involved in the propaganda effort. With domestic censorship under the direction of Ernest Chambers, Canadians absorbed a heavily sanitized and romanticized portrayal of the war. In the Second World War, information management was more extensive and nuanced. Through the Bureau of Public Information, the Wartime Information Board, the National Film Board, and the CBC, propaganda played a far more prominent role. Also, the messages were more carefully honed, such as through the use of public opinion polling. As well, those managing domestic censorship understood that the horrific costs of the First World War had resulted in a home front with a more mature understanding of war – an understanding that was poorly suited to the nanny-like approach that Chambers had taken.

The debacles surrounding the Shell Committee during the First World War demonstrated the importance of strong organization and principled leadership in munitions production. With the creation of the Imperial Munitions Board in late-1915, Canada, though an industrial neophyte, transformed itself into a major arms producer. A quarter-century later, the Department of Munitions and Supply achieved even greater results. C.D. Howe controlled profits, insisted on quality and compliance with deadlines, and did not hesitate to have government take over inefficient industries or to establish Crown corporations. Finally, the mobilization of resources necessitated a growing array of government controls. The relative lack of controls during the First World War contributed to rapid and destabilizing inflation. To prevent a repetition of this, at the outset of the Second World War, Ottawa created a Wartime Prices and Trade Board whose restrictions most Canadians accepted, especially since inflation remained low.

The broader scope and more mechanized nature of the Second World War required stronger government intervention, management, and controls. Again, the First World War provided important lessons that resulted in more effective results during the Second. Missteps during the First World War demonstrated the need for careful, rigorous, and strategic government stewardship. The Shell Committee had been a debacle because the government had not established proper administrative structures or developed the appropriate skills to manage a major mobilization. The founding of the IMB showed that it realized that greater intervention was essential. C.D. Howe built upon this approach in running the Departments of Munitions and Supply, and Reconstruction. Effective mobilization that built on the lessons of the First World War prevented destructive inflation and provided better management of scarce resources through the Wartime Prices and Trade Board. Over the course of both world wars, governments became larger, but also far more professional and effective, and this produced impressive and sometimes astonishing results when it came to total mobilization.

3

Fighting the Wars on Land

Canada sent two generations of soldiers across the ocean to fight Germany and its allies in the First and Second World Wars. In both conflicts, Canadian troops operated in close partnership with the British Army. For ordinary soldiers, many fundamentals of military service – fear, confusion, fatigue, boredom, bad weather, catastrophic injury, disease, and death – are common to every war, and certainly they were to both world wars. Like the soldiers of 1914–18, those of 1939–45 fought opponents who were highly motivated and well equipped. Soldiers of both generations lived mostly out of doors for extended periods, in all weather. In battle, they often had little sense of the larger picture, and they tended to be preoccupied with their immediate situation and surroundings.

While these parallels are significant, the story of Canada's land forces in the world wars is also a study of contrasts. On the battlefield, for example, Canadians in the First World War participated in static operations (trench warfare) on the Western Front for the better part of three years. Only during the last few months of the war did the troops see wide-ranging mobile operations (open warfare). The pace of operations in the Second World War was comparatively more rapid, albeit punctuated by phases when progress seemed painfully slow to the men on the ground. Modern technology and armaments played key roles in each conflict, but the Canadian forces of 1939–45 were much more comprehensively mechanized than those of 1914–18, a period when the horse was still the dominant engine of military logistics at the front.

There are other contrasts to consider. In the First World War, the Canadian government, led by Prime Minister Robert Borden, was eager to make a major contribution of manpower; in early 1916, Borden had pledged an overseas army of 500,000 men. The country never reached that goal, but Canada did field four fighting divisions (about 100,000 men all together) organized in a single corps on the Western Front. A fifth division of Canadians was formed in Britain but never reached the front. Instead, it was broken up to reinforce the other divisions as voluntary enlistments declined. The Borden government introduced conscription in 1917 to keep the four divisions up to effective strength.

The Second World War government of William Lyon Mackenzie King adopted a more cautious manpower policy. Wishing to avoid a major political crisis such as resulted from the 1917 conscription debate, Mackenzie King at first aimed to limit Canadian army participation in the war, and by extension, Canadian casualties. Not until the Allied invasion of Sicily in July 1943, nearly four years after the outbreak of hostilities, did Canadian troops partake in sustained operations in the field. But as in the First World War, there was little time for rest from that point until final victory was won in 1945. And despite Mackenzie King's intention to limit Canada's liability, the nation's Second World War ground forces surpassed the Canadian Corps of 1914–18 in size: five divisions and two independent armoured brigades fought in Europe between 1943 and 1945. The largest Canadian formation to serve in the First World War was a corps (a grouping of divisions). But a Canadian army (a grouping of corps) fought in Northwest Europe in 1944–5.

Canada's overseas armies, in both wars, were overwhelmingly male institutions organized according to British Army custom. The language of instruction and command was

English. During the First World War in particular, almost all instructional materials were printed in English. There were a few predominantly French-speaking battalions in the First World War, such as the 22nd (the Vandoos), and to a lesser extent the 14th. The 22nd also fought in the Second World War, as did Le Régiment de la Chaudière and Le Régiment de Maisonneuve. Outside of such units, however, English was the dominant language, and most official printed materials were still English only.

There were virtually no women in khaki in the Canadian Expeditionary Force during the First World War. The nursing sisters who served with the Canadian Army Medical Corps were key exceptions – although their uniforms were blue rather than khaki! Policies changed significantly in the Second World War with the formation of the Canadian Women's Army Corps (CWAC) in 1941. But while some "CWACs" served overseas, they were generally limited to administrative and support roles; the Canadian government did not permit women to serve in the combat arms, a state of affairs that remained unchanged until the 1980s.

The First World War began in August 1914 as a war of movement. Hoping for a quick victory, five German armies poured into neutral Belgium and northern France – a theatre of operations known as the Western Front. German plans, however, did not survive contact with the enemy. Defensive action by Belgian, British, and French soldiers delayed the Germans, who in any case lacked the logistical capacity to sustain their advance. The Allies suffered major reversals in August and September but were able to stop the German onslaught on the banks of the Marne River.

After the Marne, Allied and German troops attempted to outmanoeuvre each other in a northerly "race" towards the English Channel. Neither side could seize the advantage, and in the wake of a major clash at the Belgian town of Ypres, a series of static positions formed along a front line stretching from Nieuport, on the Channel coast, to the Swiss frontier. Troops on both sides dug in to gain protection from artillery and small arms fire. The fortifications soon assumed an increasingly permanent character. Deep trenches were arrayed in echelon, one behind the next, and joined with communications trenches carved out at perpendicular angles. The troops arranged thick belts of barbed wire in between each position, so that if one trench were to fall, the next might be held until reinforcements arrived to close the breach. The trenches were permanently garrisoned, in all weather and all seasons.

Attacks against such strong defensive positions demanded massive volumes of artillery fire, and even when they succeeded, the cost in human life and materiel was high. But gains were usually limited, local, and temporary; when one side captured portions of the enemy line, the ground was difficult to hold against immediate counterattacks. With few exceptions, trench warfare persisted on the Western Front until summer 1918, when the German armies cracked and open warfare returned. As Europe's soldiers fired their first shots in August 1914, and Canadians at home rushed to join the colours, few could have imagined the enormous scale that the war was to assume over the next four years.

Canada's first contingent arrived in the United Kingdom in October 1914, too late to participate in the inaugural battles of manoeuvre on the Western Front. Instead, the Canadians spent their first winter on the rainy Salisbury Plain, in southern England. Inclement weather hampered training, but the Canadian Division (soon to be known as the 1st Division) carried on with its exercises under a seasoned British commander, Lt.-Gen. Edwin Alderson. The following February, Alderson's Canadians embarked for France, where they received practical instruction in trench warfare from British troops in the front line near Armentières.

The Canadians witnessed limited action in February and March 1915, including the tactically significant Battle of Neuve Chapelle, before moving north to the Ypres sector. Ypres was one of the few Belgian towns that remained in Allied hands after the invasion of 1914. As a transportation hub and a popular symbol of Allied willpower, Ypres was to be defended at all costs for the rest of the war.

In April 1915, the 1st Division was holding the line along with British and French divisions north of town when the German Fourth Army launched an attack using a new weapon, chlorine gas. The poisonous gas most seriously affected French units situated to the left of the 1st Division. For several days the fate of Ypres hung in the balance as the Allies rushed reinforcements to the scene. At the centre of the action, the 1st Division suffered heavy casualties: about 6,000 men, or approximately one-third of the entire division. Chlorine gas accounted for a portion of the Canadian losses, but most of the dead and wounded were probably victims of conventional small arms and artillery fire.

Thanks in part to the 1st Division's efforts, Ypres was saved from capture. Some Canadian soldiers who survived the battle saw fit to record their exploits in heroic verse. John McCrae's "In Flanders Fields," inspired by the battle, remains one of the best-known poems of the war. Others, much more forgettable, nevertheless captured ordinary soldiers' feelings. Typical is a stanza from "The Canadians' Stand at Ypres" by Corporal Jocko Vinson:

> A hard struggle at hand, and every man they could find,
> When the cry of a general soon passed through the lines,
> "For God's sake hang on, men, it's the key to the West!"
> And the boys from dear Canada sure did their best.[1]

The Canadian veterans of the 1st Division would celebrate their stand at Ypres for years to come, but the battle was not without controversy. British officers criticized the performance of two of the division's brigade commanders, Richard Turner and Arthur Currie. Turner had ordered his troops to withdraw at an inopportune moment, and Currie had left his headquarters at the peak of action in search of reinforcements. The conduct of both brigadiers was regrettable, if perhaps understandable in the circumstances.

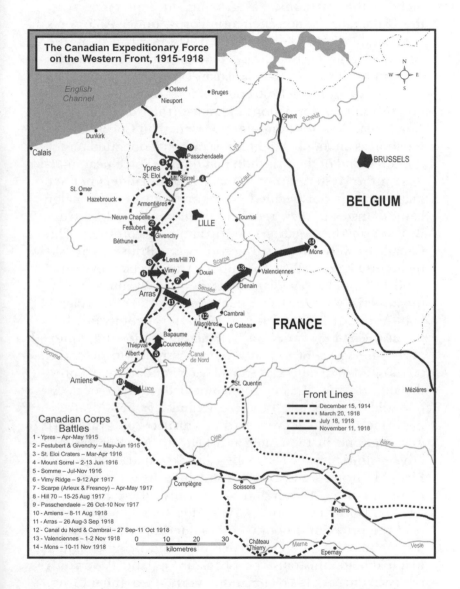

The Canadian Expeditionary Force on the Western Front, 1915-1918

Canadian Corps Battles

1 - Ypres – Apr-May 1915
2 - Festubert & Givenchy – May-Jun 1915
3 - St. Eloi Craters – Mar-Apr 1916
4 - Mount Sorrel – 2-13 Jun 1916
5 - Somme – Jul-Nov 1916
6 - Vimy Ridge – 9-12 Apr 1917
7 - Scarpe (Arleux & Fresnoy) – Apr-May 1917
8 - Hill 70 – 15-25 Aug 1917
9 - Passchendaele – 26 Oct-10 Nov 1917
10 - Amiens – 8-11 Aug 1918
11 - Arras – 26 Aug-3 Sep 1918
12 - Canal du Nord & Cambrai – 27 Sep-11 Oct 1918
13 - Valenciennes – 1-2 Nov 1918
14 - Mons – 10-11 Nov 1918

Front Lines
— December 15, 1914
••••• March 20, 1918
– – – July 18, 1918
——— November 11, 1918

0   10   20   30
kilometres

Despite the heavy losses of 1915, at Ypres and in subsequent battles at Festubert and Givenchy, Canada's investment in the war effort was growing. In September 1915 the Canadians formed their own corps, under Alderson's command, when Canada's 2nd Division arrived at the front. (An army corps comprised two or more divisions.) By the end of the 1916, the Canadian Corps had reached its maximum wartime field strength of four divisions. Like the other Dominion formations in France (the Australians and New Zealanders, for example), the Canadian Corps did not function as an independent army; rather, it operated under the command of the British Expeditionary Force headquarters on the Western Front. Canadian commanders neither made strategy nor decided where or when to fight major battles. Instead, they received operational orders from British army headquarters, and planned accordingly. The Canadians were organized according to British establishments, used mostly British equipment, and relied on British supply channels. Canadian soldiers were fully integrated in the imperial war effort, and many were proud of this fact.

In April 1916, Canada's 2nd Division fought its first battle, at the St-Eloi craters, a horrific encounter that epitomized the agony of trench warfare. Assigned to defend a series of flooded mine craters in a sea of mud south of Ypres, the men of the division could not believe their eyes. As one soldier observed, "heads, arms and legs were protruding from the mud at every yard … Thirty corpses [at least] were showing in the crater and beneath its clayey waters other victims must be lying killed and drowned."[2] Maj.-Gen. Richard Turner's 2nd Division sustained heavy losses, and it appeared that Turner and some of his subordinates had lost control of the battle. It was Alderson, however, who paid the price for a poorly orchestrated operation, losing his command of the Canadian Corps and being assigned to a token administrative post back in England. Alderson's replacement as corps commander was Lt.-Gen. Julian Byng, an energetic British officer who was to serve as Governor General of Canada after the war (1921–6).

Canadian infantrymen of the 13th Battalion consolidate a German trench
that has just been captured in the Ypres sector, July 1916. LAC, PA-000095.

In early 1916 the 3rd Division joined the Canadian
Corps. The new arrivals soon learned the harsh realities of
warfare on the Western Front, when the Germans launched
yet another attack against the Ypres sector that June. Artillery fire obliterated Canadian positions east of the town,
near Mount Sorrel and Observatory Ridge; German troops
then pressed forward to overwhelm the stunned survivors.
The 3rd Division took heavy losses (including the death of
its commanding officer, Maj.-Gen. Malcolm Mercer). But
in mid-June, the 1st Division recaptured much of the lost

ground, which demonstrated the sharp tactical acumen of its commander, Maj.-Gen. Arthur Currie.

As tragic as the Canadians' experiences had been in 1915–16, they were not uniquely difficult. All armies on the Western Front were suffering heavy losses in horrific circumstances that defy comprehension a century later. This type of warfare was new for all the forces involved. Perhaps some less than effective Canadian officers should have been sacked at the outset, but the sensitivities of Imperial–Dominion relations prevented such a course. Under Byng's leadership, however, Canadian officers and soldiers of all ranks persevered, and they would distinguish themselves in later phases of the war.

British forces on the Western Front, which had expanded significantly throughout 1915, launched a major offensive in conjunction with the French in the valley of the Somme River in July 1916. The Somme is best remembered for the carnage of 1 July; of the 120,000 British soldiers who fought that day, 57,000 were killed or wounded. These losses included the near-annihilation of the 1st Newfoundland Regiment (serving in the British 29th Division) at Beaumont-Hamel. But this was only the beginning of a gruelling five-month campaign. The Canadian Corps arrived in the sector in September 1916, in time to take part in the battle for Courcelette. It was there that tanks, a recent British invention, were employed in combat for the first time. Several of the new twenty-eight-ton machines operated in conjunction with the 2nd Division in the capture of Courcelette village.

Heavy fighting on Thiepval Ridge followed, including an infamous series of attacks against Regina Trench in September–October. The ground captured during the final stages of the campaign was of little strategic importance, yet the price had been heavy. Canadian battle casualties over a two-month period exceeded 24,000 men. Allied and German casualty figures for the entire campaign at the Somme are less certain. Estimates are that the Germans suffered about 500,000 losses, the British 420,000, and the French 204,000 (these figures include killed, wounded, and missing). The Somme came to represent the attritional reality of the Western Front: whichever side could hold out the longest would win. The losses were devastating for both sides in 1916, and time would prove that the Germans could afford them least of all.

In early 1917, the Canadian Corps – by then four divisions in strength – joined the British First Army north of Arras. The British were preparing for a major spring offensive in conjunction with French troops on another part of the Western Front. The Allies intended to break through German lines, cut off the bulk of the German Army in France, and win the war. As in 1916, it was not to be.

The Canadian objective was Vimy Ridge, to the northeast of Arras, in a sector that had already witnessed heavy fighting during the first two years of the war. French North African troops had reached the crest of the ridge in 1915 but had lacked the strength to hold the ground after costly fighting. (British troops launched no major attack against the ridge prior to the Canadian attempt.) The situation was rather different in 1917: British and Canadian forces had spent several months building transportation infrastructure and concentrating supplies and ammunition for a major push up the ridge in April. The three-month build-up for the Battle of Arras also allowed the infantry more time than usual to train for their specific roles in the coming attack, but shovel and pick were just as important as rifle and bayonet in this contest. Private James Robert Johnston, a young American who had left a lumber camp in the Maritimes to join the Canadian overseas forces in early 1916, caught his first glimpse of the front near Arras in March 1917. In the transport section of a machine gun company, Johnston was in charge of a horse team that hauled supplies up the line, often under fire. He would survive the battle unscathed, having watched many of his fellow soldiers die seemingly random deaths, the victims of unseen machine guns and distant artillery.[3]

Like other British forces on the Arras front, Byng's Canadian Corps achieved significant gains when the offensive began on 9 April; much of Vimy Ridge was under Canadian control within three days. But if the capture of the ridge was impressive from a tactical standpoint, it was also of little strategic consequence. On both the French and the British and Canadian fronts, the Allies had failed to fully unhinge German defences. At Vimy, for example, German troops simply withdrew across the Douai Plain to a new defensive position a short distance farther east. The Allies were hardly any closer to winning the war after the battle than they had been before. And the cost of limited territorial gains had been horrific: the Canadian Corps suffered some 10,600 casualties on the ridge between 9 and 14 April, including more than 3,500 men killed. How many more such victories could Canada afford?

Fighting continued in the Arras–Vimy sector throughout the summer of 1917. Byng, meanwhile, was promoted to command the British Third Army. His replacement was Maj.-Gen. Arthur Currie, a Strathroy, Ontario, schoolteacher and failed real estate speculator, who had commanded the veteran 1st Division since September 1915. Although lacking experience at the war's outset, Currie had honed his leadership and administrative skills in the two years that followed. He was the only Canadian-born officer to command the Canadian Corps during the war. His first battle as corps commander came in August 1917 with the tactically impressive capture of Hill 70, north of Arras. Like the capture of Vimy earlier that year, however, the victory at Hill 70 hardly influenced the course of the war in general terms.

After the Arras offensive, the British high command launched a new campaign in the Ypres sector. Known as the Third Battle of Ypres, and also as the Battle of Passchendaele, the fighting began in July 1917. The objective was to unhinge the German line in Flanders and liberate the Belgian ports on the English Channel. Although initial progress had been promising, heavy rains began in August, turning the battlefield into a sea of deep mud. Rather than

halt the offensive, Field Marshal Douglas Haig, command-
er-in-chief of the British forces on the Western Front, reinforced the Passchendaele sector that autumn. There was no
chance of breaking the German grip on Belgium, but Haig
wished at least to secure the limited objective of Passchendaele Ridge before winter set in.

The Canadian Corps joined the battle in time to press
the final series of attacks towards Passchendaele, against
Currie's better judgment; indeed, the corps commander
had hoped to keep his troops out of the morass. Conditions
were worse than impossible, with much of the battlefield
inundated. As one Canadian sergeant wrote, "I don't sup-
pose there is any place on earth in quite such a mess ... For
over six miles in depth the land is nothing but a sea of shell
craters, the majority of which are full of water."[4] After pausing to build corduroy roads through the mud and bring up
sufficient artillery and supplies, Currie's troops secured the
ridge in a series of limited attacks during late October and
early November.

The capture of Passchendaele cost the Canadian Corps
some 15,600 casualties. As with most actions on the Western Front, some of these men were victims of friendly
artillery fire that had fallen short. Lt. Tom Rutherford, an
infantry officer who fought at Passchendaele, believed that
his friend Jaffray Eaton had been killed by a Canadian shell.
Rutherford returned to the battlefield months later to
search for Eaton's remains. He found them. "Someone had
apparently covered him up with earth where he fell," Rutherford later recalled, "but the rains had washed his skull
clean and while I could find no identity disk I knew it was
Jaffray by his teeth which were quite distinctive. I believe
there were many more killed the same way that morning."[5]
Eaton's fate underscored the cruel reality that death came
in many forms on the Western Front, sometimes from one's
own guns.

In sum, 1917 had been a discouraging year for the Allies.
The spring offensives on the Western Front had ended

inconclusively, as had Haig's offensive in Flanders. Mutiny plagued the French Army that summer. On the Eastern Front, the Russian Army had collapsed in the chaos of revolution. The Italians (who had joined the Allies in 1915) suffered a major defeat on the Austrian front. Although the United States entered the war on the Allied side in April 1917, properly trained and equipped American soldiers could not be expected to arrive at the front in strength until sometime in 1918. The outcome of the war seemed as uncertain as ever.

As desperate as the situation may have been from the Allied perspective in late 1917, Germany's war effort was also in jeopardy. The Royal Navy had been blockading Germany since 1914, cutting its access to international trade. The Germans responded in early 1917 with an unrestricted submarine campaign against merchant shipping destined for Britain. The offensive failed to starve out the British; furthermore, it antagonized the neutral Americans badly enough to draw them into the war. German commanders were determined to settle the war in early 1918, before the American Expeditionary Force tipped the balance in favour of the Allies.

The Germans launched their final offensive on the Western Front in the spring of 1918. Artillery and assault infantry hammered British positions on the old Somme battlefields. German forces at first achieved impressive local successes, but their losses mounted quickly: the first two weeks of the battle cost the German Army some 250,000 casualties. In July 1918, French and American forces soundly defeated the Germans in the Second Battle of the Marne. Four months of heavy fighting, coupled with three years of brutal attrition, had all but destroyed the offensive capacity of the German Army.

Some smaller Canadian formations, such as the 1st Canadian Motor Machine Gun Brigade and the Canadian Cavalry Brigade, participated directly in the defensive actions of March and April 1918, often with heavy losses. But the Canadian Corps was, on the whole, spared the worst of the fighting. Currie jealously resisted British attempts to break up his formation and assign Canadian divisions to other corps. In July 1918, the Canadian forces in Europe reached their peak wartime strength of 150,000 soldiers. Among them were conscripts who had been sent overseas under the controversial Military Service Act of 1917. Consequently, the Canadians were relatively strong when the time came for the Allies to launch their own offensives in August 1918. Few could have imagined it at the time, but the war was to last only three more months. Sadly, this final stage of the conflict, known as the "hundred days" campaign, was among the most costly of the entire war for Canada. Fully 20 per cent of Canada's wartime casualties were inflicted during the Allied victory offensives of August to November 1918.

The offensives began east of Amiens, an important Allied transportation hub. The Canadian Corps, in conjunction with Australian forces, spearheaded an attack on 8 August that caught the enemy off-guard. The Battle of Amiens brought to bear the full panoply of modern arms and equipment, including artillery, aircraft, tanks, cavalry, and wireless communications. Allied troops advanced some 13 kilometres. Open warfare had returned.

German soldiers surrendered in record numbers: the Canadians alone claimed more than 9,000 prisoners, and the Allies together captured about 30,000 in the battle. Although the German high command stabilized the situation by rushing reinforcements into the area, it was evident that the morale of the German Army was broken. General Erich Ludendorff, an architect of Germany's failing strategy in 1917–18, famously wrote that "August the 8th was the black day of the German Army in the history of this war."[6]

The German Army was in crisis, but some of its field units remained capable of stiff resistance. At times they inflicted heavy losses against Allied troops when fighting rearguard actions. A Canadian junior officer described a sharp, deadly struggle against a German machine gun strongpoint at Amiens:

Fritz is on top of us ... Get the guns trained on him, make it hot for him up there! No one else will push him off this bit of hill. It is up to us. Cautiously Moreau and I raise our heads ... Crack! Moreau is hit. He falls back ... My hand is wet with blood that spurts from his chest. What a flow of blood, a fountain of blood! Moreau gasps and chokes ... then stiffens in a final convulsion and collapses. It is all a matter of a few seconds. The corpse is heavy and I push it from me.[7]

Final victory did not come cheaply to Canadian soldiers or their allies; all faced stubborn enemy defensive positions as well as ongoing logistical challenges. After three years of static warfare, the transportation system was hastily adapted to suit mobile operations. Ammunition and supply columns moved slowly over poor, overcrowded road networks.

In late August, the Canadian Corps struck the Hindenburg Line, a deep belt of defences in the Arras sector. The cost was some 12,000 Canadian casualties over about ten days. Canadian and British troops crossed the Canal du Nord in late September. To the east lay a further series of defensive lines and fortifications, barring the way to the transportation hub of Cambrai, which fell on 11 October.

After capturing Denain and Valenciennes, the Canadian Corps crossed the French border into Belgium. Even while German and Allied leaders were negotiating a ceasefire, the Canadians were fighting in Mons – the legendary site of the first encounters between British and German soldiers in the opening days of the war. More than four years later, on the morning of 11 November 1918, units throughout the Canadian Corps learned that the armistice would take effect at 11:00 am. The end did not come a moment too

soon, for in the final hundred days, the Canadians had suffered more than 45,000 casualties. The 1st and 2nd Divisions embarked on a long march into western Germany,
where they occupied a bridgehead over the Rhine under
the terms of the armistice.

Over the course of the war, enlistments in the Canadian
Expeditionary Force exceeded 619,000, including approximately 99,650 men conscripted under the Military Service
Act. About 418,000 served overseas, of whom about 47,500
were conscripts. By the most recent estimates, the war cost
more than 66,000 dead and some 173,000 wounded in the
Canadian forces. No one counted the men who returned
home emotionally broken, but the number must have been
great.

Although the Canadian Corps constituted the largest
component of Canada's overseas military effort, tens of
thousands of men served in specialist units and formations
outside of its ranks. The Canadian Forestry Corps, with a
peak strength of 31,000 men, worked in France and the
United Kingdom to supply the British war effort with vital
wood products required for troop housing, railway construction, and field works. Tradesmen serving with the
Canadian Railway Troops put their peacetime skills to work
to build transportation infrastructure in France, Belgium,
Britain, and as far afield as the Middle East. As of 1918,
nearly 14,000 men were serving with the Canadian Railway
Troops. An unknown number of Canadians also served in
regiments of the British Army.

In October 1918, 4,200 officers and men of the Canadian Expeditionary Force (Siberia) embarked at Victoria
and Vancouver to join an Allied intervention in the Russian revolution and civil war. Few Canadians witnessed
any direct action in Siberia, and by June 1919 most of the
force had returned home. After nearly four years of fighting on the Western Front, working-class Canadians – and

francophones in particular – showed little enthusiasm for intervention in a chaotic civil war.

Military historians in Canada and beyond generally agree that the Canadian Corps ranked highly among the best fighting formations in the British Empire forces. This is not to say that men in Canadian uniform were somehow braver or more committed than other soldiers. However, four years of hard experience, solid leadership, and staff work (often from British Army officers), as well as a strong sense of purpose, had welded the corps into a powerful force capable of operations on a scale few could have imagined before 1914. Of course, there was much about the war that was unanticipated. The early volunteers had envisioned a short and mobile war. Instead, they would live and die on battlefields shaped primarily by static, siege-like operations.

Just as there was no typical soldier, there was no typical veteran. Although a relative handful of men stayed on to soldier with the Permanent Force or the part-time militia after 1919, most were glad to take off their uniforms for the last time and leave army life behind. Lacking much in the way of institutional support, veterans in Canada formed their own associations, such as the Red Chevron Club, where they could revisit their war experiences in familiar company. Such groups were active well into the 1950s and 1960s. Many old soldiers, with or without physical injuries, suffered psychological trauma for the rest of their lives. Some found solace in alcohol, and perhaps others gave up on living. Most men, however, picked up the pieces of their lives in their own way. James Johnston, who had left the woods of Nova Scotia in 1916 to serve with the CEF, returned home in June 1919. After working for a time in the United States, he settled down in Moncton, New Brunswick, with his wife and children. In 1964 he travelled to France and Belgium to see his battlefields one last time. Johnston passed away in 1976 at seventy-eight years of age.[8]

Johnston and fellow veterans of the Great War likely watched with chagrin as Nazi Germany pulled the world into a second global war in 1939. This would be a different kind of war than the old soldiers of the Canadian Corps had seen. While there was never any serious doubt that Canadian soldiers would cross the ocean to fight Hitler's armies, Prime Minister Mackenzie King intended to limit Canada's human liability in the new conflict by channelling a significant part of the national effort into air and naval forces (which would, it was supposed, incur fewer casualties), as well as war production on the home front. The government's policy indelibly shaped the war experience for all three services. Canadian sailors and airmen saw action very early in the war, whereas the overseas army did not become involved in sustained fighting until 1943, nearly four years after the outbreak of war. In the meantime, Canadian soldiers spent much of the war training in Britain.

While Canada was assembling the first of its five overseas divisions in September 1939, some fifty German divisions poured into western Poland, overwhelming its defences. If the collapse of Poland was troubling for Britain and France, contemporary opinion hoped that the powerful French Army, reinforced by a small British Expeditionary Force, would be enough to halt Germany. In this context, Canada's initial overseas contingent, the 1st Division, arrived in England in December 1939, under the command of Gen. Andrew McNaughton, who had been an artillery officer in the First World War and who had served as Chief of the General Staff from 1929 to 1935.

The war had taken unexpected turns after the Polish campaign. At first, not much happened, but the so-called Phoney War of 1939–40 came to an abrupt end in April when German forces invaded Denmark and Norway. Denmark collapsed almost immediately, but British and French troops had time to intervene in Norway: elements of two Canadian battalions were slated to participate. The Canadians got as far as Scotland when their operation was cancelled. It was just as well. Norway soon capitulated to the Nazis.

German forces invaded the Netherlands, Belgium, and France in May. Allied troops rapidly fell into disarray, and the Germans soon reached the English Channel. In Operation Dynamo, Royal Navy ships and civilian craft of all descriptions evacuated some 350,000 disheartened Allied soldiers from the French port of Dunkirk. Only a small contingent of Canadian troops had set foot on the continent before the French government agreed to an armistice on 22 June. Most of the Canadian soldiers returned safely to England, having lost much of their equipment.

As France collapsed, the British people braced for a German invasion. What remained of the British Army was in a frightful state. It had abandoned its equipment in France, and its soldiers were exhausted and demoralized. In this context, McNaughton's 1st Division was among the best equipped to respond to a German landing on British shores. For more than a year after the fall of France, Canadian units stationed in the south of England, where German amphibious landings were most likely, conducted anti-invasion exercises. In a typical scenario, Canadian brigades would form up in the darkness with their motor transport and drive off in search of an "enemy" force that had come ashore. Such movements were easier said than done, as there were hundreds of motor vehicles in each brigade, and the Canadians were moving through unfamiliar territory at night. For a mechanized column, one wrong turn down a deserted country lane could take hours to sort out. The arrival of the 2nd Canadian Division in December 1940 bolstered Canadian strength in England, and the exercises expanded in scope.

Before attempting any cross-channel landing, however, the Germans needed to achieve air superiority above the English Channel. This struggle, known as the Battle of Britain, began in August and continued into late 1940. Thanks to a determined defence by the Royal Air Force, including many Canadian pilots who had volunteered in 1939, the Germans failed to seize control of the skies, making invasion unlikely in 1940. Fortunately for Britain, Hitler's pathological hatred of "Jewish-Bolshevism" and the Nazi quest for an eastern empire drew his attention to the Soviet Union. A massive group of German armies crossed the Soviet frontier in June 1941. The Nazis won a series of impressive victories during the summer and autumn, but they had underestimated the Red Army's stubborn capacity to absorb losses and continue fighting. For the next three years, much of the heaviest combat of the war took place on Soviet soil, claiming the lives of millions of soldiers and even greater numbers of civilians.

As a boy in Toronto, James Alan Roberts had followed Canadian exploits in the First World War with great interest. He eagerly enrolled in the army cadets while still in primary school, and as a young man he had served as an officer in the part-time militia. In September 1939, Roberts was thirty-two years old and working in Britain. He returned home to join the Canadian Army, albeit too late to embark with the 1st Division. In fact, there were so many volunteers for overseas service that he had to wait several months before a lieutenant's spot opened up with a Toronto regiment in April 1940. Roberts's unit sailed for Britain in 1941.

As Roberts and other Canadian soldiers stationed in Britain trained exhaustively for a German invasion that never came, the war's scope widened even further in late 1941. Japan had pursued an expansionist foreign policy in China throughout the 1930s; it now looked even farther afield for raw materials to further boost its industrial and military capacity. In December 1941, the Imperial Japanese Navy launched a preventative attack against the American naval fleet at Pearl Harbor, drawing the neutral United States into war. As a result of the Japanese offensive, Canadian soldiers were to fight their first battle of the

Second World War not against German forces but against the Japanese Army.

British statesmen and soldiers had worried about imperial security in Asia as tensions with Japan increased throughout 1940–1. In September 1941, Prime Minister Winston Churchill asked his Canadian counterpart to contribute "one or two battalions" to bolster the garrison at Hong Kong.[9] British military commanders realized that Hong Kong would fall if the Japanese attacked in strength, but hoped that Canadian reinforcements might deter Japan from further military action. Mackenzie King was willing to send troops as a deterrent. Defence Minister J.L. Ralston and senior Canadian Army commanders went along with the prime minister.

Two Canadian infantry battalions and a brigade headquarters, known collectively as C Force, arrived in Hong Kong in November 1941. The Canadians joined a weak garrison comprising British, Indian, and local troops to defend the mainland (New Territories) and the island of Hong Kong. On 7 December, Japanese forces struck on the mainland. British forces fell back to the island, where the tragedy played out.

The commander of C Force, Brigadier J.K. Lawson, was killed on 19 December in close quarters fighting, leaving Lt.-Col. W.J. Home (one of the Canadian battalion commanders) as the senior Canadian officer on the island. Home knew that a Japanese victory was inevitable: no reinforcements were expected, and the exhausted garrison had few heavy weapons. However, the British garrison commander, Maj.-Gen. C.M. Maltby, insisted that resistance must continue. It cost C Force dearly. By 25 December, when Maltby decided to surrender, some 290 Canadians were dead and 500 wounded.

The survivors suffered terribly in captivity: more than 260 Canadian prisoners of war died in Japanese hands – almost as many as had fallen in battle. After the war, some British officers claimed that the Canadians had fought unreliably. Canadian survivors retorted that Maltby had

wasted lives by continuing a hopeless struggle, the outcome of which, one Canadian officer insisted, "required
no great military genius to predict."[10] Much detail about
the Canadian experience at Hong Kong was lost with the
men who died there (or in captivity), but the weight of
evidence indicates that Canadian soldiers did the best they
could with light weapons and limited supplies of ammunition. To be sure, Hong Kong was a bitter loss for a nation
that prided itself on the exploits of its soldiers at Ypres and
Vimy in the Great War.

As the war expanded into the Pacific in early 1942, Canadians stationed in Britain soldiered on with a seemingly
endless series of anti-invasion exercises. For sure they had
had plenty of time to get acquainted with England and its
population. In the war's early months, relations between
Canadian soldiers and local civilians had been somewhat
cool. By North American standards, the British were living
under strict rationing, and they could offer little in the way
of hospitality, which the Canadians found off-putting. But
the military crisis of 1940–1 strengthened the ties between
Canadian soldiers and their hosts, who had warmed to the
newcomers. Relationships soon developed between Canadian troops and British women, leading to some 45,000
marriages as well as countless shorter liaisons.

The invasion threat subsided in 1942 as Nazi fortunes
waned in the Soviet Union. As a consequence, Canadian
Army exercises in Britain shifted from defensive operations
to offensive action and amphibious landings. The exercises may have been rigorous, but there were innumerable
problems to overcome in pursuit of effective training. For
example, as ever greater numbers of Allied soldiers concentrated in the United Kingdom to prepare for the invasion
of Europe, training space became scarce. Modern, mechanized forces required large open areas in which to conduct
realistic exercises with live fire. James Roberts, who served
with an armoured reconnaissance regiment, later recalled

that "we did have some rather ad hoc chances to test and fire our heavy weapons at a few seaside ranges but these were few and always busily occupied by many armoured units training in Britain. Even on those rare occasions we had to carefully control our firing and cease [to fire] when coastal shipping passed close inshore."[11]

Canadian troops of the 2nd Division had a chance to put their training to the test in Operation Jubilee, the controversial Dieppe Raid of August 1942. At a time when Allied forces were still too weak to launch a major cross-channel attack, raiding offered some means of striking the enemy and testing new equipment. When British authorities asked General McNaughton if Canadian troops might participate in the Dieppe operation, he detailed the 2nd Division for the role. The landing force was to secure Dieppe temporarily and complete a series of subordinate tasks: capture of prisoners, intelligence gathering, and destruction of infrastructure. If all went to plan, the troops would withdraw by sea, returning to England on the same day.

British commanders had originally scheduled the raid for July, but poor weather forced them to cancel. British and Canadian commanders agreed to remount the raid on 19 August. The British were being pressured by the Soviets to take direct action against Germany. The Canadians, for their part, were tired of training exercises and, perhaps naively, anxious to prove that they could fight as well as their fathers and uncles had done twenty-five years earlier. The final plan called for the Canadians to land infantry and tanks on the main beach in front of Dieppe, with smaller landings at Pourville, to the west of Dieppe, and at Puys to the east. British Royal Marine Commandos would attack objectives on either flank of the Canadian landings.

The German garrison almost totally destroyed the landing force at Puys on a tightly restricted beachhead that offered little cover. Anyone who visits the beach today will realize that the Canadians had little chance. At Pourville the picture was rather different: Canadian troops managed to get ashore and fight their way through the town, but lacked the time or firepower to reach all their objectives. The landings on the main beach in front of Dieppe proved largely disappointing. Only small parties of men were able to fight their way across the beach and into the streets of the town. After less than half a day's combat, naval craft evacuated survivors under punishing fire.

Fewer than half the 4,963 Canadians who embarked on the raid returned to England afterwards. Approximately 900 officers and men were killed, more than 2,400 wounded or captured. Historians continue to debate responsibility for the operation. Some argue that British officers were largely to blame for executing a flawed plan without proper authority; others contend that Canadian commanders must bear responsibility for committing their troops to the ill-advised operation.[12] This debate overlooks the fact that contemporary decision makers did not enjoy the benefit of hindsight when they launched the raid and had little sense of how a major amphibious operation of this sort might turn out. Dieppe, to be sure, taught Allied planners to avoid landing at heavily defended ports in the future – a lesson they did not forget.

British forces based in Egypt had been fighting Italian and German troops in North Africa and the Mediterranean since 1940–1. In the spring of 1943, British, American, and other Allied forces won a major victory in Tunisia, seizing complete control of North Africa. The Allies prepared to invade Sicily, with plans to unhinge Italy's faltering war effort, draw German forces away from the Soviet front, and fully open the Mediterranean for Allied shipping. The invasion, codenamed Husky, was set for July 1943. After long years stationed in England, punctuated by the disaster at Dieppe, Canada's overseas troops joined the fighting in Sicily, their first major campaign of the war.

Canadian participation in Operation Husky was no foregone conclusion. The nationalistic General McNaughton had long hoped to see his troops committed to battle all together in one army-sized formation, not as individual divisions or brigades. At the same time, segments of Canadian public opinion seemed to favour getting at least some of the troops into action. At a Vancouver meeting of the Canadian Corps Association, a veteran of the First World War expressed his concerns: "It strikes me as one of the supreme tragedies of this war that the United States, following one year in the struggle has already placed men in battle engagements in Africa while Canadian soldiers are sitting idle in England. This constitutes the greatest disgrace of the present war."[13] Such attitudes were not limited to the soapbox: Canadian soldiers themselves were tired of looking on from the sidelines. As James Roberts later recalled, the morale of young Canadian officers plummeted as they watched their British and American counterparts march off to the fighting.[14]

If a cross-channel invasion of France had been likely for 1943, or if the public had understood that a major landing was in the offing for 1944, McNaughton's nationalistic vision of committing Canadian troops to battle in a large formation might have been realized soon enough to deflect further criticism. Prime Minister Mackenzie King, although keen to limit Canadian battle casualties, accepted that some of the troops must get into action for political reasons, even if as part of a British corps. Under pressure from the Canadian government, British planners inserted the 1st Division and the 1st Canadian Armoured Brigade – some 23,000 soldiers – into the invasion plan. The 140,000-man American, British, and Canadian amphibious force landed at many points in southern Sicily on 10 July 1943.

Canadian troops came ashore with minimal losses but soon encountered strong German forces inland, where the 1st Division tackled well-defended mountain villages. Sicily's rugged terrain suited German defensive tactics throughout the campaign, but the 1st Division had trained for such challenges. The capture of Assoro was especially dramatic. Soldiers of the Hastings and Prince Edward Regiment scaled a steep cliff to take the German defenders by surprise. With effective artillery support, the "Hasty Ps" were able to hold their gains under counterattack long enough for reinforcements to arrive.

Allied troops reached Messina, across the water from the toe of Italy, in August to find that surviving enemy forces had fled to the mainland. Meanwhile, facing certain defeat in their homeland, Italian army officers staged a coup against the fascist dictator Benito Mussolini. German commanders, surmising that the Italians intended to make a separate peace with the Allies, sent troops into Italy to occupy strategic points. The stage was set for a long struggle in Italy that would last until the war's final days in 1945.

Operation Husky cost the Canadians just over 2,300 casualties, including some 560 killed. With the scars of Hong Kong and Dieppe still fresh, Canadian troops proved themselves equal to a difficult task. In addition to a stubborn opponent, the Canadians contended with blistering heat, harsh terrain, and shortages of equipment and transport. Perhaps because Sicily was situated beyond the principal Allied thrust against Germany in northwest Europe, it has never enjoyed the same prominence in Canadian popular memory as the disaster at Dieppe in 1942 or the victory in Normandy in 1944, a matter of frustration for the veterans of Operation Husky.

Husky was not the only amphibious operation to include Canadian forces in 1943. On the other side of the world, in the remote Aleutian island chain (part of Alaskan territory), Canadians participated in the invasion of Kiska. Japanese forces had occupied the small islands of Kiska and Attu in 1942. In May 1943 the US Army recaptured Attu, virtually destroying the Japanese garrison. Still smarting from the losses at Hong Kong and Dieppe, Mackenzie King was reluctant to involve Canadian troops in the Aleutian campaign. But he was also eager to please his American neighbours,

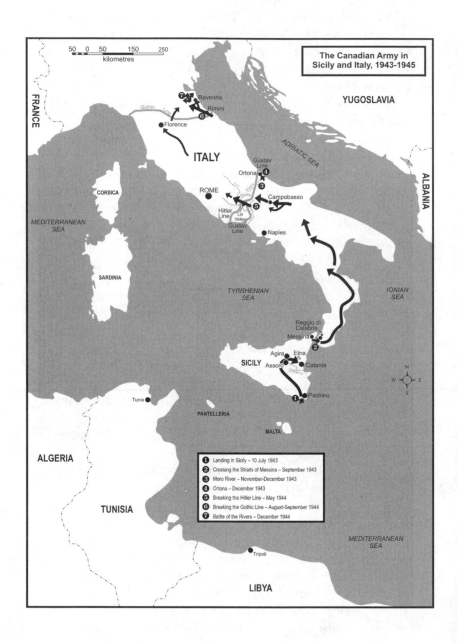

The Canadian Army in
Sicily and Italy, 1943-1945

① Landing in Sicily – 10 July 1943
② Crossing the Straits of Messina – September 1943
③ Moro River – November-December 1943
④ Ortona – December 1943
⑤ Breaking the Hitler Line – May 1944
⑥ Breaking the Gothic Line – August-September 1944
⑦ Battle of the Rivers – December 1944

and as an advocate of home defence, he was willing to commit forces to battle in the North American theatre of war. A Canadian formation, the 13th Brigade, assembled for the operation. Unlike the all-volunteer Canadian forces in Europe, the 13th Brigade included troops raised under the National Resources Mobilization Act (NRMA), a form of conscription for home defence.

The 13th Brigade was also notable because its 5,300 troops operated under American rather than British command. This was an early example of American–Canadian integration and a harbinger of closer military cooperation after 1945. The landings at Kiska proceeded in August 1943 according to plan, with one key exception: the invaders could not find any Japanese soldiers. Reluctant to repeat the bloody defence of Attu, Japanese forces had evacuated Kiska prior to the Allied landings.

Members of the American–Canadian First Special Service Force (FSSF) also participated in the Kiska operation. The FSSF had been constituted in 1942 at Fort William Henry Harrison in Helena, Montana. Its original purpose was to execute special missions against strategic targets in northern Europe, but such attacks were never carried out. After Kiska, the FSSF shipped out to the Italian front, where it engaged in heavy fighting in 1943–4.

On 3 September 1943 the Canadian veterans of Operation Husky landed in southern Italy with the British Eighth Army, gaining a foothold with little difficulty on the Italian mainland. The Italians had already agreed to abandon their German partners and make peace. But as the Allies moved into the ankle of the Italian peninsula, German commanders who had hastily occupied Italy decided to hold their ground south of Rome. The Canadians faced heavy resistance as they advanced north into the shaft of the Italian boot.

During the initial stages of the campaign, Canadian and British commanders agreed to augment Canadian strength with the 5th Canadian Armoured Division and to establish a separate Canadian corps headquarters (1st Canadian Corps) in early 1944. This was a controversial decision, for the shipping necessary to transport the 5th Division and associated corps troops from Britain to Italy was at a premium, and there was really no military requirement for a Canadian corps headquarters in Italy in the first place. Ottawa, however, was eager to underscore the role of Canadian forces: a Canadian headquarters in Italy had public relations value at home. But at the same time, the transfer of the 5th Division to Italy would reduce the strength of the First Canadian Army in England, possibly minimizing Canada's national profile in the pending invasion of France. General McNaughton, the commander of the First Canadian Army, and a nationalistic advocate for a single, independent Canadian army in the field, was unenthusiastic about a corps headquarters in Italy. His feelings on this matter, questions about his leadership skills, and personal friction with his British counterparts, were likely key factors in his decision to resign his command in December 1943. Canada's best-known army commander returned home, and in 1944 accepted a cabinet post as Minister of Defence.

In the meantime, the Canadians fought difficult battles on the Adriatic coast, most notably at Ortona. The town's narrow streets and tightly clustered buildings afforded the Germans excellent cover. Any attempt to capture the town instead of bypassing it was likely to be costly. Under pressure from higher headquarters, Maj.-Gen. Chris Vokes ordered his 1st Division troops into the town without first attempting to encircle it – an oversight that allowed the Germans to reinforce their units inside. According to historian Doug Delaney, "bashing ahead blindly cost the Canadians dearly."[15] The losses cut deeply for Vokes. One night during the battle, a divisional staff officer happened upon Vokes "having dinner all by himself in his own headquarters, and he was crying."[16]

Inside the town or beyond, the Germans were determined to hold their ground as long as they could. Canadian soldiers paid the price in a campaign marked by attrition rather than manoeuvre, not unlike in the First World War. During the first month of the Italian campaign, the 1st Division suffered 69 casualties. In December, this number climbed to nearly 4,000, including about 2,400 killed, wounded, or missing and more than 1,600 sick or suffering from neuropsychiatric disorders, known as "battle exhaustion" among the Canadians.

The 1st Canadian Corps, under Lt.-Gen. E.L.M. Burns, was organized in time to participate in the Allied advance on Rome in early 1944. Two key defensive belts, the Gustav Line and the Hitler Line, protected Rome from the south. The Canadians waited in reserve as the Allies prepared to breach the fortifications and drive up the Liri Valley to Rome. Troops from the 1st Division attacked the Gustav Line on 21 May, two days before the Eighth Army's main assault, Operation Chesterfield, was scheduled. Powerful German guns stalled the advance, leaving little choice but to dig in and wait for Chesterfield. Canadian infantry and armour broke through German lines, crossed the Melfa and the Liri Rivers, and pressed forward along the Liri Valley.

The US Fifth Army entered Rome on 4 June, ahead of the British Eighth Army. The exhausted Canadians remained in the countryside, missing the chance for a victory parade. On 6 June, just two days after the fall of Rome, the BBC announced that an Allied armada had landed an invasion force on the Normandy peninsula in France. From June 1944 until the end of the war, the campaigns in Normandy and Northwest Europe would receive first priority for resources and manpower. But the Italian campaign continued, across difficult terrain and often in terrible weather. The 1st Canadian Corps, including the 1st and 5th Divisions, remained in northern Italy until early 1945, playing a key role in breaching the Gothic Line in the north of the country. There was little the men could do but soldier on, even if important strategic developments elsewhere overshadowed their own theatre of war. They embraced a collective sobriquet: the "D-Day Dodgers," as if they had somehow avoided the "real" war in France simply to be killed or wounded on a forgotten front. Even today, Canadians are much more familiar with their army's role in Normandy than in Italy. This is perhaps ironic, given that the fighting in Italy was as bloody and unforgiving as anywhere else and that the Italian campaign was the longest in which Canadian soldiers were involved. Some 26,000 became casualties, including nearly 6,000 dead.

The Allied invasion of France in June 1944 involved amphibious landings at five beachheads, preceded by two airborne drops farther inland in Normandy. The 1st Canadian Parachute Battalion, part of the British 6th Airborne Division, helped secure the eastern flank of the Allied bridgehead during the night of 5–6 June. On the morning of 6 June – D-Day – the 3rd Canadian Division and the 2nd Canadian Armoured Brigade came ashore at three points in the landing sector codenamed Juno: Courseulles, Bernières, and St-Aubin-sur-Mer. Most of the defences on Juno had been untouched by preliminary bombardment from the air or sea; when the Royal Winnipeg Rifles came ashore at Courseulles-sur-Mer, the men discovered that naval gunfire had "failed to kill a single German soldier or silence one weapon."[17] Canadian assault troops suffered terrible losses in the battle to secure a foothold, but the casualty rate might well have been much heavier, and there was little choice but to press forward.

Allied forces immediately pushed inland across the Normandy beachhead, bracing for a counterattack. The Canadians, in their own sector, headed south towards the Caen–Bayeux highway, where they encountered elements of the 12th SS Panzer Division. The rank and file of the division were teenagers who had come of age in Nazi Germany. Their officers and senior non-commissioned officers

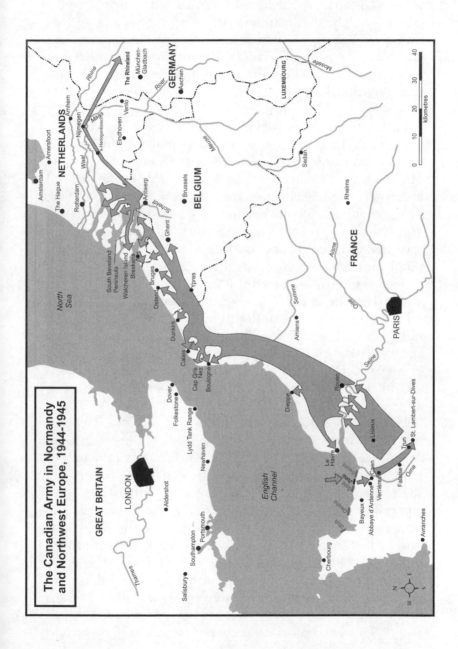

The Canadian Army in Normandy
and Northwest Europe, 1944-1945

were Nazi fanatics, hardened veterans of the brutal Soviet campaign. The commanders of the 12th SS assumed that they would easily contain and destroy the inexperienced Canadians. A stout Canadian defence proved otherwise and prevented the Germans from delivering a decisive counterstroke in the Juno sector. The Allies were in France to stay.

Early encounters between Canadian troops and the 12th SS marked the beginning of a sinister pattern: the murder of Canadian prisoners of war by 12th SS personnel. Some of the crimes occurred at the Abbaye d'Ardenne, an old monastery used as a headquarters by 12th SS commanders. Altogether, 12th SS officers and men murdered more than 150 Canadian prisoners in Normandy. According to historian Howard Margolian, "no one who has read the investigative materials relating to these crimes is apt to forget them – the crushing of several prisoners' skulls with clubs and rifle butts, the machine-gunning of dozens of POWs on a moonlit back road, the murder of the wounded, the indignities done to some of the bodies."[18] Aside from the controversial trial of Kurt Meyer, one of the SS officers implicated in the murders at the Abbaye d'Ardenne, Canada made little effort to bring the perpetrators to justice after the war.

Having failed to drive the Allies into the sea, German forces in Normandy dug in for a grinding battle of attrition. Any Canadian soldier who valued his life took care to prepare a compact slit trench, where he could seek immediate shelter from machine gun, mortar, and artillery fire. Military police prepared signs and posted them all over the battle area: "Old Soldiers Never Die! They Dig! And Fade Away into a Slit Trench!" This would have been familiar business to any veteran of the First World War. So would the other universal realities of soldiering: unsanitary conditions and the acute sickness that invariably resulted. James Roberts never forgot the bout of dysentery his unit suffered in July 1944. "This uncomfortable experience results in quick and violent diarrhea … Unfortunately, the officers' latrine had been placed on the outside (facing the enemy) of a stone wall."[19] Roberts learned to vault over the wall, do his business, and retreat to safety before German observers took note.

In July the 2nd Division joined the 3rd Division and the 2nd Armoured Brigade to constitute the 2nd Canadian Corps under Lt.-Gen. Guy Simonds, a veteran of the Italian campaign. The first task was to capture Verrières Ridge, a key terrain feature south of Caen, in Operation Spring. It was one of the bloodiest battles of the Normandy campaign. On 25 July the Canadians suffered 344 fatalities. (No other day in Normandy was more deadly for Canada, except for the landings on 6 June, which had cost 359 dead.) Under the highly stressful operational conditions of July 1944, Canadian and Allied forces suffered significant rates of battle exhaustion. In July, about one-quarter of non-fatal Allied casualties were exhaustion cases.

The fighting south of Caen, the principal urban centre and transportation hub in Normandy, ushered in the final phase of the campaign. In late July, American forces in western Normandy broke through west of Caen and poured into the open country beyond. The British and Canadian formations in the eastern sector now pressed their advance south of Caen, towards Falaise, where they could link up with American troops and encircle the surviving German forces in Normandy. August 1944 was hot and dry, and the battlefields between Caen and Falaise were often shrouded with dust thrown up by convoys of military vehicles. Many soldiers were still wearing the same clothing they had come ashore with back in June or July – uniforms that were now unspeakably filthy. In the circumstances, short visits to the army's mobile bath units were simple pleasures that any First World War veteran would also have remembered vividly.

By mid-August, the Falaise "pocket" contained the remnants of two German field armies, comprising elements of more than twenty divisions. The Canadian and other Allied units were hard pressed to contain the desperate German forces. Finally, the pocket was closed by a relative handful of troops, including soldiers under the command of Maj. David Currie at the tiny village of St-Lambert-sur-Dives. The battle for Normandy was over, with the Germans in full retreat towards the Seine. The Allies were poised to liberate Belgium and the Netherlands and press forward into Germany. Soviet forces, meanwhile, had advanced well into Poland. As the war entered its final phase, Germans braced for the invasion of the Reich itself.

Canadian forces in northwest Europe, now part of the First Canadian Army, were to play a central role in the liberation of Belgium and parts of the Netherlands in the autumn of 1944. A complex series of developments shaped the Canadian experience. By early September, the German forces in France had cracked. Allied troops, however, were running short of supplies as they advanced well beyond Normandy's limited port facilities. General Dwight Eisenhower, the American in overall command of Allied forces in Northwest Europe, aimed to secure additional ports along the English Channel coast while advancing towards Germany along a broad front. Field Marshal Bernard Montgomery, the eccentric British officer in command of 21 Army Group (and subordinate to Eisenhower), had other ideas. He argued that existing resources should be concentrated on a narrow front for a rapid advance in depth, across the Rhine into northern Germany. Eisenhower relented, agreeing to give priority to Montgomery's proposal for a combined ground and airborne offensive on a narrow front. Operation Market Garden was launched in mid-September.

In the meantime, Montgomery ordered the First Canadian Army to capture the Channel ports of Boulogne, Calais, and Dunkirk and to secure the 100 kilometre estuary leading from the North Sea to the Belgian port of Antwerp. The excellent port facilities at Antwerp had actually fallen to the Allies in early September, but the Germans continued to occupy the approaches, including the Breskens pocket (on the southern shore) and the South Beveland Peninsula and Walcheren Island (on the northern shore). Clearing these areas of German troops was no small order, especially since Montgomery had transferred away British and Polish forces that had been under the First Canadian Army's command to support Market Garden. This reallocation of troops left the Canadians with just two divisions to capture Boulogne, Calais, and the Breskens pocket. The soldiers of the 3rd Division who attacked Boulogne were actually outnumbered by its 10,000 German defenders. Most of the defensive positions were captured in close quarters fighting. The same was true at Calais.

The Scheldt Estuary assumed new significance after Market Garden failed to secure a Rhine crossing in September. The war was to continue into 1945, and the Allies required sea access to Antwerp if their armies were to be supplied efficiently. The battles for the Breskens pocket, South Beveland, and Walcheren were as difficult as anything the Canadians experienced in 1944; as the weather deteriorated and casualties mounted, Canadian soldiers' morale suffered. However, the port was finally opened to Allied shipping in the third week of November. Fighting in the Scheldt cost the Canadians in excess of 6,300 casualties, including more than 1,400 killed. As in Italy and Normandy, exhaustion cases accounted for a significant proportion of casualties.

The war of movement continued in early 1945 as the western Allies fought their way into Germany while the Soviets invaded from the east. Meanwhile, in February, in the aftermath of hard fighting for the Gothic Line the previous autumn, the 1st Canadian Corps left the Italian peninsula to join the First Canadian Army in Northwest Europe. All five of the Canadian overseas divisions and the two independent armoured brigades were now united in one theatre of war.

The veterans of the 1st Canadian Corps arrived in North-west Europe as 21 Army Group prepared for Operation Veritable, the effort to crush German defences on the west bank of the Rhine. Because the Germans were defending their home soil, the fighting was predictably heavy. After nearly a week of intense combat, Allied commanders had little choice but to halt and regroup.

As the German positions finally began to give way in late February, the First Canadian Army executed Operation Blockbuster, which was to deliver the final blow against German defences west of the Rhine. Once again, Cana-dian soldiers and officers on the firing line showed skill and tenacity in the face of a determined enemy, but they lacked adequate fire support to break through. As one offi-cer observed, that "the Canadians put up a good fight can-not be doubted, for many enemy dead were later found, but there was not sufficient direct support against well con-cealed German tanks."[20]

The First Canadian Army spent the final weeks of the war liberating the northern part of the Netherlands. Just as in October and November 1918, April and May 1945 were filled with tragedy even as victory was within sight. The war was all but lost for Germany, yet German soldiers continued to resist. Nazi administrators in the occupied Netherlands cut food supplies to Dutch civilians during the last win-ter of the war. The "Hunger Winter" had already claimed thousands of lives by the time the Canadians arrived, not a moment too soon. Fighting in the Netherlands cost 1,191 Canadian lives in April, the "cruellest month" with peace so near yet losses so high.[21] A further 114 men were killed during the last five days of the war, in early May. Reflect-ing the experience of November 1918, Canada's soldiers greeted the end of the war in May 1945 with a mixture of relief, disbelief, and anxiety. Infantryman Bob Stier recalled years later that "when the ceasefire was announced every-one unloaded their guns. That night was terrible. It was too quiet. You were so used to sleeping with shells landing all about you and machine gun fire that when it became quiet that night, nobody could sleep."[22]

After the German surrender, Canadian formations in the Netherlands were responsible for general security duties and the disarming of German divisions. The Canadians, who had suffered such heavy losses while liberating the Netherlands, found consolation in the welcome they received from the Dutch. A contemporary postcard observed: "The Germans stole our food – The Canadians our heart!" With the fighting behind them, Canadian soldiers and Dutch civilians had the chance to get better acquainted. James Roberts, then in command of a Canadian brigade, was one of many soldiers of all ranks who fell in love that summer. But wartime romances could be complicated: Roberts had left a wife back in Canada in 1941. He divorced after the war and in 1947 married his Dutch sweetheart, who joined him in Canada, one of some 2,000 Dutch women who started new lives with Canadian husbands.

Like their fathers and uncles before them, the Canadian soldiers of 1939–45 fought a different kind of war than they had expected. Except for Dieppe and Hong Kong, the overseas forces were not directly involved in combat until 1943. But for the remainder of the war, there had been little rest. Canadians were almost continuously engaged in Italy from the beaches of Sicily in July 1943 to the river valleys in the north in late 1944 and early 1945. After landing in the Juno sector, Canadian troops fought with few pauses, against steep odds, through Normandy, the Channel Ports, the Scheldt, the Rhineland, and the Netherlands. Many soldiers volunteered to continue the fight against Japan, but the war in the Pacific ended in 1945, before Canadian troops could reach that distant theatre of operations. Nevertheless, the geographic scope of Second World War operations had been considerably wider for Canadians than in the First World War.

The Canadian Army's combat experience from 1943 to 1945 was no less intense than the worst moments of the

First World War. The key difference, of course, was the generally faster pace of forward movement during the Second World War. While modern technology played a key role in both conflicts, the Second World War was much more heavily mechanized. After 1940, a single division boasted nearly as many motor vehicles as the whole of Canada's overseas forces had on hand in 1918. With few exceptions, animals were all but absent in Canada's Second World War army. The more complex technology of the 1939–45 called for better-educated troops with higher standards of technical training. Service on the front lines still demanded courage and physical endurance, but there was no substitute for technical competence.

Just over 600,000 men and women volunteered for general service in the Canadian Army between September 1939 and August 1945. The army reached its peak wartime strength in March 1945, at just shy of 496,000. In absolute terms, and also relative to the national population, the army's Second World War losses were notably lighter than in 1914–18. Nearly 53,000 soldiers were wounded, and some 23,000 died on far-flung battlefields. A comprehensive Veterans Charter ensured that survivors would be able to return to civilian life more easily than their fathers and uncles had in the 1920s.

It is fair to say that in contrast to the First World War, Canada's Second World War soldiers did not go to war happily, nor were they seeking adventure: 1939 was a long way from 1914. Unlike some of their enemy counterparts, most Canadian soldiers did not strive to be military supermen, nor did they see violence as any sound test of manhood. And yet the majority served *willingly*, in the knowledge that they were fighting for a safer and more humane world. Many did indeed believe that it was the right thing to do.

4

Life and Death at Sea

As Britain and Germany inched closer to war in early August 1914, Commander Walter Hose, the captain of the light cruiser HMCS *Rainbow*, brought his ship in to port at Esquimalt, British Columbia, to take high explosive ammunition on board. As the *Rainbow* waited for the shells to arrive, Hose received word that the powerful German cruiser *Nürnberg* was prowling somewhere off the California coast. With little time to lose, he took the *Rainbow* back to sea in the small hours of 3 August. Equipped only with old-fashioned black powder shells, the *Rainbow* would have been less than a match for an opponent like the *Nürnberg*. It was just as well that Hose's cruiser did not encounter enemy ships on its first wartime voyage, for had it been lost, there was little else available to protect Canada's Pacific coast from enemy raiders.

Although bounded by oceans on three sides, Canadians had invested little in naval defence before the First World War. Britain's Royal Navy (RN) had long provided for Canada's maritime security, but as British strategic priorities evolved in the late nineteenth century, Westminster looked to the Dominions to shoulder a greater portion of the Empire's defence burden. Between 1904 and 1906, the British closed dockyards and garrisons on either coast, at Esquimalt and Halifax, and downsized the RN's North American and West Indies Squadron (based in Bermuda).

Canada's navy was born in 1910, in a political storm that made the waters of the North Atlantic seem placid by comparison. Prime Minister Wilfrid Laurier's Naval Service Bill called for the purchase of six destroyers and four cruisers, a force that would provide for the Dominion's coastal defence and contribute to the security of merchant shipping on the British Empire's Atlantic trade routes in the event of war. The British supported Laurier's proposal, but at home in Ottawa the Conservative opposition in the House of Commons had other ideas. They argued that over the short term, Canada should forgo building its own navy and instead make financial contributions to Britain. The funds would support the construction of the RN's vaunted dreadnoughts, a new class of vessel armed with long-range 12-inch guns and driven by steam turbine propulsion systems. French Canadians tended to reject both party platforms, and the Naval Service Bill played a role in the defeat of Laurier's Liberals in the 1911 election. However, when Prime Minister Robert Borden's Conservatives attempted to pass the $35 million Naval Aid Bill for British warship construction in 1913, the Liberals used their majority in the Senate to block it. Canadians spent a lot of energy debating the "naval question," but ultimately went to war in 1914 without having built up their own oceangoing navy and without having contributed to the RN's coffers.

Canada's navy was only a little better prepared for war in September 1939 than it had been in 1914. Although Mackenzie King was much more interested in naval affairs than Borden had been during the First World War, he was reluctant to rearm too soon, lest he be accused of choosing the path of war with Nazi Germany before diplomatic alternatives had been exhausted. In stark contrast to the Borden years, however, the navy witnessed dramatic expansion after 1939; it would play a much greater role at sea in the Second World War than in the First. Indeed, naval power was a central pillar in Mackenzie King's limited liability wartime strategy, which was intended to spare heavy casualties among army troops by channelling national efforts into war production, especially cutting-edge naval and air technologies. But despite the differences in strategy between the two wars, there was one common denominator in the Canadian experience: the German submarine (*Unterseeboot* or "U-boat") threat to the merchant shipping that was the lifeblood of the Allied war effort.

Prior to each war, naval commanders in both Britain and Germany had planned for major confrontations between large fleets of heavily armed and armoured fighting ships. It was supposed that control of the seas (and merchant traffic) would be decided by the outcome of such encounters. Planners made some allowance for the raiding of enemy merchant vessels with surface ships (known as commerce raiders), but most eyes were on large fleet actions, in the tradition of Nelson's victory over the French and Spanish fleets at Trafalgar in 1805. In the event, neither world war saw truly decisive fleet actions. This was due in part to a fundamental disparity between the British and German fleets. The German surface fleets, although modern and well equipped, were relatively weaker, and German naval commanders were reluctant to risk direct confrontations with the Royal Navy. Britain, for its part, resorted to a strategy of blockade against Germany, using the strength of the Royal Navy to prevent international trade from reaching German ports. Germany's response, after its commerce raiders had been chased from the oceans, was to launch submarine attacks against Allied merchant shipping – a sort of undersea blockade.

In both wars, German submarines threatened the Allied war effort by attacking merchant shipping in the Atlantic Ocean. However, for Canadians and Newfoundlanders, the naval wars of 1914–18 and 1939–45 differed strikingly. The Royal Canadian Navy (RCN) was only in its fourth year in 1914. It lacked the infrastructure, equipment, and personnel to operate on the high seas. With Canada's military effort focused on the Canadian Expeditionary Force and the Western Front, there was little opportunity for the RCN to grow during the war. In the Second World War, by comparison, the navy expanded very quickly to meet the German threat. Unfortunately for many sailors in the Canadian and foreign merchant fleets, the RCN was not especially well equipped to protect commercial shipping from German submarine attacks, especially during the critical period between late 1941 and early 1943, when the Battle of the Atlantic hung in the balance. While RCN casualties were relatively light, hundreds of thousands of tons of merchant shipping went to the bottom, with considerable loss of life among merchant crews.

The Royal Canadian Navy, as it was known after January 1911, waged its maritime war in the shadow of the Canadian Corps' celebrated land campaigns in France and Belgium. In the first weeks of the war, Canada dispatched more than 30,000 soldiers to England, and within just two years, there were four Canadian fighting divisions in the field. The strength of the RCN paled in comparison. Canada had a handful of Fisheries Protection Service vessels earmarked for coastal patrol work; it also had HMCS *Rainbow*, stationed on the Pacific coast, and HMCS *Niobe*, on the Atlantic. The Laurier government had acquired both ships for training purposes in 1910. The *Rainbow* was a light cruiser (a small to medium-sized fighting ship) with a crew of about three hundred sailors, and displacing 3,600 tons. The *Niobe* was a powerful but dated cruiser, with a crew of seven hundred sailors, and displacing 11,000 tons.

It was perhaps just as well that the RCN had few ships, because trained naval seamen were also in short supply. In August 1914 the naval service comprised only 350 regular personnel and 250 reservists. Before the war, Canadians tended to dismiss Canada's "tin-pot" service as a poor cousin of the venerable RN. Parents of Canadian boys with naval aspirations discouraged their sons from joining the RCN, directing them instead to the British service. (One young man, James Douglas Prentice, opted for the Royal Navy under pressure from his parents. Thirty years later, Jimmy "Chummy" Prentice would distinguish himself as an officer in the RCN during the Second World War.) With volunteers few and far between, many of the sailors who manned the *Niobe* and the *Rainbow* were loaned by the RN.

The premier of British Columbia, Sir Richard McBride, took matters into his own hands when he negotiated the purchase of two submarines from an American manufacturer in Seattle, spending twice the entire annual RCN budget for 1913–14! But national defence was a federal prerogative, and McBride's rash action was a clear constitutional violation; the boats were quickly transferred to RCN control. Although delivered without armament in August 1914, the new submarines, *CC.1* and *CC.2*, deterred German raiders from operating in Canada's Pacific waters. The enemy did not know that the boats were unarmed, and no navy in 1914 was equipped with anti-submarine detection equipment. Later in the war, *CC.1* and *CC.2* were used as "tame" boats for anti-submarine training exercises on Bras d'Or Lake in Nova Scotia.

The threat of German commerce raiding off the west coast receded after the RN defeated Admiral Graf von Spee's Asiatic Squadron in the Battle of the Falklands in December 1914. The *Rainbow* missed out on the excitement, and for the next few years the little cruiser was consigned to inshore patrol work. The ship was finally laid up in 1917 when its crew transferred to Atlantic stations for more pressing duties. After 1915, Canada's naval activity focused in the Atlantic.

Naval historian Marc Milner has described Canada's war in the Atlantic as having four phases.[1] The cruiser phase, lasting into 1915, reflected more or less what had transpired in the Pacific at the same time. Operating from Halifax, the *Niobe* joined the RN's 4th Squadron in pursuit of German commerce raiders and merchant ships. Tellingly, only about forty of the *Niobe's* seven hundred sailors were from the RCN; the rest were volunteers from Newfoundland, or men on loan from the RN. Worn out by the autumn of 1915, the *Niobe* was relegated to depot duties. It was badly damaged in the Halifax Explosion of 1917 and sold for scrap three years later.

In 1915, as the Allies gradually eliminated free-ranging enemy cruisers, the German navy began to employ submarines more aggressively. Even the largest and best-armed surface ships were highly vulnerable to attacks by submarines, whose potential had been demonstrated in September 1914, when *U-9* sent three British cruisers to the bottom in a single hour's action.

The German submarine campaign of 1915 was a response to the distant blockade that the RN enforced against Germany's maritime trade. Unlike "close" blockades, distant blockades operated well beyond the hazards of the enemy's shore defences and coastal patrols, but they were still able to control the sea lanes leading to enemy ports. The British effectively restricted merchant ships' access to Germany with a minefield in the English Channel and cruiser patrols between Scotland and Norway. The blockade slowly strangled Germany's ability to fight the war by cutting off trade with neutral nations. Except for the Battle of Jutland off Denmark in 1916, the commanders of Germany's powerful High Seas Fleet made little attempt to break the blockade through direct surface action, for fear of losing their expensive ships in battle with the Royal Navy.

Germany's best alternative to fleet action was to employ submarines against merchant shipping destined for the British Isles. In February 1915 the German Navy began to implement a policy of unrestricted submarine warfare. This meant that U-boats were essentially free to attack any ship, firing torpedoes or deck guns without warning. The campaign was immediately effective but also highly controversial. For example, on 7 May 1915, *U-20* sank the liner RMS *Lusitania* off the Irish coast, killing about 1,200 civilians, including many Americans. The US government responded with strong diplomatic notes to Germany. While the Americans were not yet prepared to enter the war, their protests convinced the Germans to discontinue the unrestricted campaign temporarily.

The prospect of long-range enemy submarines prowling the western Atlantic frightened Canadians and Newfoundlanders. The submarine threat characterized the second phase of Canada's Atlantic war, from 1915 through 1917. Although no one was quite sure in 1915 how far German submarines could actually venture from their bases, London warned Ottawa that U-boats might well reach Canadian waters.

Preoccupied with the war overseas, the Canadian government hesitated to invest in a patrol force, so Admiral Charles Kingsmill, the director of the RCN, turned to private sources. He enlisted coast watchers and a number of small launches known as the Motor Craft Reserve to prevent U-boats from establishing fuel and supply caches on remote stretches of the Canadian coast. The Eaton family's yacht was commissioned into the RCN in July 1915. John Eaton arranged for the purchase of another yacht, which was armed and commissioned as HMCS *Grilse*. Aemilius Jarvis, a Toronto businessman and sailing enthusiast, helped acquire additional yachts from American sources. The newly commissioned yachts joined with Fisheries Protection Service vessels to form the St Lawrence Patrol. This "odd collection of ships" comprised the RCN's first ever wartime fleet.[2]

Anti-submarine defence in North American waters assumed greater urgency in July 1916 when the submarine freighter *U-Deutschland* completed a transatlantic journey to Baltimore, where it took on a load of raw materials for the German armaments industry. If *U-Deutschland* could complete the long journey, it seemed probable that attack submarines were not far behind. Indeed, in October 1916, *U-53* sent several merchant ships to the bottom off the New England coast. The Borden government finally ordered a dozen Battle Class trawlers to bolster Canada's anti-submarine patrol capacity for 1917. Named for battles fought on the Western Front, these vessels were about 40 metres in length and armed with 12-pounder guns and depth charges. The first of the trawlers was completed in late 1917. Crews could only be found by decommissioning the *Rainbow* on the west coast.

The third phase of Canada's war in the Atlantic coincided with Germany's renewed campaign of unrestricted submarine warfare, which began in February 1917. The Allies had intensified their naval blockade during 1916, seriously threatening Germany's food supply. With a stronger force of U-boats than it had possessed in 1915, the German navy aimed to starve out the British and force them to the peace table. There was little doubt that the submarine campaign would draw the United States into the war on the Allied side, but German commanders intended to defeat Britain before the Americans could muster an overseas expeditionary force of any consequence. The 1917 unrestricted submarine campaign did indeed inflict enormous damage on Allied commercial shipping, but it failed to end the war on German terms. The British compensated for food losses with strict rationing and began convoying their merchant ships under naval escort to discourage U-boat attacks. The convoys significantly reduced losses to submarine attacks, nullifying the German strategy.

Some Canadian patrol vessels were fitted with depth charges and hydrophones (primitive underwater listening devices for detecting submarines), but even the very best equipped were hardly up to the task of chasing German submarines on the open ocean. Despite their inadequacies, the mere presence of Canadian ships deterred the enemy from approaching merchant convoys in the western Atlantic during 1917–18.

The fourth and final phase of Canada's naval war in the Atlantic involved the defence of coastal shipping against submarine attacks in 1918, with minimal assistance from the RN or the US Navy (the Americans had entered the war in April 1917). German U-boat activity in Canadian waters peaked in the second half of 1918. That August, *U-156* set the schooner *Dornfontein* on fire, blew up several American fishing boats, and preyed on a series of Canadian schooners. One of *U-156's* larger victims was the Standard Oil tanker *Luz Blanca*, destroyed on 5 August.

Canadian anti-submarine efforts were hindered by inadequate patrol craft, poorly trained crews, and confusion over command arrangements and responsibilities on shore. Canadian patrol vessels squandered the few chances they had to actually attack a U-boat, such as when the *Hochelaga's* captain avoided contact with *U-156* later in August. The officer in question was later dismissed from the naval service.

For Canadians on the Atlantic coast, the naval war was very much a local affair rather than a distant overseas adventure. With the trauma of the December 1917 Halifax Explosion still fresh, *U-156's* rampage of August 1918 seemed to confirm the navy's ineptitude in the public imagination. But if a handful of German submarines had enjoyed more or less free range in Canadian waters, it is also true that they had claimed few ships of any significance thanks to the convoy system. It was simply too risky for a German submarine skipper operating so far from home to risk even minor damage to his boat by attacking a convoy. (Submarines of the period spent much of their time on the surface recharging their batteries, and in any case they had to surface to use their deck guns). All of this meant that, despite notable sinkings to their credit, the U-boats in the western Atlantic had relatively little to show for their efforts in strategic terms by the time the war ended. The naval war had been a close call for Canada, for if the conflict had continued into 1919, the U-boats might have operated even more aggressively in Canadian coastal waters.

At the height of the submarine campaign, from May through September 1917, German U-boats sent some five hundred British merchant ships to the bottom, threatening the lifeline of military equipment and supplies that was feeding the Allied war effort in Europe. By war's end, Germany had sunk some 7.8 million tons of British shipping, 900,000 tons of French shipping, and 450,000 tons of American shipping. Neutral countries also suffered heavily: Norway lost 1.18 million tons, Sweden more than 200,000. To compensate for such heavy losses, Canadian shipyards had built merchant vessels to order for the British Imperial Munitions Board. It is surprising that, despite the strain that shipping losses placed on international capacity, Canada made little effort to develop its own merchant navy until very late in the war. Early in 1918, the Borden government ordered a fleet of freighters from Canadian yards, to be operated by the newly established Canadian Government Merchant Marine (CGMM). In all, the government ordered some sixty-three ships of varying sizes and designs. But the role of Canada's merchant navy was even more anticlimactic than that of the RCN. The CGMM ships missed the war entirely; none entered service before early 1919. After the war, the CGMM was taken over by Canadian National Railways but failed to turn a profit as shipping demand dropped off to peacetime levels. The ships were gradually sold for bargain prices during the interwar years. By 1935, a mere ten remained in government service. By 1936, just before the last of the ships were disposed of, the CGMM had a deficit of $16.5 million on its books (nearly $277 million in 2014 dollars). Ironically, just as the Canadian government rid itself of the last of its ill-fated merchant navy of 1918–19, the nation was on the verge of a new conflict with Germany in the course of which merchant shipping capacity would be even more important than in the Great War.

The RCN had survived its first global conflict, but the years of peace between 1919 and 1939 were hardly less challenging than the Great War. Canadians lost interest in military affairs after 1918, and by the 1930s, tight budgets precluded investment in expensive naval hardware. In 1933, facing major cuts in defence expenditures, Maj.-Gen. Andrew McNaughton, the Chief of the General Staff, proposed that the RCN be scuttled all together, with the funds thereby saved going to the militia and the Royal Canadian Air Force (formed in 1924). Naval officers fought back, narrowly saving their service from annihilation.

The navy's chances improved as the international situation deteriorated. In 1935, Hitler's Germany began to rearm for war. Facing the prospect of a new conflict with Germany, and hoping to avoid the heavy casualties of the Great War, Prime Minister Mackenzie King's Liberal government favoured naval investment, although perhaps less enthusiastically than senior naval officers. In January 1939, the RCN planned for a new fleet of destroyers (speedy, manoeuvrable, long-range fighting ships), minesweepers, and anti-submarine vessels for duty on the Atlantic and Pacific coasts. Although the government scrapped this ambitious building plan before the war started, the RCN was indeed destined to expand rapidly, if not in the terms that naval officers imagined.

The January plan, revolving as it did around destroyers, was designed primarily for action against enemy surface fleets rather than anti-submarine warfare (ASW). While there was a chance the Germans might launch unrestricted submarine warfare against commercial shipping, as they had at various points during the First World War, this seemed unlikely to many naval officers in the late 1930s. After all, the 1917–18 campaign had failed to cut the Atlantic sea lanes, while angering Americans and drawing the United States into the war on the Allied side.

Even if the Germans did launch a submarine campaign in the next war, key naval experts doubted it would amount to much. Commodore Percy Nelles, the Chief of Naval Staff, did not see the submarine as a serious threat to merchant shipping.[3] Although the German submarine campaign of

1917–18 had sent a high volume of merchant shipping to the bottom, its strategic impact had been limited by a relatively simple countermeasure: the convoy system. German submarine captains launching attacks on convoys risked dangerous encounters with armed escort vessels, British or Canadian. Furthermore, the grouping of many merchant vessels together into a single convoy reduced the probability of any single ship coming into contact with an enemy submarine in the first place.

Also, from Nelles's perspective in the late 1930s, technology seemed to favour surface action. In the final stages of the First World War, the Allies had developed acoustic devices to detect submarines. By the early 1920s, a somewhat effective underwater sound locating and ranging device known as "asdic" (a name possibly derived from the Allied Submarine Detection Committee that was formed to study the problem in 1918) or "sonar" (sound navigation and ranging) was in service. But as operational experience in the Second World War was to show, asdic/sonar was fallible, and, under certain conditions, practically useless.

In fairness to Nelles and his interwar contemporaries, Nazi Germany's submarine fleet was relatively small on the eve of the Second World War. During the late 1930s, instead of focusing their naval rearmament on submarine construction, the Germans had invested heavily in powerful new surface ships. This seemed to confirm the assumptions of British and Canadian naval officers that the next naval war would be a surface war.

On the outbreak of the Second World War, the RCN faced two immediate and familiar challenges: it needed new ships, and it needed sailors to operate them. At that time, almost no training infrastructure existed to manage a large volume of naval recruits, and Canadian shipyards were restricted as to the types of vessels they could actually produce. Both factors shaped the Canadian naval experience throughout much of the war.

For political as well as military reasons, the Mackenzie King government wanted to build the ships on the navy's wish list. Shipbuilding contracts would help revitalize the Canadian economy, and naval expansion suited the prime minister's limited liability strategy. Canadian shipyards, however, could not build the Tribal Class destroyers the RCN needed to operate in conjunction with a British surface fleet. As in the Great War, British firms were too busy with their own war contracts to offer much in the way of technical assistance to Canadian yards. As well, shipbuilding capacity in Britain was too far stretched for the RCN to purchase British-manufactured destroyers in the short term.

As a stopgap, Canadian naval authorities proposed a corvette building plan. Compared to destroyers, corvettes were smaller and less sophisticated ships, and the Canadian yards could construct them. The RN had already decided to use corvettes for coastal anti-submarine duties, so it made sense for the RCN to do the same. Moreover, if Canada specialized in corvette construction, perhaps it could trade home-built corvettes for British-built fleet destroyers. In early 1940, the government contracted for fifty-four corvettes, about half of which were intended for RCN service and half for trade to the RN in exchange for new Tribals. The barter scheme fell through shortly afterwards when Canadian and British authorities failed to agree on a rate of exchange. So the RCN introduced more corvettes into service over a shorter term than originally planned.

Sailors could not be trained quickly enough for the growing corvette navy. After the first few corvette crews put to sea and gained experience, they were broken up and reassigned throughout the service to help fill out the companies of newly commissioned ships. This policy was understandable in the circumstances, but it also played havoc with operational efficiency at sea: crews changed just as they developed a capacity for teamwork. Schemes to accelerate naval training were insufficient. Given the limited Canadian training infrastructure, naval authorities agreed to "loan" recruits to the Royal Navy for training. Canada had trouble getting these men back once their training was complete, for the British were also short of personnel.

With the corvette building program under way, the RCN brought other classes of ships into service. In 1940 the navy acquired three liners for conversion to Prince Class armed merchant cruisers: the *Prince David,* the *Prince Henry,* and the *Prince Robert.* Displacing about 5,700 tons, and nearly 120 metres in length, these passenger liners were armed for convoy escort duties and later converted to infantry landing ships for amphibious operations in Europe.

As of May 1940, Canada's destroyer fleet included six River Class vessels, each displacing about 1,300 tons and 98 metres in length. That year they were augmented by six of the slightly smaller Town Class destroyers. New to the RCN, they were actually former American destroyers that had been passed to the British in the so-called Destroyers for Bases Agreement. In exchange, the Americans had received basing rights in Bermuda and Newfoundland.

Canadian sailors "seldom loved and more frequently hated" the old Town Class, but in the circumstances, any ships were better than none.[4] The British accepted Canadian orders for four Tribal Class destroyers in 1940–1, but the first of these was not commissioned until 1943. Throughout the crucial phase of the Atlantic war (from late 1941 to early 1943), the RCN operated with a relatively small number of dated destroyers, along with a fleet of corvettes that had been intended solely for coastal patrol duties.

By international standards, Canada's deep sea merchant fleet was also relatively modest during the early part of the war. In September 1939, fewer than forty oceangoing merchant ships were sailing under Canadian registry. Altogether, these vessels employed only about 1,450 men, although there were certainly many other Canadian sailors serving aboard ships of foreign registry. Canada's merchant shipping capacity gradually expanded after the war's outbreak, augmented by ships seized from the enemy, the ships of friendly occupied nations, and coastal vessels and Great Lakes freighters that were not really designed for the North Atlantic. In the mounting struggle against the U-boats, it would be the merchant crews rather than the navy seamen who suffered the heaviest loss of life. The *Erik Boye*, a Danish freighter taken over by the Canadian government in 1940, was the first of nearly sixty Canadian-flagged merchant ships to fall victim to enemy action. The *Boye*, like so many others, was destroyed by a U-boat.

On 3 September 1939, just hours after Britain declared war, the German submarine *U-30* spotted the passenger liner *Athenia* sailing to the west of the British Isles. Although Hitler's regime had elected not to pursue an unrestricted submarine campaign against commercial shipping for the time being, the *U-30* fired two torpedoes, scoring one hit. The *Athenia* did not sink immediately, but more than one hundred lives were lost during its evacuation. The *U-30*'s captain later claimed that he had mistaken the *Athenia* for a troopship or an armed merchant cruiser. Once again, the German submarine fleet threatened Atlantic shipping.

Foreseeing this eventuality, both Britain and Canada had brought merchant shipping under naval control for convoying purposes in late August. There were essentially four types of Atlantic convoys: slow eastbound (SC) convoys, fast eastbound (HX) convoys, slow westbound (ONS) convoys, and fast westbound (ON) convoys. Ships that could not manage more than 10 knots sailed with SC or ONS convoys. Ships that could make between 10 and 15 knots sailed in HX or ONS convoys. Faster ships sailed alone as independents. Canadian escorts groups were generally responsible for slow convoys – a factor in relatively high loss rates among Canadian-escorted shipping later in the war.

In the early stages of the war, escorts accompanied the convoys only partway across the ocean, since submarine attacks were most likely in coastal waters around the British Isles. Eastbound convoys, for instance, would be escorted by

Canadian ships for about two days' sailing time out of Halifax and would proceed unattended through the mid-ocean. As the convoys approached the Irish coast, they would be picked up by RN escorts.

The RCN's Atlantic war took its first major turn after German armies invaded France in May 1940. By early June, the Allies were losing the battle on the Western Front and British troops were preparing to withdraw from the continent. In the wake of Operation Dynamo (the evacuation of the British Expeditionary Force from the port of Dunkirk), Britain braced for a German invasion. Canadian River Class destroyers arrived in British waters to join the RN's anti-invasion screen.

The invasion never came, in part because the German air force failed to achieve air superiority above the English Channel. But with the French coast now under enemy control, the complexion of the naval war changed dramatically. Operating from French bases such as La Rochelle and Lorient, German submarines enjoyed direct access to Atlantic waters without having to dodge RN ships in the North Sea. Britain had been spared invasion, but Germany was in an excellent position to sever the sea lanes that carried vital war material and reinforcements to Britain from the United States, Canada, and the rest of the Empire. The submarine war began in earnest, and Canada's sailors joined the first line of defence.

As German submarines ventured into the mid-Atlantic during the winter of 1940–1 in search of merchant shipping to prey upon, convoy escort operations demanded greater effort and coordination. British and Canadian naval authorities realized that convoys needed continuous protection from Germany's aggressive submariners throughout the transatlantic journey. Merchant ships could no longer be left on their own in the mid-Atlantic.

In 1941, Britain and the neutral United States divided the globe in two strategic zones in the event that the Americans joined the conflict. The US Navy would oversee much of the Pacific and the western Atlantic, while the British covered the eastern Atlantic. For practical purposes, these terms came

Canadian sailors on convoy escort duty operate an anti-aircraft gun aboard the destroyer HMCS *Assiniboine*, July 1940. Ships from the convoy are visible in the background. LAC, PA-104057.

into effect even before the Americans entered the war. Further discussions determined that Canada would be responsible for its coastal waters and would provide five destroyers and fifteen corvettes to join US Navy forces in the western Atlantic for escort duty with the Newfoundland Escort Force (NEF).

The NEF facilitated "end to end" escort protection for the convoys, with Canadian escorts based at St John's. At a point several hundred kilometres east of St John's, they picked up eastbound convoys setting out from Halifax and escorted them into the frigid waters of the North Atlantic

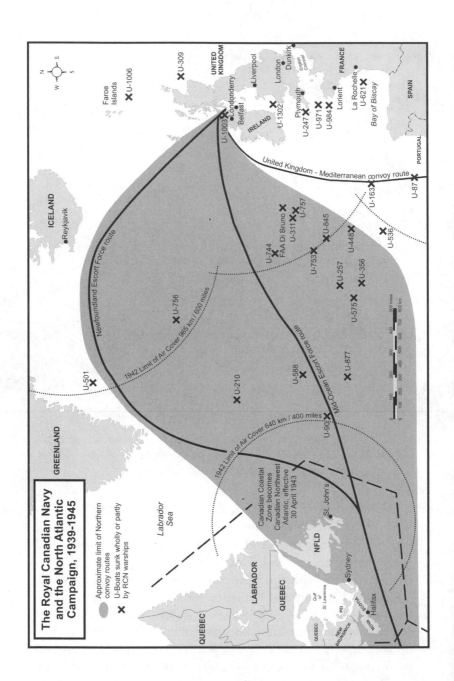

The Royal Canadian Navy and the North Atlantic Campaign, 1939-1945

Approximate limit of Northern convoy routes

✕ U-Boats sunk wholly or partly by RCN warships

on a course for Greenland. At the Mid-Ocean Meeting Point approximately 2,000 kilometres southwest of Reykjavik, Iceland, the Newfoundland-based escorts handed over the convoys to RN escorts, who ushered them the rest of the way to the British Isles. After leaving a convoy, NEF ships carried on to Iceland for fuel, repairs, and, too rarely, a short rest. From there they set out again to pick up west-bound convoys sailing out of the British Isles.

Neither Canadian sailors nor Canadian ships were especially well prepared for an anti-submarine role in the mid-ocean in 1941. The Canadian Navy was hard enough pressed teaching basic seamanship to new recruits, let alone specialized anti-submarine warfare skills. There was little opportunity for escort ships to exercise as teams against actual submarines. Canadian corvettes had originally been slated for coastal patrol and escort duties, not long voyages into the mid-Atlantic. British corvettes had been modified for deep-sea sailing; Canadian corvettes had less living space for the crew. Like British corvettes, the Canadian ships carried 4-inch guns as their main armament, but the secondary armament on Canadian ships was much weaker: machine guns instead of the 2-pounders on British ships. For the time being, Canada's corvettes were equipped with magnetic compasses that were insufficiently stable for accurate navigation or pursuit of enemy submarines. Effective anti-submarine operations required a gyrocompass for accurate navigation, but there were not enough available in Canada at the time. Asdic sets on Canadian ships were also out of date. British corvettes were fitted with breakwaters to help keep certain parts of the ship reasonably dry in heavy seas. Canadian versions lacked this modification. Given the hard lessons of the naval war during 1917–18, the poor state of Canadian ships and equipment in 1941 was especially lamentable.

To say that a transatlantic crossing in a Canadian corvette was a trying experience would be putting it mildly. With a length of about 62 metres and a beam (width) of 10 metres, the small ships gained well-deserved notoriety for pitching and rolling. More than a few green sailors suffered awfully from seasickness as they went about their duties. A naval veteran recalled standing watch on his first voyage aboard HMCS *Agassiz* in 1942: "The motion of the ship climbing up and down each rolling swell got my stomach heaving. The next thing I knew I was throwing up all over that corner of the bridge."[5] A sailor who served on HMCS *Sorel* observed that "while corvettes were very seaworthy they were the next thing to perpetual motion. That introduction made my time on [larger] ships, a destroyer and a frigate, seem luxurious."[6] Another navy man summed up the tribulations of corvette sailing very neatly, quipping that most "old corvette vets rated the enemy as follows: 1) a winter North Atlantic gale; 2) a summer North Atlantic gale; 3) the U-boat."[7] Even in the absence of the enemy, naval escort duty on the North Atlantic Run was not to be taken lightly.

With the pressing need for convoy escorts in 1941, the Canadian Navy had to use the ships and crews that were available, whatever their deficiencies. The first NEF escort group to sail with a convoy put to sea in June. That convoy, HX-129, was the first of the war to be escorted throughout its journey across the Atlantic. Although no U-boats attacked HX-129 directly, the Germans sank some ships that fell out of station. Both HMCS *Chambly* and HMCS *Collingwood* made asdic contact with enemy submarines, but search efforts broke down due to mechanical and technical problems aboard the *Chambly*. This was not the last time that technical problems thwarted Canadian efforts.

HX-129 had escaped with relatively light losses; by contrast, the fate of SC-42, which sailed the first week of September, was tragic. A small escort group was responsible for screening sixty-five merchant ships carrying steel, iron ore, lumber, wheat, oil, and motor vehicles. Two additional RCN ships set out to reinforce SC-42 as a pack of U-boats prepared to pounce.

The *Muneric*, an ore carrier, was the first victim. The ship's heavy cargo pulled it to the bottom in an instant. As the escorts rushed about picking up stragglers and looking for the U-boats, the Germans launched several more attacks. By the time British naval reinforcements and air cover arrived, the submarines had claimed sixteen vessels: one-quarter of the merchant ships in the convoy. The only consolation for the RCN was the sinking of *U-501*. Two escorts had surprised the submarine, driving it to the surface with a depth charge attack. When the submarine crew refused to surrender, the corvette *Moose Jaw* rammed the boat, sending it to the bottom.

The sinking of *U-501* was the RCN's first known submarine kill, but on balance, SC-42 had been a disaster. The attacks seemed to indicate that the escort group had been under strength (RCN escorts were outnumbered by U-boats), less than adequately trained (the fleet had expanded too quickly), and improperly equipped for ASW (RCN ships lacked effective radar to detect surfaced U-boats). According to historian Marc Milner, SC-42 "was a devastating defeat for the fledgling escort fleet and one of the salient events of Canadian naval history."[8] The losses shook British and American faith in Canada's ability to escort merchant ships, a process that continued throughout 1941–2. Unfairly, however, British critics of Canadian performance tended to focus on training shortfalls while overlooking insufficient escort strength and poor equipment.

During the first two years of the Second World War, as in the First World War, German submarines had generally operated individually and independently. As the Allies increased the strength of their escorts and closed up the gap in the middle of the Atlantic in 1941, Admiral Karl Doenitz, in command at the German submarine fleet's headquarters (*Befehlshaber der Unterseeboote*, or BdU), implemented the "wolf pack" tactics that had so ravaged SC-42. Submarines conducted their patrols in long lines astride a likely convoy route. When one of the boats sighted a convoy, the captain signalled its location and course to BdU using a high-frequency radio transmission. BdU, in turn, transmitted this information to other boats in the patrol line. While the captain who first sighted the convoy shadowed the merchant ships, the wolf pack formed up along the sailing route. Once all available boats were on station, they were essentially free to attack, without any further central direction from BdU. Small, poorly equipped escort groups like the one that sailed with SC-42 could scarcely cope with multiple submarines operating in packs.

Given the tactics employed by BdU and the general condition of the RCN at the time, there was nothing surprising about the outcome of battles such as SC-42. While the RCN wanted for many things in late 1941, it was most deficient in radar equipment. Escort ships operating without radar may seem unthinkable in hindsight, but it must be kept in mind that radar was a cutting-edge technology in 1941; its "correct" application was not yet widely apparent. As a Canadian radar specialist serving with the RN later recalled of this period, "in those days nobody really knew much about radar and you found two things happen: one, you had to convince somebody it was worth carrying and when that was achieved, you had to convince them that it couldn't tell you what kind of cigarettes a pilot was smoking when he was flying an aircraft."[9] In other words, non-specialists tended either to underrate or overrate the capabilities of radar.

At the beginning of the war, Canadian naval authorities underestimated the value of radar and, more generally, paid insufficient attention to role that science could play in Canada's effort. One historian of science has argued that the navy was the least committed of the three armed services to a scientific research program and that it did not cooperate easily with the National Research Council (NRC).[10] Only in 1940, many months after the war began, did the navy ask the NRC to design a Canadian version of the British type 286 radar set. By the time the Canadian version, known as "Surface Warning, 1st Canadian" (SW1C), was first tested at sea in the spring of 1941, it was already obsolete. The Royal Navy had since adopted the type 271, which was much more effective at detecting submarines. The NRC set out to develop its own version of 271, but it was not available until 1943 and did not work properly in any case. Meanwhile, Canada's sailors were left to fight the convoy battles at a major technological disadvantage.

If poor radar capability represented the RCN's greatest blind spot, the service also suffered from a shortage of destroyers for escort work in the mid-Atlantic. Within the escort groups, the destroyers had the speed and agility to chase off U-boat packs as they formed up along convoy routes. Sadly, the precious few destroyers in service with the RCN in 1941–2 were not especially well equipped. A key deficiency – perhaps second only to radar – was the lack of high-frequency direction-finding (HF/DF) sets. German headquarters used high frequency radio transmissions to communicate with U-boats, and these signals could be a wolf pack's undoing. The HF/DF sets in Allied hands were capable of detecting outbound transmissions from U-boats as they arrived on station and made contact with headquarters. Two or more sets operating on separate escort ships could reveal each U-boat's position through triangulation. The converging pack could then be chased off or at least kept at bay by the destroyers.

While most RN destroyers were equipped with HF/DF during 1942, the RCN lagged behind. Only one Canadian destroyer, HMCS *Restigouche*, carried HF/DF in 1942. Lt.-Com. Desmond Piers, the captain of the *Restigouche*, had acquired the set on his own initiative from British sources. It cost him a "bottle of booze," but the trade was more than fair.[11] It seemed that Naval Service Headquarters in Ottawa did not fully grasp the dimensions of the equipment shortfalls on Canadian ships.

With overworked crews and poorly equipped ships, escorts could not prevent the enemy from exacting a heavy toll on the convoys in late 1941. A new low was reached in November, when U-boats converged on SC-52 not far from Newfoundland. Fearing heavy losses, British naval authorities ordered the convoy, whose escort group comprised mostly Canadian vessels, as well as British and French ships, to return to Canada. Even then, four ships were lost to U-boat attacks, and two more ran aground in heavy fog. This was the only instance in the entire war when U-boats actually forced an Atlantic convoy to turn about. The cancellation of convoys, if it were to become commonplace, would spell the end of the Allied war effort in Europe, for Britain's survival, and its role as an advanced Allied base, depended on Atlantic supply routes. Naval Service Headquarters and the Canadian government had committed the RCN to a vital role that it was not properly equipped to perform. But the Canadian escorts had been supplied upon urgent request from the British Admiralty. In the dire circumstances of 1941, partly trained and equipped escorts were perhaps better than none at all.

Not long after the SC-52 incident, the strategic context of the naval war changed once again with the Japanese offensives of December 1941 and early 1942. The RCN had been cooperating with the still-neutral Americans in the NEF since June 1941 – evidence of the closer defence relationship between the two North American nations since 1940. Although not technically under American command, Canadian naval forces in the western Atlantic were, for practical purposes, under the "direction" of the US Navy. This somewhat irregular state of affairs was tolerable as long as the US Navy contributed to escort duties in a meaningful way. Now at war against Japan and Germany, the US Navy began to shift its strength from the Atlantic to the Pacific, leaving the British and Canadians to take up much of the convoy escort work in 1942. Meanwhile, BdU was sending its U-boats farther west than ever before, preying on shipping off the east coast of the United States with deadly effect. That spring, more than 90 per cent of the shipping lost in the Atlantic went to the bottom near the American coast. The Americans did not employ convoys to protect coastal shipping, despite having worked closely with the RN and RCN on convoy duties in 1941, and despite compelling evidence from both world wars that convoys minimized shipping losses.

To help stem the tide, the NEF supplied escorts for the new Western Local Escort Force (WLEF), which was responsible for shielding vulnerable coastal shipping on the eastern seaboard of North America. By March 1942, the WLEF was escorting convoys between Boston and Halifax, where they formed up for the Atlantic crossing. This reallocation was facilitated, in part, by redrawing the convoy routes the NEF had followed in 1941. The Newfoundland-based escorts had taken the merchant ships as far as Iceland, where they were then picked up by RN escorts; the new sailing plan for 1942 followed the great circle route. This shorter trans-Atlantic route omitted the stopover at Iceland, taking the original escorts all the way to the convoys' terminus in Northern Ireland, where there were much better basing facilities in any case. In February 1942, escort groups from the former NEF, now reorganized as the Mid-Ocean Escort Force (MOEF), began to follow the great circle route. Under the new arrangement, MOEF escorts picked up their convoys off the coast of Newfoundland.

The U-boats were inflicting catastrophic damage on Allied merchant shipping by 1942. In addition to the tonnage lost, some 25,000 merchant seamen, most of them British, had become casualties of sinkings during the first two years of the war. Reprising the Borden government's 1918 decision to form the Canadian Government Merchant Marine, the Canadian government established a new Crown corporation, the Park Steamship Company, in April 1942 to bolster Allied shipping capacity and keep the tenuous lifeline to Britain open. The 10,000-ton *Prince Albert Park,* the first of the "Park" ships (each was named after a Canadian park), was ready by June. Canadian yards delivered four more ships by year end. The rate of deliveries increased in 1943, and peaked in 1944, with nearly two ships completed per week that year. By the end of the war, 176 ships had flown the Park flag. Their crews were heavily Canadian and included men from many walks of life, from experienced sailors to teenagers who had only just caught their first whiff of the ocean.

By the time the bulk of the Park fleet was plying the trade routes in 1944–5, the Allies had brought the German U-boat threat under control. Over the course of the war, the enemy would sink only four Park ships, representing less than 7 per cent of Canadian-flagged merchant ships that were lost. Almost 90 per cent of Canadian merchant sailor casualties occurred before the end of 1942.[12] The infusion of Park ships helped offset earlier wartime shipping losses. Yet, the Park building program accounted for only a fraction of Canada's wartime ship construction. In all, Canadian yards completed more than four hundred freighters and tankers, many of them for the British merchant fleet. Canada also turned out more than 480 corvettes and minesweepers for naval service.

While the RCN was heavily engaged in convoy protection, the submarine war moved into Canada's very heart in 1942. Since the submarine crisis of 1918, Canadian naval experts had worried about the damage that submarines might inflict in the Gulf of St Lawrence and the St Lawrence River. These inland waters were ideal for submarine operations, for deep trenches offered shelter on the bottom and the shoreline was sparsely populated. Notwithstanding the dangers that U-boats posed to merchant shipping in the St Lawrence, the Canadian government decided not to implement any significant defensive measures upon the outbreak of war – a policy that remained unchanged until early 1942. The RCN was simply too hard pressed with its Atlantic escort duties to worry about the St Lawrence. As long as no U-boats appeared, merchant ships sailed independently and without escort protection.

The status quo in the St Lawrence was upset in May 1942 when *U-553* sailed into the Gulf through the Cabot Strait. During the night of 11–12 May, *U-553* sent two merchant vessels to the bottom. As the survivors came ashore in lifeboats, the RCN responded by holding shipping in port until convoys could be arranged. Canadian and American patrol aircraft scoured the surface for any sign of submarines. This flurry of activity discouraged the captain of *U-553* from making further attacks, but the navy and air force could spare few resources to maintain their presence.

A second submarine found its way into the St Lawrence in June. *U-132* ventured much farther west than *U-553*, attacking a Quebec-to-Sydney convoy and sinking three ships. HMCS *Drummondville*, a minesweeper, spotted the U-boat and gave chase, driving the boat underwater and attacking with depth charges; *U-132* went very deep to avoid air patrols. The boat reappeared in July to attack another convoy in daylight. Escorts proved unable to track down the submarine, in part because extreme temperature variations in the river water layers rendered asdic equipment all but useless.

Coming so close to home, the U-boat attacks in the St Lawrence triggered a political firestorm in Ottawa. With good cause, Quebeckers accused the government of neglecting local defences. Angus Macdonald, Minister of National Defence for Naval Service, retorted in the House of Commons that Quebeckers were too quick to complain and should face the German threat more stoically. As the Quebec press called the government to task, two more German submarines, *U-517* and *U-165*, entered the Gulf of St Lawrence. They began their work in earnest, claiming an American troopship and two merchant vessels. In early September, *U-517* sank the steamer *Donald Stewart*, narrowly escaping retribution from the corvette *Weyburn*. Once again, temperature variations in the water blinded the asdic equipment.

The two U-boats were only getting started. In September they claimed nine more ships in short order, including the armed yacht HMCS *Raccoon* and the corvette *Charlottetown*. Most of the *Charlottetown*'s crewmen were able to abandon ship. Sadly, as the *Charlottetown* sank, its depth charges exploded, killing many sailors who had not yet been pulled from the water.

One of the greatest tragedies in Canadian inshore waters came in October 1942 with the sinking of the Nova Scotia–Newfoundland civilian ferry SS *Caribou* in the Gulf of St Lawrence. Although the *Caribou* was under escort, the pitch darkness cloaked *U-69* while it made its deadly attack. Of 237 passengers aboard *Caribou*, 137 died in the sinking.

The German hunters had one or two near runs with disaster, such as when Royal Canadian Air Force patrol aircraft pounced on *U-517*, dropping depth charges but failing to destroy the boat. The RCN seemed powerless to stop the U-boats, partly because asdic equipment was so ineffective in the gulf's complex waters, and partly because there were not enough escorts available. The Atlantic battles absorbed heavy resources, and on top of that commitment, the RCN had agreed to provide seventeen corvettes for Operation Torch, the Anglo-American landings in French North Africa planned for November 1942.

With the RCN escort fleet stretched to the limit, there was little option but to close the St Lawrence to ocean traffic in September (local traffic would continue along the river until freeze-up). This was a clear embarrassment for the government, for it indicated that despite the commitment of Canadian forces overseas, the homeland was far from secure. It did not help that not a single German U-boat had been sunk during the action. The RCN could not defend home waters while shouldering the burden of Atlantic escort duty and other overseas commitments.

While the St Lawrence garnered much of the press coverage in Canada in 1942, a larger struggle was under way in the Atlantic. Early that year, the U-boats concentrated their strength against unprotected American coastal shipping. By spring the Allies had tightened up defences in coastal waters (by establishing the WLEF, for example). This prompted BdU to renew its efforts in the mid-ocean, beyond the effective range of coastal air patrols. (Almost a year would pass before the Allies introduced "very long range" (VLR) patrol aircraft to the mid-ocean in 1943.) In early 1942, furthermore, the German U-boat fleet was growing, and Allied intelligence services were no longer able to read North Atlantic U-boat signals traffic after the German navy introduced new cipher equipment in February. This intelligence deficit made it more difficult for convoys to avoid U-boat patrol lines.

The gravity of the situation was evident in the German victory against ONS-92, a slow westbound convoy, in May 1942. The escort was under the command of an American officer aboard the US Navy destroyer *Gleaves*, but there were four Canadian corvettes in the group. During the first night of the battle for ONS-92, the U-boats sank five ships. A day later, the Germans claimed two more. Although the escort commander had been warned that U-boats were in the area, he had been slow to react. The Canadian corvettes were, contrary to normal procedures, preoccupied with picking up survivors from the stricken merchant ships, and had missed opportunities to confront the U-boats. (When U-boats remained active around the convoy, it was better to drop life rafts or to leave the rescue work to designated ships in the convoy.)

While the British might criticize the Canadian corvettes for failing to engage U-boats during the battle for ONS-92, it was also true that the Canadians were now pressed beyond the limit. The advent of the MOEF made matters worse for the Canadians. NEF ships sailed only as far as Iceland; MOEF escorts followed the great circle route all the way to Ireland. The longer voyage was too much for the RCN's aged Town Class destroyers. This shifted a disproportionate share of the burden to the more capable River Class ships. The RCN simply did not have enough modern destroyers in the spring and summer of 1942.

The Royal Navy ascribed Canadian setbacks in the mid-ocean primarily to the rapid expansion of the RCN and incomplete training. This assessment was not entirely unfair, but it overlooked the technological deficits the RCN faced, as well as the shortage of modern destroyer escorts. British critics also seemed to forget that Canadian escort groups, more often than not, were responsible for shepherding slow convoys. These spent 29 per cent more time at sea than fast convoys, increasing the chances of enemy contact. Sheer chance also played a role in the Canadian experience. Through no fault of their own, Canadian escort groups were intercepted by U-boats at twice the rate of British groups. Still, further losses in December 1942 seemed to confirm British suspicions that poor training was to blame for the RCN's problems. British prime minister Winston Churchill asked Mackenzie King to withdraw Canadian escorts from the mid-ocean temporarily. In Ottawa, Naval Service Headquarters agreed that Canadian escorts would benefit from refitting and retraining but chafed at the implication that Canadian escorts were solely at fault for heavy losses. The withdrawal of Canadian escort groups was a blow to the officers and men who had sailed them under the most difficult conditions.

During the early months of 1943, the Canadian escorts rotated through a series of assignments with the Royal Navy around the approaches to the British Isles, as well as on convoys between Gibraltar and Britain. These involved shorter cycles than in mid-ocean, leaving more time for training courses and the refitting of ships. There was also less enemy activity in the eastern Atlantic than in mid-ocean. Besides calling in the ships loaned out for Operation Torch, the RCN received six refitted destroyers from the British. When the reconsolidated Canadian Navy returned to mid-Atlantic escort duty in May 1943, it was stronger and better equipped than in 1941–2.

The Atlantic campaign had changed dramatically in the spring of 1943 after senior British and American leaders agreed to allocate sufficient long-range aircraft to cover the neglected skies above mid-ocean, where U-boats had been prowling without having to worry unduly about enemy air patrols. The Allied navies also formed support groups that could bolster regular escorts in the event of U-boat encounters. By mid-year, heavy losses had forced the U-boats to withdraw from the principal Atlantic trade routes for the remainder of the war. The Atlantic shipping lanes were finally reasonably secure.

After the Canadian escorts returned to mid-ocean, they largely performed close escort roles; the mostly British support groups engaged in much of the direct action against the U-boats. As important as the close escorts were, it was the support groups that won most of the accolades. Mackenzie King was dismayed that the RCN was not garnering the recognition due to it from the British and Americans. But the prime minister, and Canadian sailors, could take some pride in the founding of the Canadian Northwest Atlantic Command, under Canadian Rear Admiral L.W. Murray, in April 1943. It was the only theatre of operations commanded by a Canadian officer in the Second World War.

Notwithstanding a series of refits in early 1943, RCN ships were on average still less well equipped than their Allied counterparts. Later that year, Angus Macdonald, the Minister of National Defence for Naval Service, ordered an investigation into the matter, which revealed what Canadian sailors already knew too well: many Canadian ships lacked gyrocompasses, effective asdic and radar, and hedgehog (an anti-submarine mortar system). Macdonald's investigation had been sparked by seagoing RCN officers who had grown frustrated with the apparent failure of Naval Service Headquarters to properly equip Canadian ships. Staff at headquarters insisted that they had indeed informed Macdonald of the navy's technical problems. A major rift between Macdonald and headquarters ensued, resulting in the dismissal of Percy Nelles, Chief of the Naval Service, in early 1944.[13] In this instance, as in many others, the government had the last word, but this did not absolve Macdonald of his share of responsibility for the fleet's wartime problems.

Throughout the harrowing years of transatlantic escort duty, the RCN had helped ensure that vital supplies and sufficient numbers of troops safely reached the United Kingdom, the strategic island base for the Allied counteroffensive against Nazi-occupied Europe. But if the RCN's primary function throughout the war had been convoy escort, Canadian sailors also distinguished themselves in surface operations. In 1944 the RCN played an integral role in Operation Overlord, the Allied invasion of Normandy. The fleet's four new Tribal Class destroyers joined an RN destroyer flotilla that January to begin clearing the English Channel of German naval traffic that threatened the final preparations for the invasion. The older River Class destroyers, meanwhile, were reassigned to anti-submarine groups in the English Channel. One of the new Tribals, HMCS *Athabaskan*, was lost in action against two German destroyers just five weeks before D-Day; 128 Canadian sailors died in the sinking.

On the morning of 6 June, Canadian minesweepers led the American assault force that landed at Omaha Beach. Later, RCN corvettes protected troop reinforcement convoys in the Channel. The armed merchant cruisers *Prince David* and *Prince Henry* operated with three flotillas of Canadian landing craft to ferry assault troops ashore in Normandy. Almost exactly four years after the British Expeditionary Force had withdrawn from Dunkirk in 1940, RCN ships were in the heat of the action as Allied soldiers assaulted the Normandy beaches. About 7 per cent of Allied naval strength in Operation Overlord was Canadian – a notable contribution, given the ongoing commitment to convoy

duty in the Atlantic. Overcoming its difficulties with training and equipment in the early years of the war, the RCN
had evolved into a powerful and effective anti-submarine
force by 1944. That spring, Canadian sailors under Murray's command, equipped with new frigates and improved
corvettes, assumed full responsibility for convoy escorts in
mid-ocean, now a truly Canadian theatre of war.

As the war against Germany reached its final phase, Canada's navy was finally commissioning the types of ships it
had wanted since 1910. In October 1944 the British transferred the *Uganda*, a light cruiser, 169 metres long, displacing 8,800 tons, and bristling with nine 6-inch guns, to the
Canadians. The following spring, a second light cruiser,
HMCS *Ontario*, entered Canadian service. In April 1945,
the *Uganda* joined the British Pacific Fleet (BPF) for operations against Japan, the only Canadian ship in that theatre
of war. At the time, no one could be sure how much longer
the war with Japan would continue; the RCN planned to
send a large force into the Pacific, including a pair of light
carriers, a pair of cruisers, seventeen destroyers, thirty-six
frigates, and eight corvettes during 1945–6.

Such a fleet would have required something like 50,000
sailors. The Mackenzie King government, always sensitive to
the political ramifications of overseas military expeditions,
wondered how the force would be generated. While the
95,000-strong RCN was an all-volunteer service, the government was reluctant to transfer tens of thousands of sailors
from the Atlantic to the Pacific upon Germany's surrender.
After much confusion, the government decided that serving RCN sailors should be asked directly to volunteer for a
new term of service in the war against Japan. "Volunteers"
from within the RCN would be granted a thirty-day leave
in Canada before joining a ship in the Pacific theatre. This
attempt to avoid political controversy at home by sending
an "all-volunteer" force to the Pacific backfired. Permanent
Force naval officers were incensed that the government had

asked them to volunteer for a specific posting in time of war when they had already accepted such duties as part of their professional responsibilities. Likewise, men who had volunteered for the RCN for the duration of the war – that is, until Germany *and* Japan were defeated – did not understand why they should be called to do so a second time. As long as Canada was at war, they were ready to remain at their posts. But if given the option, many would gladly go home.

The government's volunteering policy was especially problematic for the *Uganda,* which was the only Canadian ship in action against the Japanese at the time. (As part of the BPF, the *Uganda* had supported the April 1945 American invasion of Okinawa.) If a significant proportion of the crew refused to revolunteer, there would be little choice but to return the ship to Canada until replacements could be found. This is exactly what happened; two-thirds of the nine-hundred-man crew decided not to volunteer for continued service in the Pacific conflict, and the ship withdrew from the British fleet in July. Arrangements were made to assemble a fresh crew and to dispatch the *Uganda* and other RCN ships back to action, but the Japanese surrendered before that could happen. It is not difficult to understand why so many of *Uganda's* crew opted out – they worried about finding postwar employment, and they feared that their wives and families would become upset if they did not return home at the earliest opportunity.

Canadian involvement in the fighting at sea evolved considerably during two global conflicts. In the First World War, the Borden government channelled most of Canada's effort into the Canadian Expeditionary Force, paying far less attention to naval affairs. The nation lacked a true oceangoing navy, was unable to counter the German U-boat threat, and did not begin building a merchant fleet until the eleventh hour. By the late 1930s, the navy was much more central to Canadian defence policy. However, the service's rapid expansion and heavy commitments significantly strained its capability after 1939, drawing much criticism from the Royal Navy. Meanwhile, the sailors of the corvette navy persevered against the odds, escorting vital merchant trade to Britain throughout the darkest hours of the war. By 1944, the RCN had assumed primary responsibility among the Allies for North Atlantic convoy protection, under a Canadian theatre commander. The navy's personnel strength had increased by a factor of fifty since 1939, from 1,800 officers and men to about 95,000 all ranks. Its strength was smaller than that of the Royal Canadian Air Force (RCAF) or the army, but its strategic role was perhaps the most important of all three services, for without control of the shipping lanes, there could be no war effort overseas. By 1945, it was the world's third-largest navy, with more than four hundred ships in commission. The toll on RCN sailors was 2,300, including some 1,800 killed.

The Second World War witnessed the development of a thriving Canadian merchant navy. In the late 1930s, about 12 per cent of Canadian exports were carried on Canadian merchant ships; by 1945, 60 per cent. But with the end of the war in 1945, and a sharp decline in shipping demand over 1946–7, the Canadian government lost interest in the merchant fleet and offered the Park ships for sale to private buyers. Many of the first to be sold went to Canadian companies and remained under Canadian registry, but foreign buyers soon lined up, and the fleet gradually dissolved. Roughly 12,000 Canadians served on Canadian-flagged ships during the war. More than 670 of them lost their lives, meaning that the merchant navy suffered a much higher fatality rate than the RCN – a mark of total war. It is unclear how many Canadian merchant sailors were employed on foreign ships, but all together, between 1,100 and 1,600 died in service, including those on Canadian ships.

In the final weeks of the war against Japan, senior naval officers lobbied for a rather large peacetime force that would include two cruisers, two aircraft carriers, twenty destroyers, and 20,000 men. On the heels of a general election victory that produced yet another Liberal majority government, Mackenzie King had no intention of maintaining such a large force. The sudden defeat of Japan in August meant that the days of the 95,000-strong world-class RCN were numbered. Within two years, it counted fewer than 10,000 all ranks, with one operational cruiser and five destroyers. Yet the war at sea proved to Canadians that they did not live in a fireproof house. Enemy submarines had easily infiltrated Canadian waters – indeed, it was discovered that a German U-boat crew had landed on a remote part of the Newfoundland coast to set up an automated weather station during the war. The emerging Soviet threat, and general concerns about Canadian maritime sovereignty, rescued the naval service from oblivion. During the Cold War, it once again assumed a principal role in anti-submarine operations, echoing the Battle of the Atlantic.

Whether serving in the RCN or the merchant fleet, most sailors were glad to return to civilian life – and dry land – after the war. Still, few would soon forget their years at sea, and it is fair to say that the experience was life-changing for many. After serving as an officer on corvettes, Thomas Holland Burdon happily went to work for Zellers. But following naval tradition, he christened his first-born son in a ship's bell. And he named his eldest daughter after an RCN corvette.[14]

5

Battles in the Air

In the winter of 1909, J.A.D. McCurdy coaxed his biplane, the *Silver Dart*, into the sky for a short jaunt over Baddeck Bay, Nova Scotia. The *Dart* was a product of the Aerial Experiment Association, formed in Halifax two years earlier by inventor Alexander Graham Bell. The *Dart*'s ascent over Baddeck was more than a personal triumph for a small group of pioneers: it was also Canada's first successful powered airplane flight. That summer the Department of Militia and Defence permitted McCurdy and associates to demonstrate their flying machine at Camp Petawawa, Ontario, a military training camp that had been established in 1905. The trial flights went well at first, until the fragile aircraft was badly damaged during a heavy landing. It was an uncertain beginning for Canadian military aviation, but Canadians were destined to play key roles in the air wars of 1914–18 and 1939–45.

The first half of the twentieth century witnessed advances in powered flight that added a third dimension to warfare. From a tactical perspective, aircraft filled vital roles in support of ground forces in each war, although the machines of 1939–45 were much more powerful and reliable than their 1914–18 predecessors. In strategic terms – that is, in the use of air forces to strike directly at the enemy's home front and population – the First World War efforts were relatively limited compared to those of the Second World War. Due to evolving technology and ideas about the primary function of airpower, strategic operations tended to eclipse tactical ones during the Second World War.

Setting aside key advances in aviation technology, any comparison of Canada's air experiences in the two world wars raises institutional and organizational contrasts. Canada fielded no air force of its own during the First World War. Instead, young Canadian men with a taste for flight joined the various British air services, and some distinguished themselves in the public imagination as bold fighter pilots. The Canadian government created the RCAF only in April 1924, nearly six years after the war ended. Throughout the interwar period, the RCAF was a small organization whose very survival seemed at times to be in doubt. This changed on the eve of the Second World War, when Prime Minister Mackenzie King's government looked to the air force (much as it did to the navy) as a suitable instrument of limited liability. That is, it would spare Canada from high numbers of army casualties like those suffered during the First World War.

While Canada's Second World War airmen served widely in all branches of the air force (with Royal Air Force [RAF] and RCAF units and formations), few individual aviators achieved the enduring myth status of their First World War predecessors. Perhaps this was partly because most of Canada's airmen in the Second World War served with RAF Bomber Command in the strategic air campaign against Germany. Unlike the aerial warfare of 1914–18, the strategic bombing campaign of 1939–45 was a collective effort, one that focused less on individual exploits. Contrary to Mackenzie King's projections, the strategic air war proved to be very costly, both for the airmen and for the civilians whose cities were destroyed. To a greater extent than the battles on land and at sea, the strategic air war's legacy is one of enduring controversy.

In the last years of peace before 1914, Militia Headquarters in Ottawa showed some interest in forming an aviation section, but the government did not allocate funds for this purpose. As the official Canadian air historian later observed, Prime Minister Robert Borden's policy "towards aviation, and particularly towards the idea of the formation of a Canadian air force, was variously negative, indifferent, inconsistent, and puzzling."[1] Consequently, Canada, unlike Britain, went to war without an air service in 1914. As the conflict intensified, Ottawa was so heavily preoccupied with Canada's commitment of ground troops in the Canadian Corps that air matters rarely received much official attention. Canadians joined the British air services, but Canada did not field a distinct national air force of its own during the war – a notable contrast to the Canadian Corps on the ground.

Canadians may have been uninitiated to war in the sky, but aerial warfare was not completely new in 1914. During the Italo-Turkish War of 1911–12, Italian pilots flew airplanes on reconnaissance missions and bombing attacks against enemy forces in Libya. At the outset of the First World War, the major powers immediately employed aircraft for reconnaissance purposes, sometimes with dramatic consequences. For example, timely reports on German troop movements from a reconnaissance pilot instrumentally shaped the Allies' response to the invasion of France in 1914. There was little air-to-air combat during the first months of the war, however, as aircraft were unarmed, except for personal small arms carried by crewmen.

As the war on the Western Front entered its static phase in 1915, aircraft came to play increasingly important reconnaissance and intelligence-gathering roles. Airborne spotters helped direct artillery fire by searching for targets and reporting on the effects of fire. Aircraft equipped with cameras provided timely information for mapping enemy defences, artillery emplacements, and transportation infrastructure. Early aerial photographers flew haphazardly at low altitudes, capturing distorted oblique images with handheld cameras. As the art of aerial photography progressed, cameras were mounted on the sides of airplane fuselages so that images could be captured at higher altitudes with the lens aimed perpendicular to the ground. Such images, less distorted than oblique shots, were essential to accurate large-scale map making. In this manner, aircraft played a vital role in Canadian soldiers' war on the ground.

From the opening of hostilities, lavishly illustrated news periodicals published detailed images of military aircraft in action for a reading public fascinated with the latest technology. Canadian soldiers serving in or near the firing line had front row seats, often pausing in their daily routines to observe aerial encounters. In a typical engagement in late 1915, soldiers watched a British aircraft tangle with a German opponent. At an altitude of just one hundred feet, the German's engine stalled. By the time he restarted it, the plane was well within range of infantry small arms fire, which brought it down, killing both the pilot and his companion observer. In another instance from those early days of the war, a German Albatross shot down a British airplane above Canadian lines. Soldiers rushed to the scene and found the observer wounded but the pilot somehow uninjured. Most aviators who crashed were not so lucky.

The novelty of such incidents punctuated the monotony and tedium of trench life. At the same time, however, the troops began to take enemy aircraft more seriously. Hostile aircraft posed only a limited threat of direct attack; much more dangerous were the prying eyes of aerial observers and photographers. The Allies and the Germans alike responded by developing special anti-aircraft mounts for machine guns and field artillery. These weapons were sometimes fitted to motor trucks for rapid response when enemy planes appeared. Despite these adaptations, Canadian officers in the trenches complained of insufficient anti-aircraft defences throughout 1915.

Most of the early aircraft were slow and awkward two-seaters, carrying a pilot and an observer. Faster aircraft armed with machine guns soon took to the skies to attack observation and reconnaissance craft. The first British aircraft designed for air-to-air combat, the Vickers FB5, reached the Western Front early in 1915. Known as the "Gun Bus," and fitted with a forward-firing machine gun, the FB5 was a two-seater pusher aircraft, meaning that its propeller faced rearward, with the engine behind the crew compartment. Tractor aircraft, with engines mounted in front of the crew compartment, and with forward-facing propellers, gradually superseded the pushers for combat roles. The better-streamlined tractor aircraft were capable of higher speeds than the pushers.

A key technological problem remained to be solved before the tractor airplane could become an effective fighting platform: how to mount and operate a forward-firing machine gun without shooting up the propeller. In early 1915 a French pilot developed a simple if imperfect solution by fastening metal plates to the propeller blades to protect them from bullets passing through the propeller arc. A breakthrough came that spring with the new German "interrupter" gear, a mechanism that synchronized a forward-firing machine gun (mounted on the cowling) with the propeller so that the gun did not fire at the instant when a propeller blade passed directly in front of the muzzle. For the better part of a year, until April 1916, German pilots enjoyed this advantage in aerial combat before the Allies began to incorporate similar devices into their own craft.

The Western Front offensives of 1916 and 1917 witnessed an escalation in air operations. On the Somme, for example, the British initially committed some 426 pilots to the battle, of whom more than 300 were killed or injured. In April 1917, during the Arras offensive, the Germans introduced the D.III, an effective fighter that inflicted heavy losses. As new technologies and machines appeared, the initiative passed back and forth between the Germans and the

Allies. With casualties mounting in the British air services throughout 1916–17, opportunities for Canadians to take to the skies increased.

Canadian aviators played a limited role during the opening phase of the war. Just two Canadian flyers and a single aircraft – comprising the Canadian Aviation Corps – embarked for England with the first overseas contingent in 1914. This was a short-lived venture: one of the pilots soon returned to Canada; the other, Lieutenant W.F. Sharpe, was killed in a training accident early the next year. Apparently, only one Canadian pilot, Captain Frederick A. Wanklyn, saw any action in 1914. Wanklyn, a 1909 graduate of the Royal Military College of Canada, served in the British Army. He was seconded to the Royal Flying Corps (RFC) in 1912, which helps explain his early introduction to air operations on the Western Front. All told, probably fewer than two dozen Canadians served with the RFC on the Western Front throughout 1914–15. Pioneers like Wanklyn joined the RFC – or its naval counterpart, the Royal Naval Air Service (RNAS) – directly from the British Army or the Royal Navy. In time, additional Canadian volunteers stepped forward from CEF units.

In 1915 the British authorities approached the Canadian government in search of qualified pilots who might be enlisted directly in Canada or the United States for service with the RFC. They stipulated that recruits must hold an aviation certificate (earned at the applicant's expense) from a reputable civil flying organization and must be medically fit, with normal vision. The RNAS implemented a similar scheme. Only a handful of volunteers came forward, given that few Canadian men held aviation certificates in 1915. A newly established private flying school in Toronto soon opened its doors to would-be naval aviators, who could earn their certificates at a steep cost of $400. Canadian involvement in the air war gradually intensified between 1915 and 1917. It helped that British authorities relaxed their recruiting standards as the demand for aircrew spiked. As of late 1915, for example, an RFC candidate recruited in Canada no longer required an aviation certificate if he was a commissioned officer. Together, the RFC and the RNAS recruited some seven hundred flyers in Canada during 1915–16.

Heavy losses among aircrew convinced British authorities that certificates earned in civilian schools held little practical military value. More important than soliciting additional volunteers, the air services needed to develop a proper military aviation training system. The establishment of Royal Flying Corps Canada (RFC Canada), a British organization responsible for recruiting and training pilots in Canada, represented a key shift in air training. Between May and December 1917 alone, RFC Canada netted perhaps 2,400 cadet pilots. Recruits attended ground school at the Cadet Wing, housed at the University of Toronto. Additional training stations operated at fields around Toronto, as well as at Camp Borden and in Beamsville, Hamilton, and Deseronto, Ontario. After the United States entered the war in April 1917, Canadian and American aviation officials developed joint training plans, with Canadian cadets learning to fly in Texas during Canada's inclement winter months. Throughout the final two years of the war, the number of Canadian aviators in the air war increased significantly.

As their numbers swelled, some Canadian airmen garnered considerable fame for their exploits in the skies above the Western Front. The best-known aviators were the aces: according to French practice, an *as*, or "ace," was a pilot who had shot or forced down five or more enemy aircraft. By the end of the war, ten of the twenty-seven top aces in British service were Canadians. According to official sources, Major W.A. "Billy" Bishop was Canada's highest-scoring ace, with seventy-two victories. A native of Owen Sound, Ontario, Bishop volunteered for overseas service as a cavalryman. Arriving in England in 1915, he applied for transfer to the RFC, trained as an observer, and joined a squadron in early 1916. Later that year he qualified as a pilot and joined 60 Squadron in time for the Arras offensive.

Bishop is remembered best for his alleged solo attack on a German aerodrome in June 1917. He claimed four German aircraft and was decorated with the Victoria Cross. Bishop often flew alone during his operational tours, so there was no concrete evidence to corroborate many of his claims, including those of June 1917 that won him the Victoria Cross. Nor were there any witnesses. Consequently, historians have long debated how many enemy aircraft Bishop actually destroyed.[2] During the difficult war years, such technicalities mattered little to a public eager for good news. Bishop's exploits fit the bill, and he achieved unrivalled fame and status as a hero of the air. Among other honours, a mountain peak in the Canadian Rockies was named for him. So is Toronto's downtown commuter airport.

Tactical air operations normally involved the direct support of ground forces at the combat front. Strategic air operations targeted an enemy's home front and civilian population. Beginning in 1915, German bombing raids against British or French cities and Allied raids against targets inside Germany were components of an intensifying strategic air war. Germany's air offensive against British cities began with the famous zeppelins. These slow and vulnerable dirigible airships caused hundreds of civilian casualties with their bombs, but otherwise did little damage to the British war effort. Major Raymond Collishaw, another of Canada's successful pilots, first saw action in 1916, patrolling British skies in search of German intruders. He later participated in strategic air raids against German targets such as the Mauser rifle factory at Oberndorf am Neckar.

In 1917 the Germans began to employ Gotha bombers, capable of carrying 1,000-pound payloads, against British targets. British defences (including observation posts, warning sirens, anti-aircraft batteries, and fighter squadrons) brought the German bombing campaign to an inconclusive end in May 1918. The British replied to the Gotha raids with attacks against Germany, executed by the RAF. (In April 1918, the RFC and RNAS had combined to form a third, separate service, the RAF.) By the standards of the Second World War, the RAF did little significant damage to German cities. Even so, strategic air attacks shocked and terrified people on the ground. One frantic German from Mannheim wrote in August 1918: "My eyes won't keep open while I am writing. In the night, twice into the cellar and again this morning ... One air raid after another ... That is no longer war but murder."[3] The Germans allocated valuable resources to air defence on the home front, as the British had done earlier in the war. The limited strategic air campaigns of the First World War foreshadowed much larger and vastly more destructive efforts twenty years later.

At the end of the war, there were about 290,000 men (all ranks) in the RAF. Official sources indicate that, among this number, about 24 per cent of the officers (some 6,600) and 6 per cent of the other ranks (some 15,700) were Canadians. Beyond this snapshot in time, there is no definitive statistic to indicate how many Canadians joined the flying services throughout the war. Canadian airmen followed any number of pathways into the British flying services: some joined directly in Britain, some were seconded from the CEF, and others were recruited in Canada. Without hard statistics on Canadian participation, there can be no conclusive tally of Canadian fatalities. However, based on available evidence, 1,500 is a reasonable estimate.[4] In a conflict that killed millions of anonymous soldiers in grinding campaigns on the ground, the air war seemed to offer a refreshing alternative: free-spirited individuals like Bishop or Collishaw could escape the deadlocked trenches and win fame as aces in the skies. As exciting as it all might have seemed, combat and death in the air war were no less horrific than the fighting on the ground had been.

For much of the war, the Canadian government had been determined not to form a separate Canadian air service. This arrangement permitted the Borden government to invest heavily in the Canadian Corps and other ground forces, but it also denied Canadians the valuable administrative and organizational experience that would have come with a separate Canadian air service. After months of discussion and debate among Canadian officers and government officials, the British Air Ministry authorized the Canadian Air Force in August 1918. Two squadrons (one fighter squadron and one bomber squadron) were formed in England, but the war ended before they began operations. The Canadian squadrons were stationed in Britain until 1920. The organization was re-formed in Canada that year, and lasted until 1924, when the Royal Canadian Air Force came into being.

Like the Royal Canadian Navy, the RCAF struggled for survival during the lean interwar years. Perhaps the lowest point came under Prime Minister R.B. Bennett's Conservative government in 1932. In that year's so-called "Big Cut," the RCAF lost nearly half its 1931 budget and one in five of its personnel. The skeleton RCAF's role was limited to forest fire prevention and occasional air mail delivery. If not for these civilian duties, the RCAF might have ceased to exist altogether during the Great Depression. Canadians might relish the exploits of Bishop and the other aces, but economic hardship discouraged meaningful investment in a peacetime air force.

Aviation technology in Europe and North America made significant advances during the 1920s and 1930s with respect to range, speed, payloads, and overall reliability. In this context, few people, in or out of uniform, doubted that long-range aircraft would play a prominent role in the next war. Political and military leaders and ordinary civilians alike feared that bombers would annihilate urban populations with chemical weapons. Such threats demanded well-orchestrated civil defence plans, including the manufacture of respirators (gas masks) for every man, woman, and child in Europe, and ultimately in Canada as well.

Some military air theorists and politicians viewed strategic air power as an alternative to the massive infantry casualties of the First World War. Why bother to fight the enemy's army on the ground when a force of strategic bombers could attack their homeland and means of production? As one American airpower advocate imagined early in the Second World War, "invading aerial giants strike at the nerve centre and jugular veins of a great nation. Unerringly they pick their objectives: industrial centers and sources of power, government seats and fuel concentrations ... The havoc they wreak is beyond description."[5] Many believed that, in the words of Stanley Baldwin (a former prime minister of Britain) in 1932, "the bomber will always get through" in the next war. Bombing attacks indeed killed or displaced millions of people throughout the war, but optimism regarding the decisive potential of strategic airpower proved to be misplaced.

Interwar discussion of the role of strategic bombing in future warfare did not mean that tactical airpower was consigned to history. On the contrary, the 1930s witnessed the development of some excellent fighter aircraft – such as Britain's Supermarine Spitfire – that would win great fame in the Second World War. Based on the experience of open warfare in 1918, tactical airpower assumed key support roles in the land campaigns of 1939–45. It often proved difficult, however, to integrate tactical air forces effectively with army units on the ground.

Prime Minister Mackenzie King's Liberals returned to the government benches in 1935 and looked skyward in their defence planning. Canada's heavy commitment of ground troops to the Western Front during the First World War had precipitated a conscription crisis in 1917–18 that tested the nation's social fabric and fractured the Liberal Party.

With this experience seared into his mind, Mackenzie King hoped to pursue an air-minded strategy that would cost fewer Canadian casualties in a future war. In April 1939, Mackenzie King declared that the "first line of defence for Canada must be the air force."[6]

Canada was in an excellent position to assist the Allied war effort in the skies. The Dominion's factories could turn out high-quality aircraft, and its vast geographic expanses offered an ideal training ground for aircrew. In late 1939, British, Canadian, Australian, and New Zealand representatives discussed a joint training scheme to be conducted in Canada. They hammered out an agreement that December for the British Commonwealth Air Training Plan (BCATP). The RCAF was to establish and operate a series of specialist training schools and airfields across the country. The original goal was to train 25,000 Commonwealth airmen each year. Between 1940 and March 1945, more than 131,000 students graduated from the program, including nearly 73,000 RCAF personnel. Air force training facilities in Canada were staffed in part by members of the RCAF Women's Division. One of them was Jackie Bishop, daughter of Billy Bishop. The younger Bishop trained airmen in Morse code.

Perhaps the legend of Billy Bishop and the other aces of the First World War had prompted young Canadians to volunteer for the air force in 1939. But the RCAF at that stage of the war was too modest in size to accommodate everyone who wished to fly. Consequently, many Canadians turned to the RAF, and by the end of the year, more Canadians were flying with the RAF than with the RCAF. A few of these pioneers, such as Flight Lieutenant George "Buzz" Beurling, who joined the RAF in 1940, followed in Bishop's footsteps and became famous fighter pilots. Among other exploits, in 1942 Beurling destroyed more than two dozen enemy aircraft during a two-week period in the Mediterranean theatre. But the majority of Canadian pilots, whether in the RAF or the RCAF, served with less fanfare.

An all-Canadian RAF squadron, No. 242, was formed and participated in the Battle of France and the Battle of Britain in 1940. It maintained its Canadian designation until September 1941, by which time most of the Canadian members had become casualties or had transferred to other units. Throughout the war, individual Canadian pilots and aircrew – including many from the first wave of BCATP graduates – flew with Canadian and British Commonwealth squadrons in all operational theatres, including Alaska, North Africa, and Southeast Asia (China–Burma–India). In the latter theatre alone, about 7,500 Canadian airmen served throughout the war. Some flew transport or coastal patrol craft in Canadian squadrons; others were radar technicians. About one-quarter of the pilots in British Commonwealth squadrons in Southeast Asia were Canadian.[7] One of them, Flight Sergeant Harry Gill, had been decorated for his role in an attack on German warships in the English Channel in February 1942. Gill, who flew a Hurricane, was transferred to India shortly afterwards to fight the Japanese. He was killed near the Indian–Burmese border in January 1943.[8] The air war took many Canadians, like Gill, far and wide.

Air forces are highly technical services; long maritime air patrols and night-time bombing raids comprising hundreds of aircraft would have been unsustainable without expert maintenance on the ground. Many Canadian airmen, in fact, spent all of their time on the ground as maintenance personnel. Leading Aircraftsman Arthur Myers was one of thousands of volunteers who joined the RCAF, not to fly, but to repair and maintain aircraft. Myers had grown up along the Eastern Passage in Nova Scotia, so he knew enough about the North Atlantic to opt out of naval service. Perhaps his father, who had been conscripted for overseas service in 1917, had convinced him to choose the RCAF over the army. Myers enlisted at nineteen in 1942 and trained as an aero-engine mechanic. He excelled at his trade and would adapt his technical skills to a career in agricultural machinery manufacturing when peace returned. Countless other Canadian airmen followed similar paths.

After France capitulated in June 1940, German forces prepared to invade Britain. But before German commanders could seriously contemplate an amphibious landing, they needed to achieve air superiority. The British were very hard pressed at this stage of the war, but they possessed excellent fighter aircraft (the Spitfire and the Hurricane) and an effective defensive radar network known as Chain Home. Between July and September 1940, British skies witnessed heavy aerial combat during daylight hours as fighter squadrons scrambled to intercept German fighters and bombers.

No. 1 (Fighter) Squadron arrived from Canada just in time to participate in the Battle of Britain during the desperate summer of 1940, and was the first RCAF unit to engage the enemy. Equipped with Hurricane fighters, Canadian pilots of No. 1 Squadron fought their inaugural air battle against a German bomber formation in late August, downing three and damaging four enemy planes. Two Hurricanes were damaged, and one destroyed, with the death of its pilot. The squadron scored one of its greatest victories in late September during the German air force's last major daylight bombing attack. Thirteen pilots of No. 1 Squadron brought down or damaged fifteen enemy aircraft. In the face of such heavy losses, the Germans gave up on their invasion plans that autumn and switched their efforts to night-time bombing raids against British cities and industrial targets. RAF Fighter Command was poorly equipped to repel night raids, but the German bomber forces were not strong enough to achieve a decisive strategic impact.

Despite the Canadian government's initial enthusiasm for airpower, the larger British effort subsumed Canada's front-line contributions to a degree, especially during the first part of the war. This was partly because there was no separate, distinct Canadian air command operating overseas. And by

1941, Canadian overseas squadrons were too few to absorb the influx of Canadian BCATP graduates, which drew many to British units instead. The terms of the BCATP were later revised to create twenty-five new RCAF squadrons in Britain, at British expense. Additional squadrons were authorized subsequently. All together between May 1941 and 1944, more than forty new RCAF squadrons were formed for overseas service.

The air war evolved in late 1940 and 1941. The German air force abandoned daylight operations in favour of night-time bombing raids against British cities. RAF Fighter Command, meanwhile, adopted an offensive posture, attacking German airfields in occupied France. The idea was to carry the war to the enemy and draw German aircraft into battle. This policy of "leaning forward into France" was not especially successful. When fighting over their own ground, German pilots held the upper hand, as the RAF (and RCAF) had done when defending British airspace during the Battle of Britain.

RAF Bomber Command also changed its approach during 1940–1. In the first six months of the war, British (and by extension Canadian) bombing policy had been "deliberately non-provocative."9 Bomber Command missions included long-range reconnaissance, "leaflet raids" (dropping bundles of propaganda pamphlets over Germany), and daylight attacks against military targets such as enemy shipping and naval bases. The daylight operations proved too costly in aircraft losses to justify the limited results achieved. Night operations, by contrast, afforded some protection against German fighter and anti-aircraft defences; however, the darkness rendered accurate navigation extremely difficult. In early 1940, RAF experts estimated that only 50 per cent of crews could locate targets under even the best conditions (high visibility, and when the target area was situated on a coastline or near a large body of water). In poor conditions, it was difficult for any crew to find its target during the night. Bomber Command nevertheless shifted its focus to night raids against key economic targets such as oil production facilities. When the war escalated in the spring of 1940 with the German invasions of Denmark and Norway, officials at RAF Bomber Command urged attacks against enemy civilian targets. The British government was not prepared to take that step because the enemy's air force had not yet bombed Britain. So, during the battle for France and the Low Countries, Bomber Command engaged mainly in ground support (tactical) operations.

A turning point came during the Battle of Britain. On the night of 24–5 August 1940, German aircraft inadvertently bombed the centre of London instead of their prescribed target. Prime Minister Churchill ordered the RAF to retaliate with a raid on Berlin. The next night, about fifty RAF crews, including a number of Canadians, set out for the German capital. Although the attack was rather inaccurate, a line had been crossed. German bombers replied with further attacks on London and other British cities throughout the autumn of 1940. RAF Bomber Command raided German cities in kind. The British had abandoned any pretence of avoiding civilian targets.

Germany's control over the European continent in 1940 and its invasion of the Soviet Union in June 1941 necessitated an aggressive bombing strategy, in British thinking. It would be some time before the western Allies could muster the strength to send an expeditionary army back to the continent. In the meantime, a bombing offensive was the only way to strike directly at enemy's heartland as the Red Army struggled to stem German advances deep inside Soviet territory. However, the impact of bombing raids against Germany during 1941–2 was limited by technological deficiencies. Simply put, Britain went to war with a line-up of bomber aircraft that proved less than ideal for long-range operations. On paper, for example, the massive four-engine Stirling, which first flew in 1939, might have seemed ideal for delivering heavy bomb loads. Among other technical problems, however, the Stirling's wingspan was too short to lift its heavy fuselage to reasonably safe operating ceilings. The excellent Lancaster, capable of carrying a 14,000-pound bomb load, and perhaps the best-known aircraft flown by Bomber Command, did not enter service until early 1942, about halfway through the war. Nearly 7,400 Lancasters were built, and the aircraft was flown on 156,000 sorties over Europe. But even after the Lancaster's debut, Canadian aircrew continued to fly older planes like the Stirling, or the Halifax, which could manage a 13,000-pound bomb load but suffered from ongoing technical problems. There were simply not enough of the newest and best aircraft available to re-equip all units at once.

Even the most reliable bomber aircraft were of little use if their crews failed to locate their targets. Evidence mounted in 1941 that a significant proportion of bombers were missing their targets by wide margins. That summer, economist D.M. Bensusan-Butt examined some 650 bomb release photographs taken during June and July. His conclusions were sobering. Of those aircrews that claimed to have bombed their targets, only one in three (on average) actually dropped bombs *within five miles* of the prescribed target. Air historian Randall Wakelam notes that this "was the average, but the results varied based on weather conditions; for example in full moonlight two attackers in five got within five miles of the target, but in thick haze that ratio dropped to one in fifteen."[10] Target location also influenced accuracy. In Germany's Ruhr valley, a centre for heavy industry and power plants, only one aircraft in ten dropped its bombs within five miles of the target. Again, these ratios included only the crews that reported successful attacks. Just 66 per cent of the sorties that Bensusan-Butt examined fell into that category – in other words, in 34 per cent of sorties, crews admitted that they had not reached their target in the first place.

The "Butt Report" sent shockwaves through the British government, the Air Ministry, and Bomber Command.

Clearly, not *all* bombers were getting through. Electronic navigation aids offered a partial solution to the target-finding problem, although bombers might still be pushed off course by enemy fighters or anti-aircraft fire. Because of the difficulties involved in hitting precise targets such as factories, power plants, and other infrastructure, Bomber Command refocused on "area" targets. In contrast to precision targeting, area bombardment placed less emphasis on pinpoint accuracy. Instead, it went after generally defined targets, such as an entire city district rather than a particular group of buildings. In the aftermath of Bensusan-Butt's study, Bomber Command increasingly practised area bombing, with the goal of undermining German morale, crippling war industries (which were usually situated in urban areas anyhow), and drawing enemy resources such as fighters and anti-aircraft artillery away from other theatres of operations to the German homeland.

Bomber Command continued to develop area bombing techniques under the leadership of Air Marshal Arthur Harris, who assumed command of the organization in February 1942. The basic destructive technique was to mix high explosive bombs with incendiary types. The high explosive bombs blew out doors and windows and tore roofs apart, opening up pathways for powerful drafts that fed oxygen to the many fires started by the incendiaries. During a clear night in March 1942, for example, some four hundred tons of bombs damaged more than 60 per cent of Lübeck's mostly wooden buildings. The Germans responded with "Baedeker" reprisal raids against British cities. There was a key difference in scale, however. The number of German bombers involved was counted in the dozens. Bomber Command, by contrast, launched its first 1,000-aircraft raid in May 1942, against Cologne. This aerial armada delivered some 1,500 tons of bombs. Any visitor to Cologne today will find that few traces of the old city survived the war.

In the early stages of the air war, Canadian airmen serving overseas had been most active in Fighter Command. By

1941, however, authorities were channelling the swelling ranks of aircrew trainees towards the bombers. This trend would continue throughout the war. As early as October 1942, there were enough operational RCAF bomber squadrons overseas to form No. 6 (RCAF) Group, an all-Canadian bomber group. As of 1944, about one-fifth of the personnel in Bomber Command were Canadian.

No. 6 Group was not at first especially popular with Canadian aircrew, who had grown accustomed to the culture and routines of RAF groups and now chaffed under the harder-edged discipline in their new organization. Air Marshal Harris was also dissatisfied with the Canadian group, albeit for different reasons than his airmen. He feared that a "national" group comprising squadrons from a single Dominion would create unnecessary friction within his command. Furthermore, he argued that some of the Canadian officers promoted to higher levels of command with No. 6 Group lacked the requisite experience. Given the scope of Canada's air commitment, however, there was fair justification for an all-Canadian bomber group. No. 6 Group remains the largest Canadian air formation ever committed to battle in any war.

No. 6 Group joined operations in January 1943, at a key moment in the strategic air war. British and American leaders had agreed to coordinate their efforts in what became the Combined Bomber Offensive. The primary targets were submarine construction yards, aircraft plants, transportation networks, oil refineries, and other industrial facilities. As much as possible, submarine bases on the French coast and the city of Berlin itself were to be targeted. The RAF continued to bomb by night, while the US Army Air Force bombed during the day. The Americans continued to pursue precision bombing, which was more likely to succeed in daylight.

Throughout 1943 and into 1944, No. 6 Group suffered rather heavy losses in exchange for mixed results on various types of operations. For example, attacks on submarine bases on the French coast were not particularly effective

against the massive concrete "pens" that sheltered the
U-boats. Poor accuracy was also an ongoing challenge. During one raid against Lorient in February, just 37 per cent of
crews bombed within three miles of their targets. Later in
1943, the emphasis shifted to the Ruhr industrial area. No.
6 Group's loss rate was among the highest in Harris's command during this phase, rising from 2.8 per cent in March
to 7.1 per cent in June. As in the Royal Canadian Navy,
where expansion had occurred too rapidly, inexperience
played a role in No. 6 Group's losses, but so did technology. It did not help that some Canadian squadrons continued to fly outmoded Halifax aircraft after the Lancaster
had entered service. Improved German defences, including radar-equipped night fighters, also took their toll in
1943. Although the Canadian group participated in some
highly destructive raids, such as those that created a major
firestorm in Hamburg in July 1943, aircrew morale sank.
Declining spirits were hardly difficult to fathom: only one
in ten crews could expect to survive a thirty-mission operational tour.

Spirits lifted in No. 6 Group during the spring of 1944,
as Bomber Command shifted its sights from German cities to French, Belgian, and Dutch targets, in support of the
imminent Allied invasion of Normandy. Furthermore, the
high tempo of raiding in 1943 had depleted the strength
of the German air force, allowing Allied bombers to strike
transportation infrastructure in the occupied countries
with relatively light losses. During the Battle of Normandy,
the bomber force occasionally operated in direct support of
Allied troops on the ground, albeit with mixed results.

In 1945, Bomber Command turned once again to area
raids over Germany. No. 6 Group had improved significantly
during the summer of 1944 and achieved excellent results
during the final months of the war, which witnessed some
of the most destructive raids of the entire conflict. These
attacks – against Dresden and Hildesheim, for example –
were intended to dislocate Germany's last ditch defences,
which they likely did, but to a degree that is difficult to assess. ·

At this late stage of the war, some Allied leaders, including Churchill, began to question whether such intense bombing was really necessary.

Long after the fires have been put out and the cities rebuilt, the big four-engine aircraft of Bomber Command, such as the Halifax and Lancaster, continue to capture popular imagination and inspire debate. But these machines meant nothing without their crews. Who were these men, and where did they come from? At twenty years old, Gordon Gross served on a Halifax crew in 1944. Gross later remembered his fellow flyers as "typical of the diverse group of airmen that manned the heavy bombers."[11] The pilot, Tom Prescott, was a New Brunswicker who had left college to join the RCAF. Bill Caton, the navigator, had been a Toronto businessman before the war. The bomb aimer, Dave Harris, was much older than his mates at 30! He had been a high school teacher in Whitby, Ontario. Hank Gilpin, who served as the wireless operator, air gunner, and at times radar operator, was a farmer who ran a general store in Alberta. The tail gunner was Jimmy Willet, an outdoorsman from New Brunswick. Gross was the Halifax's mid-upper gunner. He had left high school to work in an armaments plant in Hamilton, Ontario, before joining the RCAF in 1943. He earned his high school diploma after the war, went on to university, earned a doctorate in geology, and joined the Geological Survey of Canada. The lesson here is that men from every walk of life put their civilian pursuits aside to participate in the deadly contest in the skies.

Canadian airmen endured incredible stress in the air war. They flew mission after mission against steep odds, watching in horror as planes and crews in their units were lost in action. Fear was their constant companion, but RAF policy classified any airman who refused to fly in the absence of a recognized medical explanation as a "waverer" who was "lacking in moral fibre." Waverers were stripped of rank and flying badges and typically put to the most menial tasks on the ground until transferred to the army or consigned to hard labour in Britain's coal mines. The RCAF implemented a somewhat more moderate policy with respect to possible "lacking in moral fibre" cases. Charles "Chubby" Power, Canada's Minister of National Defence for Air, insisted that any RCAF man who was suspected of wavering be returned to Canada for physical and mental health assessments. It was ultimately up to Power to decide whether an airman should be stripped of rank and flying badges and/or dismissed from service.

At least one Canadian airman, pilot Murray Peden, believed that the RAF's tough regulations were "necessary simply because the strain was so great. If there had been an easy and graceful way to abandon operational flying, many crews would have found the temptation hard to resist."[12] As controversial as the policy may have been, by the end of the war, fewer than 3,000 British Commonwealth airmen (from all air commands) had been classified as waverers, which was only about 0.2 per cent of those who served. It seems that the great majority of aircrew somehow carried on until they became casualties or their tours were complete. As a Canadian Lancaster pilot serving with an RAF squadron later recalled, "it was a relentlessly sad business. It was a great strain on the crews, but you just dealt with it. You put it out of your mind and just went on. Before you knew it, there would be a replacement on the squadron and you were getting on with the job."[13]

In sum, the strategic air war against Germany and occupied Europe defied some predictions while realizing others. It was indeed destructive, inflicting massive damage against German cities and infrastructure and killing some 600,000, including about 410,000 German civilians, 23,000 German police and civilians attached to the German armed forces, 32,000 foreigners and prisoners of war, 128,000 displaced persons, and about 60,000 Italians.[14] By the same token, losses to aircrew were frighteningly heavy. About 45 per cent of the aircrew (of all nationalities) who served in Bomber Command lost their lives. Some 40,000 RCAF airmen served in Bomber Command. One in four of these was killed, a staggering fatality rate.

An RCAF Lancaster bomber that has returned home safely to Canada at the end of the Second World War sports typically provocative nose art, Greenwood, NS, 1945. Authors' collection, photograph by Arthur Myers.

The impact of the strategic air campaign on the war's outcome was, and is, difficult to assess. The bombing campaign did significantly disrupt the German economy, as well as the lives of civilians and soldiers – cities were devastated, factories were damaged, transportation infrastructure was crippled, and millions were left homeless. Civilians who managed to survive a night attack physically unscathed were exhausted by lack of sleep when returning to work the next day. Soldiers at the front worried about the well-being of their wives and children at home. German authorities redeployed significant military resources, including fighter aircraft, anti-aircraft guns, and all of the associated personnel and supplies from the fighting fronts to defend the home front. Yet despite these costs to German society and the war economy, industrial output continued to increase between 1940 and 1944, albeit likely at a slower rate than if there had been no bombing.

The Allies' massive investment of scarce materials, such as aluminum and rubber, in aircraft production must be factored in; so must the large numbers of personnel who were involved in the bombing campaign. There was also the opportunity cost of using long-range bomber aircraft for offensive actions against Germany rather than for defensive purposes, such as convoy protection at sea. Had it not been for the safe passage of convoys carrying troops and war materiel, the Allies could never have returned to the continent to defeat Germany on the ground. Given the great complexity of the bombing campaign, and the high cost in human lives (in the air and on the ground), the controversy is unlikely to abate any time soon.

During the interwar years, the RAF had made a strong effort to develop strategic air doctrine. The tactical sphere – how air forces might cooperate with ground troops in battle – had received less attention. Germany's 1940 victory over France prompted the British to revisit the matter of tactical air support. By 1943–4, when the western Allies returned to the offensive in Europe, the RAF had developed techniques for the close support of ground troops. Air force doctrine identified two types of support: direct and indirect. Direct support had an immediate impact on the course of a battle. For example, if a body of German troops and tanks was moving to counterattack a Canadian infantry unit, fighter aircraft might be called to descend upon the Germans with cannon fire, rockets, or bombs. Such missions were reactive in nature and therefore could not be easily planned ahead of time. Indirect support was less immediately concerned with the outcome of a particular tactical engagement; rather, it aimed to influence the general course of a ground campaign. This might be achieved, for example, by systematically striking enemy railway and road infrastructure so as to disrupt logistics and the flow of reinforcements to the battlefield.

The British 2nd Tactical Air Force, which included Canadian squadrons, supported Allied operations during the campaigns in Normandy and Northwest Europe in 1944–5. The impact of tactical air power during these campaigns remains a matter of debate. On the one hand, Canadian and other Allied army officers claimed that the tactical air forces were too slow to provide direct support when or where it was most urgently needed. On the other, virtually all German commanders insisted that enemy aircraft were responsible for their setbacks.[15]

There is some truth to both perspectives. As historian Terry Copp has written, the "2nd Tactical Air Force waged a separate war against the enemy's air force, lines of communication, and targets of opportunity" with overwhelming success, "but this was not the same campaign the army was waging."[16] In other words, the air force provided reasonably effective indirect support but fell short when it came to close direct support. Tactical air power, then, aggravated German logistics but was not the decisive factor in the Normandy campaign. While air–ground coordination improved to a degree later in 1944, poor weather often limited the ability of air forces to participate fully in the Northwest Europe campaign during the final winter of the war.

The majority of Canadian airmen who served overseas did so in Bomber Command, with Fighter Command placing second. A smaller number of Canadians participated in the anti-submarine war in home waters under Eastern Air Command or overseas as part of RAF Coastal Command. For much of the war up to 1943, Coastal Command squadrons flew outdated machines with limited ranges, as Bomber Command was reluctant to surrender its long-range aircraft for anti-submarine operations. The British government intervened in late 1942, determining that convoy protection required at least forty "very long-range" aircraft in the eastern Atlantic.

Successful air attacks against U-boats were relatively rare, but the very presence of air patrols was enough to discourage German submariners from getting too close to convoys. Besides escorting convoys, Coastal Command squadrons attacked German submarines as they returned to base in the Bay of Biscay or along the Norwegian coast. In one such instance, an RCAF Sunderland flying boat depth-charged *U-489*. As the submarine began to sink, its crew returned fire with anti-aircraft armament, forcing the Sunderland into the sea. A passing Allied destroyer picked up the Canadian aircrew and the German sailors in the water. For the most part, however, Coastal Command patrols were characterized by long hours of boredom with no enemy sightings at all. Consider the following account from a typical patrol:

The day drags on. Periodically, the radar operator picks up something that turns out to be a surface vessel. Or two or three grey corvettes, which from 2,500 feet and six or seven miles could be mistaken for submarines ... a submarine-sighting is something merely hoped for and rarely attained (a large proportion of aircrew complete a whole tour of 800 hours without seeing a submarine).[17]

RCAF aircrew based at home in the Maritimes participated in the war against the U-boats as part of Eastern Air Command. With little practical experience to summon and an imposing geographical area to defend, the flyers of Eastern Air Command did not destroy any U-boats during the early part of the war. However, as the convoy battles moved into the western Atlantic in 1942, Eastern Air Command units made increasing numbers of contacts and were ultimately responsible for damaging three U-boats and destroying six others. No. 162 Squadron, a unit that began its war with Eastern Air Command, went on to distinguish itself in the eastern Atlantic, on loan to RAF Coastal Command as of

January 1944. The squadron claimed its first U-boat in April and destroyed five more in June. Aircraft of the RCAF came to play a key role in the contest against the U-boats.

In common with Coastal Command, the role of RAF Ferry Command is often overlooked in the history of the air war. Established in August 1941, Ferry Command was the result of an initiative to transport military aircraft from North American manufacturing plants to Britain by flying them across the Atlantic rather than shipping them in freighters. William Maxwell Aitken (Lord Beaverbrook), the Canadian-born newspaper magnate who served as Britain's minister of aircraft production, secured London's support for the idea. Civilian and commercial pilots and navigators flew newly manufactured aircraft from the Atlantic Ferry Organization base in Montreal through Gander, Newfoundland, and on to Britain. It was a controversial scheme, given the dangers and unknowns of transatlantic aviation at the time. Still, the risk paid off. By the end of the war, ferrying operations had delivered 10,000 aircraft of at least seventeen varieties to operational theatres, saving valuable shipping space and potential losses to U-boats. The ferry operations not only delivered war material but also ushered in the age of long-range strategic air supply, establishing the infrastructure that "formed the basis of the international grid of civil air routes throughout the world."[18] Perhaps more important, Ferry Command radically changed the psychological dimension of travel over the North Atlantic. Crossing the ocean by air – once an exceptional feat – had become a normal routine for Ferry Command. During the First World War, politicians, diplomats, and other high-profile travellers had taken a week or more to cross the Atlantic. Thanks to Ferry Command, it was possible during the Second World War to have "breakfast in Scotland and dinner in Canada" on the same day.[19]

Transatlantic air traffic helped keep up the morale of Canada's overseas soldiers through expedited mail delivery.

Rather than consign personal correspondence to slow shipping, military authorities used air transport to carry mail,
significantly shortening the turnaround time for letters
between soldiers and their loved ones. The RCAF's No. 168
(Heavy Transport) Squadron, based at Rockcliffe, Ontario,
for example, provided mail delivery service across the Atlantic. This squadron's headquarters, like many other air units
based at home and overseas, was staffed in part by members
of the RCAF Women's Division.

Canada's experience of flight in the two world wars was, in
many respects, an exercise in contrasts. The nation went to
war in 1914 with no air force to speak of, and the Borden
government showed little interest in developing one until
very late in the First World War. Mackenzie King, by contrast, looked to air power as something of an alternative to
a large army in the field and the high casualties it might suf-
fer. At home, Canada hosted the BCATP, a training scheme
that surpassed expectations and that was a major component of the national effort. No comparable investment had
been made in aviation on the home front during the First
World War – indeed, during the winter months, Canadian
cadets had gone to Texas for training!

The airplanes of 1939–45 were radically different from
their 1914–18 predecessors. Long-range bombers capable
of carrying more than 4,500 kilograms of ordnance were
available in large numbers in the Second World War, and
fighter aircraft were capable of longer ranges, higher
speeds, and dazzling manoeuvrability. Both wars witnessed
extensive use of aircraft for tactical and strategic purposes,
but strategic air power had become more important by the
1930s as aviation technology improved. This would make
an indelible mark on the Second World War, especially on
the home fronts.

From a cultural perspective, the heavy bomber, with a
crew of six or seven men, played a much more significant

role in the Second World War than had been true of bombers a generation earlier. While the popular media still celebrated individual fighter aces, Second World War pilots and aircrew were less likely to become national household names as Bishop had done in 1917–18. With high loss rates among aircrew, and many more planes aloft than in the First World War, the campaigns of 1939–45 lost some of the romantic character of Billy Bishop's war on the Western Front – real or imagined. Yet for many young men, the chance to fly during the First and Second World Wars was a transformative experience, notwithstanding the great risks they undertook. That is a common thread linking the two conflicts. Perhaps the majesty of flying is best captured in "High Flight," a poem written by Pilot Officer John Gillespie Magee, an American who served in the RCAF:

> Oh, I have slipped the surly bonds of earth
> And danced the skies on laughter-silvered wings;
> Sunward I've climbed and joined the tumbling mirth
> Of sun-split clouds – and done a hundred things
> You have not dreamed of – wheeled and soared and swung
> High in the sunlit silence. Hov'ring there,
> I've chased the shouting wind along and flung
> My eager craft through footless halls of air.
> Up, up the long delirious, burning blue
> I've topped the wind-swept heights with easy grace,
> Where never lark, or even eagle flew;
> And while with silent, lifting mind I've trod
> The high untresspassed sanctity of space,
> Put out my hand, and touched the face of God.[20]

At nineteen years of age, Magee died in a mid-air collision over England in December 1941. After Magee's death, "High Flight" achieved enduring fame. President Ronald Reagan recited excerpts of the poem in his speech to the

American people following the loss of the space shuttle *Challenger* in 1986.

More than 20,000 Canadians joined the British flying services during the First World War, but the RCAF (and RAF) absorbed a greater proportion of Canada's military human resource pool in the Second World War. In September 1941, for example, there were 6,800 RCAF personnel posted overseas. By March 1945, the number overseas was 58,000, including more than 1,300 members of the Women's Division.

On the eve of war, Prime Minister Mackenzie King hoped that the RCAF would represent Canada while sparing Canadians the heavy casualties of the First World War. In fact, the air war was much deadlier than Mackenzie King had imagined. More than 18,500 RCAF personnel became casualties. That figure included an incredible 17,100 fatalities, an absolute figure equal to about 75 per cent of the Canadian Army's 23,000 dead. So Mackenzie King, like many others, had forecast air force casualty rates less than accurately. He did, though, succeed in avoiding much of the political controversy that had surrounded the Military Service Act in 1917, while making an important contribution to the Allied war effort.

The strategic bombing of the Second World War was intended to carry the war to the enemy while putting fewer soldiers at risk on the ground. But it also thrust civilians much more directly into harm's way, a harbinger of things to come after 1945. In sum, the military history of the twentieth century suggests that wars cannot be won solely through airpower, but that airpower may help to win wars. Its precise impact in both wars, but especially the second, remains controversial. Was tactical airpower instrumental in the defeat of German ground forces in Normandy? Was the material and human investment in strategic bombing worth the cost? Did it shorten the war? These questions will continue to occupy historians for years to come.

6

Society and Morality

Politicians and societal leaders portrayed them as Canada's best, and Minister of Militia and Defence Sam Hughes was determined to keep it that way. Yet shortly before the First World War, Hughes learned that drunken militiamen at the Niagara training camp were terrorizing townsfolk. A staunch temperance advocate, he responded with a decree that prohibited the sale of alcoholic beverages in army canteens. The policy elicited praise from the powerful Dominion Alliance for the Total Suppression of Alcohol, the YMCA, and the Women's Christian Temperance Union, groups that had long campaigned for prohibition as a cure-all for social ills. But Hughes was denounced by "his boys," as he liked to call them, who smuggled alcohol into camps and went on binges while off duty.

In the fall of 1914, Hughes again learned of drunk and disorderly conduct, this time by Canadian troops in England, where wet canteens were standard and community pubs abounded. On the Salisbury Plain, where the Canadian Expeditionary Force was encamped and where constant rain and cold weather made for utterly miserable conditions, he ordered that the training facility go "dry" (alcohol-free). However, British Lt.-Gen. Edwin Alderson, who commanded the Canadian troops, ignored the order, a decision that endeared him to the men. Hughes, of course, was outraged. At the front, Canadian soldiers

wrote reverentially of their daily rum ration, which provided warmth, needed levity, comradeship, and the courage
to endure the hardships and terrors of war. Indeed, when
the war ended, it was returning soldiers who led a successful campaign to end prohibition in Canada, casting it as
contrary to the British liberties they had pledged to defend.

Prohibition was not imposed during the Second World
War, but rationing of alcohol started in 1942, and some
places stayed dry. One was Halifax, even though the rest of
Nova Scotia permitted government liquor stores starting in
1929. Halifax had long housed sailors, merchant marines,
and soldiers, who were known to partake in heavy drinking.
Inundated during the war with shipyard workers and military personnel, Halifax's population exploded from 60,000
to 100,000. Everything was hopelessly overcrowded: housing, restaurants, trams, and even brothels, such as a well-
known establishment on Hollis Street where the line-up
often stretched for more than a block. Relations between
locals and military personnel grew strained, though many
civilians opened their doors to offer a meal or volunteered
at canteens run by service organizations. Those canteens,
however, remained dry, prompting many men to turn to
bootleggers and moonshiners. Sailors and soldiers complained about being bored, about sleeping in shifts at places
like the YMCA, and about standoffish civilians.

One person who empathized with the sailors was Janet
"Dolly" McEuen, the wife of HMCS *Stadacona* medical
officer Lt.-Com. Stuart McEuen. In 1941, she purchased
a vacant mansion and convinced the military and local
authorities to have it converted into a hospitality centre,
which she named the Ajax Club, where sailors could buy
a meal for twenty-five cents and a glass of beer – up to a
maximum of five – for a dime. Although wildly popular with
naval personnel, its presence drew fire from the Fort Massey
United Church, located right across the street. Within a
year, the special liquor licence was revoked and the Ajax
Club closed. In 1944, Halifax's mayor, Joe Lloyd, remarked

that antagonism between civilians and uniformed personnel was "strong and mutual." Indeed, on the very day Germany surrendered, 7 May 1945, over 1,000 sailors formed the vanguard in a riot that witnessed the looting of some five hundred stores and the theft of 65,000 quarts of booze. The event had been triggered by restaurants closing early and preventing military personnel from having a celebratory meal, but more broadly, as pointed out in a Royal Commission report, by a desire for revenge among many in uniform towards Halifax.[1]

Total war profoundly shaped social relations and moral norms. This is not to say that the wars overturned existing structures or mores. Debates around temperance long predated the wars, as did concerns about the conduct of servicemen. The same was true with respect to other themes that became more prominent in wartime, such as women's rights, the sanctity of marriage, and the spread of prostitution and venereal disease. The difference in wartime was that such issues grew more intense and often generated the need for decisive action. In both conflicts, change was quick and often significant, sometimes intensifying transformations towards a more liberal society, but also raising fears and generating backlash, such as the one by the Fort Massey United Church against the Ajax Club.

All wars place intense strain on families. Husbands, wives, boyfriends, girlfriends, and parents and children become separated. During both wars, hundreds of thousands of Canadians moved to seek employment or to undertake military training. Often lonely in their new communities, missing their loved ones, or embarking on an uncertain future – perhaps never to return again – many lived for the moment. This raised concerns about the stability of marriage. Yet during the First World War period, with Canada still very much a British nation (demographically and temperamentally) that shared Victorian moral codes, this was not something for general conversation. Indeed, there was virtually no public commentary about marital strain or unfaithful spouses. Divorce was an aberration; women who pursued it had to prove life-threatening abuse or bigamy. The legal dissolution of marriage required a parliamentary decree. (In this context, abandonment, mainly by men of women, was the norm. Women whose husbands left them often fell into great poverty.) At the outset of the First World War, there were fewer than one hundred divorces granted per year. By 1919, that number had topped 370. Even during a time of strict propriety, the strains caused by long absences, hastily pursued marriages, and difficulties of reconstituting relationships when soldiers and spouses eventually reunited began to chip away at the bedrock of marriage, at least its public face.

Public commentary on the First World War emphasized the theme of societal uplift resulting from a righteous crusade. For many people, proof lay in prohibition, long championed by religious leaders and moral reformers. Temperance advocates portrayed the consumption of alcohol as a key factor in crime, family breakdown, and debased conduct. Wartime provided the right sort of backdrop for those who campaigned against "demon rum" to achieve victory. They cast booze as particularly deplorable during war, because it made workers less productive, corrupted soldiers, and prompted men to squander money on drink rather than using it to support the war effort. And since alcohol was a key material in certain war industries, it was easier than ever to vilify drinking.

Wartime prohibition started in Manitoba with the 1915 election of the T.C. Norris's Liberals. The new government, as promised, undertook a referendum and with strong public endorsement adopted prohibition on 1 June 1916. Before the end of the year, Saskatchewan, Alberta, and British Columbia also went dry. The Maritimes had long exhibited social conservatism on this issue: Prince Edward Island had been dry since 1901, as had Nova Scotia since 1910, with the exception of Halifax, though that exception ended in 1916. In 1917, Newfoundland (not yet a Canadian province), New Brunswick, and Ontario adopted prohibition; the last-named saw a petition bearing more than 800,000 signatures demanding it as a wartime necessity. Quebec hesitated, reflecting the Catholic Church's long-established distance from the Protestant-led temperance crusade. The Catholic Church, like the Anglican, stressed individual over social redemption and used wine for communion services. Catholics opposed prohibition as an unwarranted intrusion of the state into church affairs. Only in early 1918 did Quebec's legislature endorse a ban on retail sales of liquor, but it was not to take effect until 1 May 1919. Federal prohibition began on 1 April 1918, mainly to stop the manufacture of liquor for interprovincial or international shipment; it would remain in effect for one year after the end of the war.

Although many areas reported dramatic declines in alcohol-related offences, within a year after the war's end, governments in British Columbia and Quebec were back in the business of collecting taxes and fees from liquor sales, and the federal government repealed its prohibition legislation. By the mid-1920s, widespread rule breaking had convinced nearly all provinces to abandon prohibition. Social activists who saw the war effort and prohibition as instruments for improving civilization were dismayed when former soldiers, led by the Great War Veterans Association (GWVA), called for an end to prohibition.

The belief that liquor consumption, by lowering inhibitions, abetted the spread of venereal disease (VD) bolstered the wartime campaign for prohibition. Although a taboo topic for general conversation, rising VD rates raised concerns, particularly among military, medical, and church authorities. In the era before antibiotics, VD, especially syphilis, physically incapacitated and sometimes killed those who were infected. Among Canadian troops, incidence of VD reached nearly 29 per cent, the highest rate among the

British Empire forces and more than ten times higher than the rate recorded by Health Canada in 2008. Certainly contributing to such high figures was the fact that military authorities, determined not to be seen as encouraging sex, provided men with no protection, such as condoms.

Restricting prostitution represented one line of attack against high VD rates. Crackdowns on prostitution were launched in many communities. Toronto and Montreal hired policewomen to better detect and handle the arrest of prostitutes and women whose behaviour seemed promiscuous. Disease prevention also resulted in one of the earliest conditional federal grants (meaning that the money came with stipulations), in 1917, when modest funding was made available to provincial governments to establish VD clinics and to provide information to the public. Educational materials developed by private groups like the Canadian Social Hygiene Council, whose membership included religious leaders, stressed that "gonorrhoea ... cause[d] sterility in women, blindness in children, and many still-births, while syphilis brought deformed babies, and insanity and death to adults." Ontario introduced new rules providing the police with the right to enter establishments and to order the examination and quarantine of those found to be infected with VD. In July 1918, another measure in Ontario compelled those infected to receive treatment and established penalties up to $500 for anyone who knowingly infected another with the disease – a measure adopted by every other province by 1920 except Quebec and Prince Edward Island. The new fines were intended to prevent a postwar VD epidemic with the return home of servicemen from Europe. In April 1919, when the federal government established a Department of Health largely to deal with the Spanish flu pandemic, it included a VD Division to continue work with the provinces on prevention. Still, governments' willingness to adequately address sexually transmitted disease proved limited. Federal funding never exceeded $100,000 annually (or $1.3 million in 2015 dollars) and was discontinued in 1932 as a cost-saving measure during the Great Depression.

The campaign against VD constrained the public conduct of women; at the same time, the world wars involved them in other, arguably liberating ways. The First World War raised the possibility of fundamental changes in women's roles. Adult women achieved the vote in most parts of the country. Some undertook work they would not have done otherwise, and others found new outlets for their charitable endeavours.

Wartime voluntarism reflected a view of women as performers of secondary roles; still, they received considerable praise – and notoriety – for their strong involvement and even leadership in campaigns deemed essential to Canada's war effort. Women raised funds for Belgian Relief and the Canadian Patriotic Fund; knitted warm clothing to send overseas; collected reading materials and sports equipment for the armed forces; and packed comforts for men training in Canada and Britain or fighting or held captive in Europe. Typically led by middle- and upper-class women who had more free time and important social connections, groups like the Imperial Order Daughters of the Empire arranged fund-raising tag days, lectures, luncheons, concerts, dances, bazaars, and theatrical productions. Much of the volunteer work for the Canadian Red Cross Society, including knitting and sewing garments and packing medical supplies for shipment overseas, was organized by young women at universities. With more men in the armed forces, women came to form a larger proportion of the student body, though they remained confined to the arts, household science, nutrition, and social work programs. As the war drew to a close, Prime Minister Borden credited women with raising as much as $50 million for the war effort. In March 1918, the federal government organized a Women's War Conference in Ottawa. Delegates discussed wartime challenges, the transition to peace, and the federal government's plans to enfranchise all British female subjects.

The world wars were not *responsible* for greater women's rights; the campaign for those rights pre-dated each conflict and continued after it. Still, conditions created by the wars certainly hastened change. Many women pointed to patriotic volunteerism to further justify their right to the provincial and federal vote. Leading suffragists said this campaign should take a back seat to the war effort; ironically, this made the suffrage movement appear more respectable and convinced more Canadians that women would use the vote to bolster the war effort and to build a better country in peacetime. Writer and social reformer Nellie McClung, Manitoba's most prominent suffragist, worked tirelessly for both the war effort and the vote. In January 1916, Manitoba became the first province to extend the franchise to women following T.C. Norris's election as premier on a platform that included women's suffrage. Alberta's Emily Murphy, another prominent suffragist, whose province followed Manitoba later in 1916, played a leading role in registering women for war-related volunteer campaigns. In the June 1917 Alberta election, Louise McKinney and Roberta MacAdams became the first women in the British Empire to win seats in a legislative assembly. A petition signed by 11,000 supporting female enfranchisement on the basis that women had "raised patriotic funds, knitted socks, rolled bandages, cared for the wounded, took up jobs that released men to go to the front, and surrendered husbands, fathers, and sons to the battlefields"[2] convinced Saskatchewan to extend voting rights to women. British Columbia and Ontario followed in 1917, after the opposition parties in those provinces endorsed female suffrage.

Suffrage supporters argued that it was especially unacceptable in wartime that women of British background were denied the vote while male immigrants, including those from enemy countries, enjoyed this privilege. This changed with the September 1917 Wartime Elections Act. Rammed through Parliament by closure – which cut off debate – this legislation extended the federal franchise to the wives, sisters, daughters, and mothers of men in the armed forces while denying it to those assumed to be disloyal – namely, conscientious objectors and those of enemy background who were naturalized as British subjects of Canada after March 1902. In April 1918, the Women's Franchise Act followed, granting to those twenty-one and older who were British subjects of Canada the right to vote in federal elections (though Asian and Aboriginal women were excluded until after the Second World War). The same year, Nova Scotia women received the provincial franchise, as did those in New Brunswick in 1919 and Prince Edward Island in 1922. Quebec held out until 1940: the powerful Catholic Church adamantly opposed female enfranchisement, arguing that it would distract women from their primary role as guardians of the family.

For many women and men, women's suffrage was seen as a way not of changing gender roles but rather of ensuring that women's views would either reinforce their husbands' or contribute to broader moral and social uplift because of women's presumed maternal and high moral qualities. The issue of women in the labour force was rather different. With military recruitment removing men from the civilian labour market, some 30,000 women took jobs in munitions plants, with over 80 per cent concentrated in southern Ontario and southern Quebec. Although amounting to less than 10 per cent of the number of women hired for similar positions in the Second World War, still this trend sparked controversy. Many opinion leaders claimed that work in munitions factories and other heavy industries would undermine femininity and that the higher pay in such establishments would lure women away from the domestic sphere. To make unconventional jobs seem less threatening, newspapers feminized them by using terms like *munitionette*. Many employers resisted hiring women workers, claiming that they would be unable to perform physically demanding jobs. Described as "diluted," women's work was remunerated at lower rates than men's, and almost no women occupied management positions. Still, women entered establishments and performed jobs from which they had previously been excluded. In Montreal,

some 2,300 worked for railway, steel, and cement companies, and Kingston became the first of several communities
to hire women as street railway conductors. Some historians
argue that more women entering and proving their skills in
the wartime workforce boosted support for improvements
such as minimum wage legislation for women. The first
measure came in Manitoba in 1918, and several other provinces followed by the early 1920s. But these were modest
initiatives; besides paltry minimum wage rates, there were
virtually no inspectors to enforce the rules, and loopholes
existed – for example, women could be kept indefinitely in
lower-paid apprenticeship roles.

Women were expected to back the war effort but certainly not to engage in combat. With the exception of
nurses, whose involvement with the Canadian Army Medical Corps stretched back to the 1885 North-West Rebellion,
Canada's armed services were exclusively male. Still, a small
number of civilian women performed quasi-military roles
as members of Home Guard units that guarded infrastructure and border areas against enemy saboteurs. They were
under orders to avoid violent encounters. If they detected
any threats, they were to contact authorities and not to confront the enemy, especially since they remained unarmed,
even those recruited from women's rifle associations, as was
the case in Hamilton and Winnipeg.

The closest women got to the actual fighting overseas
was as nurses – or "nursing sisters," as they were called until
after the Second World War – or as lesser trained members
of Voluntary Aid Detachments (VADs). Although nursing
sisters were commissioned officers and both they and VADs
faced dangers, such as from enemy artillery fire or bomber
aircraft, these roles were deemed appropriate because they
drew upon women's supposedly innate nurturing qualities. Lower-ranking servicemen were not required to salute
nursing sisters. In popular imagination, nurses were self-
sacrificing and saintly. Their uniform – ankle-length dress,

long white apron, long sleeves, high collar and headdress – made them look like nuns.

The 2,000 Canadian women who served with VADs assisted army nursing sisters and undertook traditionally male tasks, such as driving ambulances. Canadian nursing sisters numbered 2,504 during the First World War and served in Canada, Britain, France, and the eastern Mediterranean. Many worked at casualty clearing stations, sometimes within range of enemy guns, performing triage and dealing with ghastly wounds and dying men. Approximately fifty nursing sisters lost their lives to disease or enemy action, including six who died in German aerial bombardments of various hospital facilities in France in May 1918, and fourteen who drowned after a U-boat attacked the hospital ship *Llandovery Castle* in June 1918.

Canada's nursing sisters honed their skills under the most difficult circumstances. Their experiences in the war led many of them to spearhead efforts for the professional accreditation of nurses, a step that, between 1916 and 1922, seven provinces joined Nova Scotia (1910) and Manitoba (1913) in implementing.

The world wars also shaped the experiences of Canadian children. Schools cultivated patriotism, organizing fund-raising for charities like the Red Cross and Belgian Relief, sometimes by putting on concerts or plays. Children brought in change to schools to purchase War Savings Stamps, each of which cost a quarter, with sixteen being required to trade for a War Savings Certificate that after seven years would mature at $5. High schools established cadet corps, with most of the costs covered by the Department of Militia and Defence.

Assigned reading materials provided schoolchildren with propagandistic explanations of the issues at stake and accounts of the fighting overseas. One such source was *The Children's History of the War*, which was printed in fifty-six instalments (fifty to sixty pages each) between 1915 and

1918. Produced by the well-known British textbook writer, Sir Edward Parrott, it presented the war as an adventure, as a clash between good and evil, and as a succession of Allied triumphs.

In classrooms and school assemblies, soldiers who died in battle were lionized by teachers and school administrators as heroes. In English Canada, high school senior classes became overwhelmingly female as lads were made to feel shame if they were not in uniform. With some recruiters turning a blind eye, an estimated 20,000 Canadians under the legal enlistment age of nineteen made it into uniform; one was just twelve. More than 20,000 high school students joined the Soldiers of the Soil program, which sent them to work on farms for up to four months with no academic penalty. After the war, schools established honour rolls of former pupils who had enlisted, paying special tribute to those who had lost their lives. Students raised funds for memorials and sometimes helped design them. Such was the case at Toronto's Jarvis Collegiate, which commissioned two large murals titled *Patriotism* and *Sacrifice*.

But it was service personnel who were most affected by the world wars. Nearly 620,000 volunteered or were conscripted during the First World War, and about 1,000,000 in the Second, 97 per cent of whom were men. Many men of military age remained in Canada and benefited from the thriving war economy. In large parts of the country – especially in English Canada – they encountered harsh criticism for staying home, and attempts were made to humiliate them into military service. To spare these men from harassment, the government issued special tags for those who had tried to enlist but had been turned down, such as for medical reasons.

Political and social leaders spoke of the country owing those who enlisted a tremendous debt for their service. However, the still prevalent philosophy of limited government and the need to promote self-reliance also shaped the experiences of First World War veterans. As the war ended, the *Montreal Star* insisted that for their own sake, veterans must not become "unlimited creditors of the state to be supported in idleness."[3]

Canadians greeted the armistice on 11 November 1918 with grand, spontaneous celebrations. Local welcoming committees were formed to fête returning soldiers and to help them find them accommodation and jobs. Men were returning to a country eager to praise them, but also to one whose federal government wanted to reduce a $2 billion war debt ($29 billion in 2015 dollars).

In June 1915, shortly after Canada suffered 6,000 casualties at the Second Battle of Ypres, the federal government established the Military Hospitals Commission to deal with medical care and to set pensions for the injured. In 1918, many of the commission's activities were folded into in a new Department of Soldiers' Civil Re-establishment (DSCR). Veterans received a gratuity in the form of a payment for each month of military service, with higher rates for time spent overseas. The average payout was $240 (just over $3,500 in 2015 dollars); the highest possible award for a married private was $600. This provided veterans with a cushion to get restarted, but once the money was claimed, the government absolved itself of further responsibility for those who did not qualify for other programs. Between 1917 and 1919, the federal government spent $181 million on veterans programs ($2.6 billion in 2015 dollars). At just over 8 per cent of total government expenditures, this was an unprecedented sum for welfare costs; but it was not nearly enough. Government programs left many First World War veterans dissatisfied and angry. Canada's federal government accurately trumpeted the fact that its military pensions were more generous than in other parts of the British Empire. Pension costs mounted quickly, from $17 million in 1918 to $30 million the following year. However, only 7 per cent of pension claimants received the maximum award, which for a private, at $40 monthly, was less than the annual salary of an unskilled labourer. By contrast, 71 per cent of claimants received 20 per cent or less of the maximum.

The federal government provided 26,249 veterans with civil service jobs, but the vast majority of these were low paying. Veterans could apply for training in numerous occupations that ran the gamut from agricultural worker to X-ray technician. However, only those whose wartime injuries were judged as preventing a return to their pre-war line of work qualified for such retraining – a policy that resulted in more than 34,000 rejected applicants. Many of those who were accepted griped about poor facilities, equipment, instructors, and courses, as well as inadequate financial support while retraining. In all, 52,603 men started courses, and 43,357 completed their training.

Another program trumpeted by the government was the Soldier Settlement scheme, under which veterans could start a farm. The applicant was required to put down 20 per cent of the land's value and could borrow at 5 per cent interest up to $4,500 for the property and $2,000 for livestock and equipment. Land costs were repayable in twenty-five annual instalments, and the other money in four annual payments starting three years after receiving the funds. By 30 November 1920, 59,331 veterans had applied; 43,063 were approved, but only 19,771 settled on farms. About one-third of the property was expropriated from Aboriginal communities, something made possible by a 1918 amendment to the Indian Act enabling the transfer of otherwise "unproductive" reserve lands. The average grant of land and equipment to veterans amounted to $4,266. Most of the land was obtained in 1919 and early 1920, at a time when property and commodity prices were high; after this, there occurred a steep decline. Faced with more veterans abandoning farms, in 1922 the federal government allowed the consolidation of loans into a single account amortized over twenty-five years, which lowered payments. Still, the percentage of veterans who abandoned farms climbed from 14.5 per cent in fiscal 1922–3 to 21 per cent a year later.

Although programs for veterans of the First World War constituted an unprecedented foray by government into social welfare – especially given that state intervention in this area had been practically nil before the war – thousands who had served their country spoke of being betrayed. Indeed, some estimates in Winnipeg suggested that as many as half the veterans who returned to that city, out of anger and disillusionment, sympathized with strikers involved in the 1919 General Strike. Many veterans of the Second World War – often children of those who had fought in the First – cited the difficult experiences of these older veterans when demanding a better deal from government.

The First World War had thrust many men, women, and children into situations that challenged long-established norms. The Second World War witnessed much greater public discussion of such trends. This built on growing sexual freedoms during the interwar years as exemplified by the popular culture of the "Roaring 20s," which ushered in the first Hollywood sex symbols, the risqué flapper style for women (shorter skirts, bobbed hair), and talk of "flaming youth" (a term popularized by a 1923 film that included a famous skinny-dipping scene shot in silhouette). The greater demands on industry generated by a more mechanized Second World War drew far more women into the workforce. Further affecting the scope of change was the determination not to repeat the mistakes of the First World War and its aftermath. Veterans were the main beneficiaries of this general desire.

Popular memory of the First World War is linked to the idea of lost innocence and idealism; this does not easily embrace the notion of people letting loose and living for the moment. That notion does, however, play a role in Second World War nostalgia. It was a time associated with whirlwind romances, some of which involved the nearly 50,000 war brides that Canadian servicemen brought home from overseas. Ninety per cent of these brides came from Britain, where as many as 300,000 Canadian servicemen had been stationed during the first three years of the war. Canadian troops did not spend nearly as much time in Britain during the First World War, though 20,000 marriages still resulted, most of them while men were awaiting repatriation to Canada.

Intimate relationships between servicemen and civilians occurred beyond Britain, of course. St John's, Newfoundland, a city of some 40,000 at the outset of the Second World War, hosted over 7,000 American and 6,000 Canadian servicemen to support naval convoy and air ferry service to Britain. This led to port improvements, new airfields, roads, and buildings, and more than 20,000 civilian jobs. Partly in response to the massive American presence – the United States had assumed control over several British bases in Newfoundland under the Lend-Lease program – Canada established a High Commission in St John's in 1941. There were other consequences besides this to the "friendly invasion" of Newfoundland. Local officials blamed military personnel for doubling the rate of criminal prosecutions between 1939 and 1941. Among the socially and religiously conservative Newfoundlanders, anxiety abounded over young women dating men in uniform, who were thought to be only after sex. The VD rate among Americans stationed at Fort Pepperill, just outside St John's, rose to 30 per 1,000, the highest rate in the Eastern Defence Command, which covered most of Atlantic Canada.

Most Canadian communities welcomed the armed forces. Servicemen brought business, parades, military shows, sporting teams (with many former professionals in uniform), and headline performers, who came to entertain the troops. But the unruly conduct of servicemen also encouraged much tongue-wagging. Military authorities declared some areas off limits to uniformed personnel after drunken brawls. There were sensationalist press accounts of "camp followers," that is, women who hung around military bases, actively pursuing servicemen and even rationalizing having sex with them as a patriotic gift to those facing a hazardous future.

At the same time, more people were getting married – and divorced. The marriage rate per 1,000 climbed from a 1938–9 average of 7.9 to 10.2 in 1943. Newspapers commented about couples deciding to marry without serious forethought, the result of whirlwind wartime romances. Several clerics refused to marry such couples, predicting that the trend would result in more divorces. Despite narrowly defined grounds, the figures for divorce rose from 14.4 per 100,000 in 1936 to 20.8 in 1940 and to 27.7 in 1943. *Saturday Night* wrote as early as 1941 that divorce had become an "infant industry."[4]

Venereal disease again became a huge problem. Many servicemen were barely out of adolescence and for the first time in their lives were away from their parents and communities. Like tourists, soldiers on leave pursued their desires because they could leave behind everything they did. Communities were inundated with women war workers on their own, or women whose husbands, fiancés, or boyfriends had left for overseas. At its peak in 1940, the VD rate for the Canadian Army in Canada stood at 55 per 1,000.

The highest VD rates were in Quebec. Despite the Catholic Church's strong influence, Quebec's major cities had had red light districts since the early nineteenth century. Montreal and Quebec City, being port cities, saw multitudes of visiting sailors, who provided a steady clientele for sex trade workers. Since the 1920s, when prohibition prevailed throughout North America except in Quebec, Montreal had become a major entertainment centre with many nightclubs; in the public mind, it was the "Paris of North America"; in the eyes of its critics, it was "Sin City." In Montreal's red light district, an estimated eighty brothels were crammed into six downtown city blocks (the present-day site of the Université du Quebec à Montréal). In Quebec

City, most brothels were in the Palais district in the city's older Lower Town.

In Quebec between 1940 and 1943, around 3,000 women were arrested every year for being found in a bawdy house – more than in any other province. But many brothel managers were tipped off in advance of police raids, and many arrests were shams. A typical scenario saw a couple of women in the lobby arrested – whose fines were subsequently covered by the brothel management – while sex trade workers and their clients remained in the rear of the building in rooms that officers purposely avoided. Many authorities, and not just in in Quebec, preferred brothels in red light districts to street prostitution. Still, military leaders grew so frustrated with the loss of men to VD that they told municipal leaders in Montreal and Quebec City that if things did not improve, leaves by servicemen to those cities would be suspended. Maj.-Gen. E.J. Renaud, the commander of the military district that encompassed both Montreal and Quebec City, insisted that civilian authorities revoke the operating licences of rooming houses, hotels, restaurants, dance halls, and clubs identified as contact points in the transference of VD. The police closed down a few of the larger and better-known bawdy houses. As local officials had predicted, many women responded by taking their business to the streets, where they were more difficult to control.

More education and action helped bring down the incidence of VD. For the army, the VD rate across Canada declined from 55 per 1,000 in 1940 to 26 per 1,000 in 1944. Lectures, literature, posters, and films warned soldiers about the dangers of VD. In a change from the First World War, the army also distributed condoms to servicemen, as well as prophylactic kits containing a soap-impregnated cloth and tubes of nitrate jelly and calomel ointment to be applied to the genitals following intercourse. Early in the war, men who contracted VD were segregated from other hospital patients in order to stigmatize and humiliate them. They also faced fines. Medical staff eventually concluded that the punitive approach did not work. Rather than reforming behaviour, it prompted men to try to hide the disease, ultimately making it more difficult to treat. Many officers continued to categorize VD as a self-inflicted wound that warranted punishment. By mid-1942, however, penalties were generally discarded in favour of simply treating the infected soldier and returning him to duty.

Servicemen with VD faced pressure to provide answers about who had passed the disease to them. Brigadier G.B. Chisholm of the Royal Canadian Army Medical Corps ordered investigating officers: "Don't accept an answer about being too drunk to remember. Repeated sincere questioning will produce the truth." Provincial health officials would be supplied with leads, whereupon the alleged facilitator would receive a letter demanding, under the threat of a heavy fine, that she "present [her]self before a duly licensed and qualified physician ... to procure ... a report or certificate ... as to whether or not [she was] suffering from venereal disease."[5]

Canadians were provided with more information about VD and better treatment facilities. In 1942, British Columbia's Department of Venereal Disease Control gave over 170 public lectures and distributed more than 135,000 pieces of literature. That same year, Ontario distributed over 200,000 pieces of literature on VD prevention. *Chatelaine*, Canada's most prominent women's magazine, remarked that the "taboos, ignorance and fear" surrounding VD were "losing strength."[6] In 1944 the federal government established a Venereal Disease Control Division within its Department of Pensions and National Health. That same year, it distributed over 700,000 pieces of literature and also raised public awareness by declaring 7 February National Social Hygiene Day. With federal money, provincial governments expanded their anti-VD campaigns. In Ontario, Manitoba, and Saskatchewan, programs were introduced to supply sulpha drugs; soon after, in 1943, penicillin was being used overseas with great effect to treat VD. More VD clinics opened, including in remote areas, such as Peace River and McLennan, Alberta. Clearly, conditions created by the war compelled more extensive and realistic strategies to combat VD.

Canadian women during the Second World War largely accepted an enhanced role for the state as it related to issues such as health and family. They also expressed their support for the war effort through volunteerism, just as they had as in First World War. For instance, by the end of 1940, the United Church had mobilized 60,000 women volunteers, who produced for shipment overseas 267,372 pairs of socks, 50,223 sweaters, 18,552 pairs of wristlets, 33,275 scarves, and 22,024 pairs of gloves and mitts. As in the First World War, women assumed leadership roles through voluntarism. For example, Mona Wilson had served as a nurse in France in the First World War. Having risen through the ranks of the Canadian Red Cross Society during the interwar period, in 1943 she was tasked with coordinating more than three hundred Red Cross volunteers in Newfoundland, an appointment that further underscored Canada's increasing involvement on the island. In 1940, the federal government, recognizing the crucial role played by female volunteers, established a Women's Voluntary Services Division within the Department of National War Services. It established forty-four female-run branches across Canada to better promote and coordinate patriotic efforts undertaken by women's groups.

Between June 1939 and the beginning of 1944, some 370,000 women obtained paid work in fields directly connected to the war effort. The number of women with jobs outside the home peaked in 1944 at 1.35 million – a workplace participation rate of 33.1 per cent compared to 22.7 per cent in 1939. By mid-1942, the need for wartime labour had prompted the federal government to introduce income tax breaks for working couples as well as state-run subsidized child care. In September, National Selective Service, which to that point had focused on identifying men, organized a national registration of women.

Much commentary, such as in the press, stressed that women were taking paid work in order to release men for action overseas and that following victory, women would return to home life. In Quebec, priests denounced women's work outside the home as contrary to the principles of the church. A 1943 petition in the province demanded that mothers with children under sixteen be prohibited from working outside the home. It gathered 120,000 signatures.

Many employers portrayed women's employment in heavy industry as impractical because their inferior physical strength made them less productive than men. This claim, and the view that women were less skilled and competent than men, resulted in most women being assigned simpler and more repetitive tasks and being excluded from managerial positions. Although some women did well financially – such as those working in the aircraft sector, who in 1944 averaged nearly $1,500 per year, which was comparable to a good male wage – the average annual pay among women rose from $594 to $1,051 over the course of the war, a marginal improvement from 56.3 to 59.7 per cent of the average male rate. The press sometimes linked the jobs women performed to housework to make them seem more natural. Some comparisons were absurd, such as when large metal-turning lathes were likened to sewing machines.

Yet, with so many women performing wartime jobs well, accounts of female strength and skill also abounded. This perspective was especially evident in stories by female journalists. Among the most upbeat was Lotta Dempsey, future editor-in-chief of *Chatelaine*, who predicted: "This was the time and the place it really started, the honest-to-goodness equality of Canadian women. It began to happen that hour when Canadian girls left desks and kitchens ... stepped into overalls and took their places in the lines of workers at lathes and drills."[7]

But it was the trend towards more working mothers that generated the most trepidation. In June 1942, Ottawa introduced the jointly funded Dominion–Provincial Wartime Day Nursery program, but it never came close to meeting demand. Ontario opened twenty-eight facilities with 1,085 spaces, which met only 20 per cent of the potential demand among war workers. In Quebec, only six facilities opened in Montreal, offering fewer than two hundred spots. Alberta's Social Credit government initially announced it would join the program, then backed out after widespread criticism that it was encouraging mothers to shirk their family responsibilities. The press coined phrases such as "eight-hour orphans" and "latch-key" children. One director with the Canadian Welfare Council, a publicly subsidized policy think tank, bemoaned children, even in kindergarten, "let[ting] themselves into their homes at all sorts of hours, and snatch[ing] what food they can."[8]

As politicians faced postwar reconstruction, they pressured women to leave the workforce. In mid-1944, C.D. Howe, who by then was changing portfolios from Munitions and Supply to Reconstruction, insisted that most women "would prefer to stay at home once the war [was] over."[9] The federal government helped this process along: it stopped financing day care and eliminated the tax breaks that had helped draw wives and mothers into the workforce. Between 1944 and 1946, Canada's rate of female employment participation plunged from 33.1 to 25 per cent, though this was still higher than at the outset of the war.

Many women happily settled into domestic life. After years on their own, they wanted to marry and start a family. They accepted the message that their employment had been an emergency wartime measure and that veterans were more deserving of civilian jobs. Others were exhausted after years of the "double day" of paid work and domestic responsibilities. Canada's marriage rate climbed from 9.0 per 1,000 in 1945 to 10.9 the following year. The fertility rate per 1,000 women also rose, from 24.3 in 1945 to a postwar peak of

28.9 in 1947, ushering in the Baby Boom. Still, soon after
the war, women's workforce participation again rose, suggesting reverberations from the period. Throughout the late
1940s, the aggregate number of women in paid work each
year remained higher than it had been except for 1943–5.
Their workforce participation rate was greater than at the
outset of the decade, and the number of married women
with jobs rose from 85,600 in 1941 to 349,000 in 1951.

As in the First World War, women did not take up arms.
But in the Second, they did expand their military roles.
Some 3,656 nurses served with the Royal Canadian Army
Medical Corps, 481 with the Royal Canadian Air Force
Nursing Service, and 343 with the Royal Canadian Navy
Nursing Service. With the increasing professionalization of
nursing, Canada established no Voluntary Aid Detachments
during the Second World War.

Although military nurses, such as those posted to Sicily
only five days after Allied troops landed there, confronted
highly stressful and harrowing situations, they received comparatively little press coverage, as their job was not unusual
for women. Far more attention focused on the fact that
the Canadian government had established other female
military services, starting with the Canadian Women's Army
Corps (CWAC) in June 1941, whose numbers ultimately
reached 21,624. In July 1941, the Canadian Women's Aux-
iliary Air Service was announced, which the following February was renamed the Royal Canadian Air Force Women's
Division (RCAF WD), whose numbers reached 17,018. The
Women's Royal Canadian Naval Service (WRENS) followed
in July 1942, ultimately reaching 6,781 personnel. Overall,
women's presence in the armed forces increased more than
tenfold over the First World War, though this was still less
than 15 per cent of the number of women who took on war-
related civilian jobs.

These new uniformed roles for women precipitated much
unease. One poll found that only 58 per cent of Canadians
thought that a woman who donned a military uniform would

Recruiting parade for the Canadian women's services in Shawinigan, Quebec. McCord Museum, MP-1986.19.2.15.

not "restrict [her] chances of marriage."[10] What the armed forces dubbed as a "whispering campaign" spread about servicewomen, in which they were portrayed as masculine, as lesbians, or as sexually promiscuous. One military communiqué responded to such rumours by assuring the public that "Canadian mothers can cease worrying about their daughters the moment they enlist ... The reason being that [their] sergeant ... acts as a second mother."[11] For those who fretted over servicewomen looking too masculine, the military pointed out that women's military uniforms had been "planned and executed with the aid of Canada's foremost designers."[12]

Servicewomen initially earned two-thirds of the male service pay rate, the justification being that they did not see combat. Yet this pay differential did not apply to servicemen who saw no action. Most women performed lower-grade jobs deemed appropriate for them; for instance, 62 per cent of CWACs were administrative clerks and 8 per cent were cooks. But as more men went overseas, a greater range of positions opened up for women. When the CWAC was established, some thirty trades were listed for women; by the end of the war, some fifty-five were listed, including jobs such as draughtsman, mechanic, and technician. In 1943, to attract more recruits, servicewomen's pay was increased to 80 per cent of the male rate, and raises for qualifying for trades were provided on an equal basis with men.

Once victory was in sight, plans were developed to disband the three female military auxiliaries, a process completed by the end of 1946. Servicewomen were eligible for veterans' programs. Nearly three-quarters opted for the gratuity based on their length of service, though it was set at 80 per cent of the male rate. Servicewomen took retraining in eighty-five areas – including pharmacy and architecture – but over 55 per cent qualified as secretaries, beauticians, or dressmakers. The Second World War, more than the First, provided new opportunities for women. Much of this came to a halt as the war ended. Still, the broad trajectory of change towards greater equality had accelerated.

Many Canadians would recall the war as the backdrop to an exhilarating childhood. One Nova Scotia woman remembered that she "longed to be one of those WRENS in their snappy little hats," or better yet, a spy foiling German plans. Young Canadians tuned in to radio shows such as *L is for Lankey*, which portrayed the heroic exploits of Allied bomber crews.

As in the First World War, the schools cultivated patriotism. Saluting the flag, singing "God Save the King," and swearing allegiance to the Crown became mandatory; twenty-seven Mennonite children who refused were expelled from Kitchener schools in 1940. Children achieved impressive results in patriotic campaigns. By the end of 1944, Ontario students had raised nearly $1.4 million ($19 million in 2015 dollars) for the Red Cross and other war charities by means such as canvassing door-to-door and organizing rummage and bake sales, movie and dance nights, and plays and carnivals.

Children foraged through attics, garages, and barns for reusable scrap. In late 1942, Rotarians in Yarmouth, Nova Scotia, working in conjunction with elementary schools, turned the salvaging effort into a war game, moving students up in rank for every fifty pounds they collected. In industrial arts classes, boys made items such as wooden splints and test tube holders for the Canadian Army Medical Corps, cribbage boards and ping-pong paddles for servicemen's recreation centres, and model aircraft for Commonwealth Air Training Plan recognition classes. Boys from twelve to seventeen enlisted in the Royal Canadian Army Cadets, Sea Cadets, or Air Cadets. Boy Scouts assisted with Air Raid Protection drills by running messages and watching for violators during blackouts. Girl Guides and Rangers pitched in as nurses' aides, for which they received a special badge. Starting in spring 1941, schoolchildren as young as fourteen took paid work on farms to compensate for shortages of agricultural labour.

But unlike the First World War, the Second witnessed considerable public commentary on the potentially negative psychological impact of the conflict on youth. The interwar years had seen the rise of psychology as a respected professional field. In January 1918, the Canadian National Committee for Mental Hygiene was established; much of its early work focused on First World War veterans. The 1920s saw the first separate university psychology departments at the University of Toronto and McGill. Connected to the growing stature of psychology was the rise of child care experts. In 1925, the St George's School for Child Study was established at the University of Toronto; it was soon expanded and renamed the Institute for Child Study. One of its principal researchers was Dr William Blatz, who during the Second World War would be among a group of experts quoted in newspapers as suggesting that parents should show caution in sharing their anxieties about the war with children.

Many Canadians came to link the war with delinquency. Court appearances by juveniles across the country rose from 9,497 in 1939 to 13,802 three years later. There are no equivalent statistics for the First World War period, for juvenile courts were not widely adopted before the 1920s. Juveniles at that time were not seen as members of a separate category.

Press commentary abounded with regard to inadequate parental supervision in wartime. Politicians and child care workers weighed in. *Saturday Night* magazine claimed that with the "chief disciplinarian" in uniform, many children took advantage of the "kind-hearted" mother.[13] A Toronto *Star* editorial concluded, without evidence, that if the father was away, delinquency increased, but if the mother also worked outside the home, "it doubled." A Catholic group in Quebec claimed that "three quarters of juvenile delinquents come from the homes of working mothers."[14] A June 1942 report on Verdun, an industrial suburb of Montreal, estimated that some 5,000 ill-governed youth lived within its borders. Such concerns helped convince Quebec policy makers to implement compulsory school attendance in 1943, though the fact that it only extended to age fourteen presumably missed most teenaged delinquents.[15] The Second World brought children adventure and new responsibilities, but also considerable public anxiety and efforts to reassert traditional family life to ensure control over their activities.

Planning for the postwar period – specifically, for the return of veterans – started early. Many recalled the difficulties faced by veterans of the First World War and the anger they had felt. Only one month after the Second World War began, Canada's Minister of Pensions and National Health, Ian Mackenzie, a former GWVA vice-president, advised Prime Minister Mackenzie King to begin planning for demobilization and rehabilitation. The result, which took full form in 1946, became known as the Veterans Charter, a name chosen to convey its historical importance, with its echoes of the 1945 United Nations Charter.

In December 1939, a Cabinet Committee on Demobilization and Re-establishment began studying policy recommendations. It created fourteen subcommittees comprising deputy ministers and experts drawn from the armed forces, the Royal Canadian Legion, and the private sector. Instrumental in setting overall direction was the executive secretary of the subcommittees, Robert England, a twice-wounded veteran of the First World War, recipient of the Military Cross, and former director of the Canadian Legion Educational Services. Another key figure was Walter Woods, the Associate Deputy Minister of Pensions and National Health, the government department initially responsible for administering veterans' programs. Wounded in the First World War, Woods recalled receiving poor assistance when returning to Canada in 1918.

Applying lessons from the post–First World War reconstruction, the Canadian government granted Second World War veterans a gratuity of $7.50 per month for time served in the Western Hemisphere and $15 per month for time overseas. For veterans who did not claim other benefits, more cash was available, up to a level matching the gratuity in the form of a Re-establishment Credit to help purchase, furnish, or equip a home or business. The Reinstatement in Civil Employment Act affirmed healthy veterans' right to resume their civilian jobs, or comparable posts with their former employers, at a rate of pay equivalent to what they would have earned had they not enlisted. The government made grants and subsidized loans available for those who wished to start their own business, to enter commercial fishing, or, under the Veterans Land Act (VLA), to farm full-time or (expanding on the Soldiers Settlement Act) to start a maximum two-acre hobby farm, for which no agricultural experience was required. Self-employed veterans who struggled financially before revenue started flowing could apply for an Awaiting Returns Allowance, which paid, for up to one year, from $44.20 monthly for a single veteran with no dependents to a maximum of $120.40 for those married with six dependents under seventeen years old. The Vocational Training Coordination Act provided an allowance for any veteran who sought to retrain – and this was not just for the injured, as was the case for First World War veterans. In what was perhaps the greatest expansion of opportunities, veterans could obtain free university education with the living allowance on the basis of one year for each year of military service, though it was common that good students received support for their entire degree, and even graduate studies, well beyond the number of years they had spent in uniform. To help veterans qualify (at the time, fewer than half of Canadians had completed high school, compared to nearly 90 per cent in 2013), provision was made for them to obtain a high school diploma in as little as six months under a special accelerated program. After March 1944, the new Department of Veterans Affairs (DVA) coordinated these and other programs. Between 1945 and 1948, the federal government spent $1.6 billion ($21.6 billion in 2015 dollars) on veterans' programs. This was the largest ever social welfare initiative, claiming over 13 per cent of all federal government expenditures. Certainly, it was a vast increase over what had been provided for First World War veterans.

Over seven hundred Citizen Committees organized "welcome home" ceremonies and helped veterans find housing and employment. Like their fathers' generation, most Second World War veterans quickly reintegrated into civilian life, but others struggled to readjust. In 1946, divorces in Canada stood at 7,683; the following year they reached 8,199, compared to just 2,068 in 1939. Many veterans struggled to reconnect with their wives and children. Some children who had built up expectations of their father while he was away felt disappointment soon after he returned. Others felt trepidation about welcoming a man who had been so long absent from their lives. "He always felt like a stranger [who] had come and taken over my life and my mother's house," said one man in later years, who for some time after the war called his father Mr Palmer. Bitterness sometimes developed when a veteran attempted to re-establish fatherly authority. "I didn't like the way my dad ran our home like an army barracks," recalled one woman, who felt that her father never shook off his former role as a sergeant major. And then there were those who remembered not understanding why their father "blew up" at the slightest provocation.[16]

Overall, Canada's Second World War veterans were less embittered than those of the First World War, a glad result of the Veterans Charter. Counsellors from the DVA, many of whom were veterans, acted as advocates rather than as gatekeepers, making it clear that as long as a veteran qualified, it was his or her right to pursue any program. Approximately two-thirds of veterans opted for maximum cash payouts. The average gratuity was $488 ($6,600 in 2015 dollars). They filed nearly one million claims for Re-establishment Credits, 98 per cent of which were approved. The DVA arranged retraining for 81,418 former service personnel in over one hundred occupations. Nearly 17,000 veterans obtained allowances to help them start businesses. At more than thirty VLA offices established across Canada, just over 120,000 men received a low-interest loan of up to $6,000 to buy land and buildings, and up to $1,200 to obtain livestock, feed, seed, and equipment. Only 10 per cent of applications were refused. The veteran was required to make a 10 per cent down payment, but subsequent payments were based on two-thirds of the amount loaned, and the mortgage was fixed for twenty-five years at just 3.5 per cent interest. One black mark was that in British Columbia, 768 VLA farms came through the forced sale of property formerly owned by Japanese Canadians.

Canadian enrolment in universities doubled between 1944 and 1947 with an influx of 54,000 veterans. This included some 3,000 former servicewomen. Most women entered arts disciplines, especially disciplines traditionally dominated by women, namely social work and household science. Still, women gained a greater foothold in non-traditional areas – for example, nearly eighty ex-service-women who took degrees in business administration and commerce.

Compared to pensions paid to Great War veterans, or even to the average annual male salary of about $1,750 in 1945, Second World War pensions were quite good. At the 10 per cent disability level, they ranged from $756 per annum for a single person to $1,574 for a married veteran with six dependents under seventeen years old. At the 100 per cent disability level, they ranged from $1,260 to $2,364. By the end of 1945, pension boards, increasingly staffed by veterans, were approving support in 86.3 per cent of cases. Programs for First World War veterans had been Canada's first national social welfare initiative, but they had been constrained by the notion that welfare encouraged dependency and resulted in crippling government debt. The planners of the Veterans Charter enjoyed the benefit of hindsight and a more supportive atmosphere in which to pursue social welfare.

Wartime Canadian society changed at an accelerated pace, but in several areas that trend seemed matched by efforts to turn back the clock. War brought moral panic, reflecting the instability induced by the departure of so many men from home. But war also created opportunities for some groups to shepherd into existence social reforms they had long sought, such as women's suffrage, prohibition, and social welfare policies.

The federal government had learned a great deal from the First World War and applied those lessons in a largely successful reconstruction of the Canadian economy and society after 1945. This process was grounded in wider patterns relating to the relationship of the state to Canadians: the Second World War saw the introduction of Unemployment Insurance, the Baby Bonus, new collective bargaining rights for labour, and the adoption of Keynesian economic strategies to ensure low unemployment and stable incomes. The end of First World War had seen the country saddled with crippling debt and bitterly divided; the end of the Second saw the country wealthier. "We remember the postwar years as a time of unprecedented affluence," wrote historian Desmond Morton of the period after 1945. This was largely due to a "series of wartime policies"[17] that helped a pre-war depression give way to an unprecedented economic boom. Despite 42,000 dead, this fostered a lasting image of the Second World War as the "Good War."

Conclusion

Wyndham Colquhoun of Brantford, Ontario, was not yet twenty-one years old when he volunteered for overseas service in 1916. Two years later, he was wounded during the crossing of the Canal du Nord. Evacuated to a military hospital in England, he seemed poised to recover; evocative photographs of Colquhoun from the private album of another officer depict a young man of slight build, up and around town while convalescing in October 1918. Sadly, Colquhoun fell seriously ill with influenza. He died on 8 November, just three days before the armistice.

As a matter of official policy, Canadian war dead were not to be repatriated during either world war. Those whose bodies were not eviscerated by a high explosive shell or simply trampled into the mud after falling wounded were buried together with other British Empire or Commonwealth casualties in cemeteries maintained by the Imperial War Graves Commission (today the Commonwealth War Graves Commission). But there were exceptions; Colquhoun's father was a senior officer and was able to bring his boy home, and give him a soldier's funeral in Brantford that December. The local newspaper reported that "seldom has a military funeral attracted such universal interest; a vast concourse of people turning out to pay a last tribute of respect to the departed hero. At the [Colquhoun] house and along the thoroughfares, thousands of people gathered with bowed heads while at Greenwood cemetery the religious service and the military ceremonial drew forth a great throng."[1]

Coming as close to the return of peace as it did, Wyndham Colquhoun's death reflects the cruel, random tragedy that underpinned both world wars. That his family brought him home for burial reminds us of the ongoing tension between the private and the public, the personal and the political, and the local and the national imperatives that defined Canadians' experiences of war during 1914–18 and 1939–45.

The opening chapter of this book explored the related themes of politics and recruitment in the First and Second World Wars. Certain trends were revealed: the federal government assumed expansive powers to coordinate increasingly complex war efforts. Such measures as taxation, internment, compulsory military service, and social welfare programs reshaped the lives of ordinary people. Despite the continuity of many of these trends through both conflicts, there were also clear contrasts between the wars, such the differing approaches of Borden and Mackenzie King towards conscription. In each conflict, however, regional interests and economic considerations influenced the agendas of national leaders.

The second chapter examined the mobilization of Canada's material resources, as well as the bodies and imaginations of Canadians themselves. There were key similarities between 1914–18 and 1939–45. In each war, for instance, grassroots organizations played important roles in national mobilization. Both conflicts transformed the Canadian economy. Yet there were also stark contrasts. Learning from the Borden government's missteps during the First World War, Mackenzie King's government immediately involved itself in all facets of the war effort, from the coordination of military production to wage and price controls. Government policy restrained the free market to some extent, but it also protected ordinary Canadians from abuses, such as high rents.

The third chapter followed two generations of Canadian soldiers through the gruelling land campaigns of two global wars. The Canadian Expeditionary Force expanded rapidly during the early part of the First World War, and soldiers of the Canadian Corps played prominent roles in most of the key British campaigns on the Western Front. In 1919, many Canadians emerged from the war full of pride in the contribution they had made to the British Empire's victory. In the early part of the Second World War, Mackenzie King's more cautious manpower policies played a role in keeping Canadian ground forces out of action, but only for a time. Germany's far-reaching victories during 1939–41 rendered limited liability unsustainable, and from mid-1943 until the end of the war, Canada's fighting divisions were heavily engaged. Not until the final months of the war, however, did all Canadian formations finally come together to constitute one Canadian Army in the field.

The fourth chapter recounted the birth of the Royal Canadian Navy in 1910, and contrasted its limited role in the First World War with its far-reaching participation in the Second. While the naval policies of Borden and Mackenzie King differed dramatically, there are also common threads to be found: in both wars, the navy suffered from inadequate equipment, shortages of trained personnel, and a generally poor state of initial preparation. But in the Second World War, it expanded from humble beginnings to play a major role in convoy escort duties, a vital strategic element in the most destructive total conflict the world has ever seen.

The fifth chapter showed that Canada's two wars in the air followed, to a degree, the transformation the navy had undergone. During the First World War, Canada had no national air force in the field, although thousands of Canadians joined the British flying services. In the Second World War, the Royal Canadian Air Force was a key component of Canadian defence policy, as the navy had also become. Through the British Commonwealth Air Training Plan, the strategic bombing campaign, and anti-submarine operations, Canadians were at the centre of an air war that shaped the total nature and global scope of the Second World War.

The final chapter underscored fundamental shifts in Canadian attitudes, social norms, and gender roles between 1914 and 1945. While some of these developments, such as women's enfranchisement, would likely have occurred independently of the world wars, there is little doubt that Canadian participation in the two conflicts accelerated change. Canadian veterans clearly enjoyed greater benefits and opportunities after 1945 than had been the case twenty-five years earlier – an important difference. This is not to say that every social consequence of the Canadian war experience was positive, progressive, or complete, but clearly, the 1914–18 and 1939–45 years were essential stepping stones between early-twentieth-century Canada and the nation we know today.

Of course, the aftermaths of each conflict bring sharp contrasts into relief. As the First World War ended, the Spanish flu ravaged communities across Canada, killing an estimated 50,000 people, nearly as many Canadians as had died in battle overseas. No such tragedy befell the nation after 1945. In the years after 1918, political turmoil was the norm, beginning with the Winnipeg General Strike, and this led to the rise of the Progressives and the Co-operative Commonwealth Federation. Compared to that, the Canadian political arena was calm in the late 1940s and the 1950s. The peace of 1918–19 was an uneasy one that lasted only twenty years: a poor return for the huge investments in blood and treasure that the First World War had absorbed. Those who lived through the post-1945 era were spared such uncertainty, at least for a time. True enough, the Cold War robbed Canadians of the long-term security they desired, but at least a Third World War was avoided.

Did Canada achieve a new national identity by fighting in these conflicts? Popular rhetoric aside, there is no simple answer to that question. The period certainly witnessed an evolution in Canada's culture, and in its relationships with Britain and the United States. In the nineteenth century, British military power was Canada's most important source of security, and the United States its most threatening potential adversary. The decline of the British Empire during the world wars gradually brought the North American nations closer together in war and in peace, not only in matters of defence, but also in economic and cultural terms.

However we choose to measure the wars' impact on our collective identity, it is essential not to lose sight of individual Canadians and their personal and immediate experiences within these two national war efforts. At home or abroad, Canadians of all persuasions participated in the world wars. Whether on foreign battlefields, on the rolling seas, in the air, on prairie farms or factory floors, or in their homes huddled around a humming radio, the wars touched all Canadians. And Canadians, in their turn, left their mark on the twentieth century.

Notes

1 Politics and Recruitment

1 Quoted in Jim Blanchard, *Winnipeg's Great War: A City Comes of Age* (Winnipeg: University of Manitoba Press, 2010), 37.
2 Sandra Gwyn, *Tapestry of War: A Private View of Canadians in the Great War* (Toronto: HarperCollins, 1992), 61.
3 Ronald Haycock, *Sam Hughes: The Public Career of a Controversial Canadian, 1885–1916* (Waterloo: Wilfrid Laurier University Press, 1986), 146; Tim Cook, *The Madman and the Butcher: The Sensational Wars of Sam Hughes and General Arthur Currie* (Toronto: Allen Lane, 2010), 174.
4 Metropolitan Toronto Library, Baldwin Room, World War One Broadside Catalogue, n.p.
5 Blanchard, *Winnipeg's Great War*, 107.
6 Library and Archives Canada (LAC), RG 24, Department of National Defence records, vol. 4479, file 25-1-20, Secretary of the Montreal Citizens' Recruiting League to O.C. of M.D. # 4, n.d.
7 Robert Laird Borden, *Robert Laird Borden: His Memoirs*, vol. 2 (Montreal and Kingston: McGill–Queen's University Press, 1969) 45.
8 Robert Craig Brown, *Robert Laird Borden: A Biography*, vol. 2 (Toronto: Macmillan, 1980), 81.
9 LAC, MG 26 H, Robert Borden papers, vol. 41, Union Government Publicity Committee Pamphlets.

10 *Alberta in the 20th Century,: A Journalistic History of the Province in Twelve Volumes,* vol. 4, *The·Great War and its Consequences* (Edmonton: United Western Communications Ltd., 1994), 96.

11 Brown, *Robert Laird Borden: A Biography,* vol. 2, 128.

12 *Revised Statutes of Canada,* 10 George V, Chapter 146, 7 July 1919.

13 *Globe and Mail,* 4 September 1939, 9; *Gazette* (Montreal), 4 September 1939, 11.

14 Canada, House of Commons, *Debates,* 8 September 1939, 12.

15 *Order in Council,* PC 882, 13 October 1942.

16 J.L. Granatstein, *Canada's War: The Politics of the Mackenzie King Government, 1939–1945* (Toronto: Oxford, 1975), 94.

17 Ivana Caccia, *Managing the Canadian Mosaic in Wartime: Shaping Citizenship Policy, 1939–1945* (Montreal and Kingston: McGill–Queen's University Press, 2010), 97.

18 Patricia Roy, J.L. Granatstein, Masako Iino, and Hiroko Takamura, *Mutual Hostages: Canadians and Japanese during the Second World War* (Toronto: University of Toronto Press, 1990), 91.

19 *Canadian Unionist,* September 1942, 82–83.

20 Peter McInnis, *Harnessing Labour Confrontation: Shaping the Postwar Settlement in Canada, 1943–1950* (Toronto: University of Toronto Press, 2002), 22.

21 Granatstein, *Canada's War,* 247.

22 Tim Cook, *Warlords: Borden, Mackenzie King, and Canada's World Wars* (Toronto: Allen Lane, 2012), 365–357.

2 Mobilizing for Total War

1 Quoted in Michael Bliss, *A Canadian Millionaire: The Life and Business Times of Sir Joseph Flavelle, Bart., 1858–1939* (Toronto: University of Toronto Press, 1978), 295.

2 Ottawa *Journal,* 7 April 1916, 1.

3 Library and Archives of Canada (LAC), RG9, Department of Militia and Defence, File H.S. 27–1-2, Despatch, 29 March 1916.

4 LAC, RG9, Department of Militia and Defence, vol. 1921, file 124–4; vol. 4732, file 138–10.

5 Quoted in Ian Miller, *Our Glory and Our Grief: Torontonians and the Great War* (Toronto: University of Toronto Press, 2002), 47.

6 House of Lords Record Office, Lord Beaverbrook papers, Series 137, Neil Family papers, R.H. Neil to his parents, 15 September 1915.

7 LAC, RG6, Secretary of State, Chief Press Censor papers, file 207–5, Chambers to Field, 23 September 1915.

8 Metropolitan Toronto Library, Baldwin Room, Broadside Collection.

9 LAC, RG19, Department of Finance Records, vol. 4005, form letter from White dated 1 October 1918.

10 Bliss, *A Canadian Millionaire*, 371.

11 Rod Millard, "'The Crusade for Science': Science and Technology on the Home Front, 1914–1918," in *Canada and the First World War: Essays in Honour of Robert Craig Brown*, ed. David Mackenzie (Toronto: University of Toronto Press, 2005), 307, 316; James Hull, "'A Stern Matron who stands beside the Chair in every council of war or industry': The First World War and the Development of Scientific Research at Canadian Universities," in *Cultures, Communities, and Conflict: Histories of Canadian Universities and Wars*, ed. Paul Stortz and E. Lisa Panayotidis (Toronto: University of Toronto Press, 2012), 164.

12 Spencer Dunmore, *Above and Beyond: The Canadians' War in the Air, 1939–1945* (Toronto: McClelland & Stewart, 1996), 53.

13 Wallace Reyburn, *Some of It Was Fun* (Toronto: Thomas Nelson and Sons, 1949), 136.

14 Wilfrid Eggleston, *Scientists at War* (Toronto: Oxford University Press, 1950), 507.

15 David Zimmerman, *The Great Naval Battle of Ottawa* (Toronto: University of Toronto Press, 1989), 167.

3 Fighting the Wars on Land

1 Andrew Iarocci, *Shoestring Soldiers: The 1st Canadian Division at War, 1914–1915* (Toronto: University of Toronto Press, 2008), 190.

2 Tim Cook, "The Blind Leading the Blind: The Battle of the St. Eloi Craters," *Canadian Military History* 5, no. 2 (Autumn 1995): 26.

3 James Robert Johnston, *Riding into War: The Memoir of a Horse Transport Driver, 1916–1919* (Fredericton: Goose Lane Editions, 2004), 41–2.

4 Tim Cook, *Shock Troops: Canadians Fighting the Great War, 1917–1918* (Toronto: Viking Canada, 2008), 318.

5 Jason Adair, ed., "The Battle of Passchendaele: The Experiences of Lieutenant Tom Rutherford, 4th Battalion, Canadian Mounted Rifles," *Canadian Military History* 13, no. 4 (Autumn 2004): 70.

6 D.J. Goodspeed, *Ludendorff: Genius of World War I* (Toronto: Macmillan, 1966), 259.

7 James H. Pedley, *Only This: A War Retrospect, 1917–1918* (Ottawa: CEF Books, 1999), 218.

8 Johnston, *Riding into War*, 10.

9 Paul Dickson, "Crerar and the Decision to Garrison Hong Kong," *Canadian Military History* 13, no. 1 (Spring 1994): 97.

10 Cited in "The Controversy over Maltby's Hong Kong Dispatch," *Canadian Military History* 2, no. 2 (Autumn 1993): 116.

11 James Alan Roberts, *The Canadian Summer: The Memoirs of James Alan Roberts* (Toronto: University of Toronto Press, 1981), 41.

12 See Brian Loring Villa, *Unauthorized Action: Mountbatten and the Dieppe Raid* (Toronto: Oxford University Press, 1989); Peter Henshaw, "The Dieppe Raid: A Product of Misplaced Canadian Nationalism," *Canadian Historical Review* 77, no. 2 (June 1996): 250–66.

13 Similar feelings were expressed in newspapers and public forums across the country. See G.W.L. Nicholson, *Official History of the Canadian Army in the Second World War*, vol. 2: *The Canadians in Italy, 1943–1945* (Ottawa: Queen's Printer, 1956), 20–1.

14 Roberts, *The Canadian Summer*, 55.

15 Douglas E. Delaney, *The Soldiers' General: Bert Hoffmeister at War* (Vancouver: UBC Press, 2005), 99.

16 Cited in G.C. Case, "Trial by Fire: Major-General Christopher Vokes at the Battles of the Moro River and Ortona, December 1943," *Canadian Military History* 16, no. 3 (Summer 2007): 26.

17 Cited in Terry Copp, *Fields of Fire: The Canadians in Normandy* (Toronto: University of Toronto Press, 2003), 49.

18 Howard Margolian, *Conduct Unbecoming: The Story of the Murder of Canadian Prisoners of War in Normandy* (Toronto: University of Toronto Press, 1998), x.

19 Roberts, *The Canadian Summer*, 64.

20 Cited in Terry Copp, *Cinderella Army: The Canadians in Northwest Europe, 1944–1945* (Toronto: University of Toronto Press, 2006), 240.

21 Copp, *Cinderella Army*, 261.

22 David Kaufman and Michiel Horn, *A Liberation Album: Canadians in the Netherlands, 1944–45* (Toronto: McGraw-Hill Ryerson, 1980), 110–11.

4 Life and Death at Sea

1 Marc Milner, *Canada's Navy: The First Century* (Toronto: University of Toronto Press, 1999), 44–56.

2 Milner, *Canada's Navy*, 48.

3 Michael L. Hadley, *U-Boats against Canada: German Submarines in Canadian Waters* (Montreal and Kingston: McGill–Queen's University Press, 1985), 11.

4 Marc Milner, *North Atlantic Run: The Royal Canadian Navy and the Battle for the Convoys* (St Catharines: Vanwell Publishing, 2006), 23.

5 Mac Johnston, *Corvettes Canada: Convoy Veterans of World War II Tell Their True Stories* (Mississauga: John Wiley and Sons Canada, 2008), 95.

6 Johnston, *Corvettes Canada*, , 47.

7 Johnston, *Corvettes Canada*, 47.

8 Milner, *Canada's Navy*, 96–7.

9 Stuart E. Paddon, "With HMS *Prince of Wales* and HMS *Warspite*: The Adventures of a Canadian Radar Officer in the Royal Navy," *Canadian Military History* 6, no. 2 (Autumn 1997): 91–2.

10 David Zimmerman, *The Great Naval Battle of Ottawa* (Toronto: University of Toronto Press, 1989), 10.

11 Milner, *Canada's Navy*, 319n21.

12 Robert G. Halford, *The Unknown Navy: Canada's World War II Merchant Navy* (St Catharines: Vanwell, 1995), 27.

13 Richard Oliver Mayne, "Bypassing the Chain of Command: The Political Originals of the RCN's Equipment Crisis of 1943," *Canadian Military History* 9, no. 3 (Summer 2000), 20.

14 Shirley Burdon, "Lives Lived: Thomas Holland Burdon, 1919–2013," *Globe and Mail,* 28 June 2013, S8.

5 Battles in the Air

1 S.F. Wise, *The Official History of the Royal Canadian Air Force,* vol. I: *Canadian Airmen and the First World War* (Toronto: University of Toronto Press, Department of National Defence), 21.

2 For contending perspectives, see Brereton Greenhous, *The Making of Billy Bishop: The First World War Exploits of Billy Bishop, VC* (Toronto: Dundurn, 2002); and David L. Bashow, *Knights of the Air: Canadian Fighter Pilots in the First World War* (Toronto: McArthur & Company, 2000), for contending perspectives.

3 Air Ministry, "Results of Air Raids on Germany Carried Out by British Aircraft, January 1st–September 30th 1918," D.A.I., no. 5, October 1918, 30, Canadian War Museum.

4 See Appendix C, "Statistical Analysis of Canadians in the British Flying Services," in Wise, *The Official History.*

5 Major Alexander P. De Seversky, *Victory through Air Power* (New York: Simon and Schuster, 1942), 8.

6 Allan D. English, *The Cream of the Crop: Canadian Aircrew, 1939–1945* (Montreal and Kingston: McGill–Queen's University Press, 1996), 18.

7 Atholl Sutherland Brown, "Victory in Burma: The Role of Canada and the Air Force," *Canadian Military History* 14, no. 4 (Autumn 2005): 76.

8 Brent Wilson, ed., *Hurricane Pilot: The Wartime Letters of W.O. Harry L. Gill, D.F.M., 1940–1943* (Fredericton: Goose Lane Editions, 2007).

9 David L. Bashow, *No Prouder Place: Canadians and the Bomber Command Experience, 1939–1945* (St Catharines: Vanwell Publishing, 2005), 24.

10 Randall T. Wakelam, *The Science of Bombing: Operational Research in RAF Bomber Command* (Toronto: University of Toronto Press, 2009), 23.

11 Gordon Gross, "A Trip to Remember: An Airman's view of D-Day," *Canadian Military History* 10, no. 2 (Spring 2001): 75.

12 Cited in Brereton Greenhous, Stephen J. Harris, William C. Johnston, and William G.P. Rawling, *The Official History of the*

Royal Canadian Air Force, vol. III: *The Crucible of War, 1939–1945* (Toronto: University of Toronto Press, Department of National Defence, 1994), 786.

13 Blake Heathcote, *Testaments of Honour: Personal Histories of Canada's War Veterans* (Toronto: Doubleday, 2002), 158.

14 Bashow, *No Prouder Place,* 474–5.

15 Paul Johnston, "Tactical Air Power Controversies in Normandy: A Question of Doctrine," *Canadian Military History* 9, no. 2 (Spring 2000): 59–60.

16 Terry Copp, *Fields of Fire: The Canadians in Normandy* (Toronto: University of Toronto Press, 2003), 259–60.

17 Cited in Greenhous et al., *The Official History,* vol. III, 404.

18 Carl A. Christie and F.J. Hatch, *Ocean Bridge: The History of RAF Ferry Command* (Toronto: University of Toronto Press, 1997), 306.

19 Jonathan F. Vance, *High Flight: Aviation and the Canadian Imagination* (Toronto: Penguin, 2002), 258.

20 *Canada at War,* no. 34, *Special Pictorial Edition* (Ottawa: Wartime Information Board, 1944), 33.

6 Society and Morality

1 Stephen Kimber, *Sailors, Slackers, and Blind Pigs: Halifax at War* (Toronto: Doubleday, 2002), 80–1, 211, ch. 6.

2 James Pitsula, *For All We Have and Are: Regina and the Experience of the Great War* (Winnipeg: University of Manitoba Press, 2008), 94.

3 Desmond Morton, *When Your Number's Up: The Canadian Soldier in the First World War* (Toronto: Random House, 1993), 263.

4 *Saturday Night,* 6 September. 1941, 3.

5 Library and Archives Canada (LAC), RG 24, Department of National Defence Papers, vol. 6617, file 8994–6, pt 3, *Public Health Act,* Form II; vol. 10,924, file 239 C1.7(D19), First Cdn Army, Medical Instructions, 28 July 1945; Ottawa, Department of Pensions and Health, *Annual Report,* 1943, 97.

6 *Chatelaine,* February 1944, 18.

7 *Women at War* (Toronto: Maclean-Hunter, 1943), 6.

8 LAC, MG 28 I10, Canadian Council on Social Development CCSD, vol. 87, file 1856, "Children in a World at War," May 1943.

9 Ramona Rose, "Keepers of Morale: The Vancouver Council of Women, 1939–1945," MA thesis, University of British Columbia, 1990, 97.

10 Ruth Pierson, *They're Still Women After All: The Second World War and Canadian Womanhood* (Toronto: McClelland and Stewart, 1985), 159.

11 *Montreal Gazette*, 22 May 1942, 4.

12 *Saturday Night*, 12 May 1942, 2

13 *Saturday Night*, 16 September 1944, 5.

14 Diane G. Forestell, "The Victorian Legacy: Historical Perspectives on the Canadian Women's Army Corps," PhD diss., York University, 1986, 164; Doug Owram, "The Cult of the Teenager," ms, University of Alberta, 1993, 12.

15 Dominique Marshall, *The Social Origins of the Welfare State: Quebec Families, Compulsory Education, and Family Allowances, 1940–1955* (Waterloo: Wilfrid Laurier University Press, 2006).

16 William Horrocks, *In Their Own Words* (Ottawa: Rideau Veterans Home Residents Council, 1993), 226; Ben Wicks, *When the Boys Came Marching Home: True Stories of the Men Who Went to War and the Women and Children Who Took Them Back* (Toronto: Stoddart, 1991), 91; Patricia Galloway, ed., *Too Young to Fight: Memories from Our Youth During World War II* (Toronto: Stoddart, 1999), 91.

17 Desmond Morton, "Living with the First World War, 1914–19: History as Personal Experience," private ms, 2013, 25.

Conclusion

1 "Interred With Full Military Honors Here – Remains of Lieut. Wyn. Colquhoun Tenderly Laid at Rest in Greenwood Cemetery," *Brantford Expositor*, 9 December 1918. The authors thank Geoffrey Moyer, of the Brantford Public Library, for sharing this source.

Selected Further Reading

Overviews

Bercuson, David. *Maple Leaf A\against the Axis: Canada's Second World War.* Toronto: Stoddart, 1995.

Granatstein, J.L., and Desmond Morton. *Marching to Armageddon: Canadians and the Great War, 1914–1919.* Toronto: Lester & Orpen Dennys, 1989.

– *A Nation Forged in Fire: Canadians and the Second World War, 1939–1945.* Toronto: Lester & Orpen Dennys, 1989.

Granatstein, J.L., and Dean Oliver. *The Oxford Companion to Canadian Military History.* Toronto: Oxford University Press, 2011.

Gwyn, Sandra. *Tapestry of War: A Private View of Canadians in the Great War.* Toronto: HarperCollins, 1992.

Stacey, Charles Perry. *Arms, Men, and Government: The War Policies of Canada, 1939–1945.* Ottawa: Department of National Defence, 1970.

Regional and Local Studies

Armstrong, John Griffith. *The Halifax Explosion and the Royal Canadian Navy: Inquiry and Intrigue.* Vancouver: UBC Press, 2002.

Blanchard, Jim, *Winnipeg's Great War: A City Comes of Age.* Winnipeg: University of Manitoba Press, 2010.

Durflinger, Serge. *Fighting from Home: The Second World War in Verdun, Quebec.* Vancouver: UBC Press, 2006.

Kimber, Stephen. *Sailors, Slackers, and Blind Pigs: Halifax at War.* Toronto: Doubleday, 2002.

Miller, Ian Hugh Maclean. *Our Glory and Our Grief: Torontonians and the Great War.* Toronto: University of Toronto Press, 2002.

Pitsula, James. *For All We Have and Are: Regina and the Experience of the Great War.* Winnipeg: University of Manitoba Press, 2008.

Rutherdale, Robert. *Hometown Horizons: Local Responses to Canada's Great War.* Vancouver: UBC Press, 2005.

Thompson, John Herd. *The Harvests of War: The Prairie West, 1914–1918.* Toronto: McClelland & Stewart, 1978.

Politics

Brown, Robert Craig. *Robert Laird Borden: A Biography.* 2 vols. Toronto: Macmillan of Canada, 1975, 1980.

Cook, Tim. *The Madman and the Butcher: The Sensational Wars of Sam Hughes and General Arthur Currie.* Toronto: Penguin Canada, 2010.

– *Warlords: Borden, Mackenzie King, and Canada's World Wars.* Toronto: Penguin Canada, 2012.

Granatstein, J.L. *Canada's War: The Politics of the Mackenzie King Government, 1939–1945.* Toronto: Oxford University Press, 1975.

Granatstein, J.L., and J. Murray Hitsman. *Broken Promises: A History of Conscription in Canada.* Toronto: Oxford University Press, 1977.

Morton, Desmond. *A Peculiar Kind of Politics: Canada's Overseas Ministry in the First World War.* Toronto: University of Toronto Press, 1982.

Stevenson, Michael D. *Canada's Greatest Wartime Muddle: National Selective Service and the Mobilization of Human Resources during World War II.* Montreal and Kingston: McGill–Queen's University Press, 2001.

Science and Economy

Avery, Donald. *The Science of War: Canadian Scientists and Allied Military Technology during the Second World War.* Toronto: University of Toronto Press, 1998.

Bliss, Michael. *A Canadian Millionaire: The Life and Business Times of Sir Joseph Flavelle, Bart., 1859–1939*. Toronto: Macmillan, 1978.

Bothwell, Robert, and William Kilbourn, *C.D. Howe: A Biography*. Toronto: McClelland & Stewart, 1979.

Hatch, F.J. *The Aerodrome of Democracy: Canada and the British Commonwealth Air Training Plan*. Ottawa: Directorate of History, 1983.

Coates, Ken, and W.R. Morrison. *The Alaska Highway in World War II: The U.S. Army of Occupation in Canada's Northwest*. Toronto: University of Toronto Press, 1992.

Zimmerman, David. *The Great Naval Battle of Ottawa*. Toronto: University of Toronto Press, 1989.

Society, Social Policy, and Culture

Caccia, Ivana. *Managing the Canadian Mosaic in Wartime: Shaping Citizenship Policy, 1939–1945*. Montreal and Kingston: McGill–Queen's University Press, 2010.

Dempsey, James. *Warriors of the King: Prairie Indians in World War I*. Regina: Canadian Plains Research Center, 1999.

Kealey, Linda. *Enlisting Women for the Cause: Women, Labour, and the Left in Canada, 1890–1920*. Toronto: University of Toronto Press, 1998.

Keshen, Jeffrey. *Saints, Sinners, and Soldiers: Canada's Second World War*. Vancouver: UBC Press, 2004.

Lackenbauer, P. Whitney. *Battle Grounds: The Canadian Military and Aboriginal Lands*. Vancouver: UBC Press, 2007.

Marshall, Dominique. *The Social Origins of the Welfare State: Quebec Families, Compulsory Education, and Family Allowances, 1940–1955*. Waterloo: Wilfrid Laurier University Press, 2006.

McGeer, Eric. *Words of Valediction and Remembrance: Canadian Epitaphs of the Second World War*. St Catharines: Vanwell Publishing, 2008.

Morton, Desmond. *Fight or Pay: Soldiers' Families in the Great War*. Vancouver: UBC Press, 2004.

Morton, Desmond, and Glenn Wright. *Winning the Second Battle: Canadian Veterans and the Return to Civilian Life, 1915–30*. Toronto: University of Toronto Press, 1987.

Neary, Peter. *On to Civvy Street: Canada's Rehabilitation Program for Veterans of the Second World War.* Montreal and Kingston: McGill–Queen's University Press, 2011.

Pierson, Ruth. *They're Still Women After All: Canadian Women and the Second World War.* Toronto: McClelland & Stewart, 1986.

Tippett, Maria. *Art at the Service of War: Canada, Art, and the Great War.* Toronto: University of Toronto Press, 1984.

Vance, Jonathan. *Death So Noble: Meaning, Memory, and the First World War.* Vancouver: UBC Press, 1997.

Toman, Cynthia. *An Officer and a Lady: Canadian Military Nursing and the Second World War.* Vancouver: UBC Press, 2007.

Civil Liberties

Bourrie, Mark. *The Fog of War: Censorship of Canada's Media in World War II.* Toronto: Douglas & McIntyre, 2011.

Kaplan, William. *State and Salvation: The Jehovah's Witnesses and Their Fight for Civil Rights.* Toronto: University of Toronto Press, 1989.

Keshen, Jeffrey A. *Propaganda and Censorship during Canada's Great War.* Edmonton: University of Alberta Press, 1996.

Roy, Patricia, J.L. Granatstein, Masako Iino, and Hiroko Takamura. *Mutual Hostages: Canadians and Japanese during the Second World War.* Toronto: University of Toronto Press, 1990.

Shaw, Amy. *Conscientious Objectors: Conscientious Objectors in Canada during the First World War.* Vancouver: UBC Press, 2008.

Socknat, Thomas Paul. *Witness against War: Pacifism in Canada, 1900–1945.* Toronto: University of Toronto Press, 1987.

Swyripa, Frances, and John Herd Thompson, eds. *Loyalties in Conflict: Ukrainians in Canada during the Great War.* Edmonton: Canadian Institute of Ukrainian Studies, 1983.

Sunahara, Ann Gomer. *The Politics of Racism: The Uprooting of Japanese Canadians during the Second World War.* Toronto: James Lorimer, 1981.

Army

Cook, Tim, *No Place to Run: The Canadian Corps and Gas Warfare in the First World War.* Vancouver: UBC Press, 1999.

- *At the Sharp End: Canadians Fighting the Great War, 1914–1916.* Toronto: Viking Canada, 2007.
- *Shock Troops: Canadians Fighting the Great War, 1917–1918.* Toronto: Viking Canada. 2008.

Copp, Terry. *Fields of Fire: The Canadians in Normandy.* Toronto: University of Toronto Press, 2004.
- *Cinderella Army: The Canadians in Northwest Europe, 1944–1945.* Toronto: University of Toronto Press, 2006.

Copp, Terry, and Bill McAndrew. *Battle Exhaustion: Soldiers and Psychiatrists in the Canadian Army, 1939–1945.* Montreal and Kingston: McGill–Queen's University Press, 1990.

Crerar, Duff. *Padres in No Man's Land: Canadian Chaplains and the Great War.* Montreal and Kingston: McGill–Queen's University Press, 1995.

Delaney, Douglas E. *Corps Commanders: Five British and Canadian Generals at War, 1939–45.* Vancouver: UBC Press, 2011.

Delaney, Douglas E., *The Soldiers' General: Bert Hoffmeister at War.* Vancouver: UBC Press, 2005.

English, John. *The Canadian Army and the Normandy Campaign: A Study of Failure in High Command.* Westport: Praeger, 1991.

Granatstein, J.L. *The Generals: The Canadian Army's Senior Commanders in the Second World War.* Toronto: Stoddart, 1993.
- *Canada's Army: Waging War and Keeping the Peace.* Toronto: University of Toronto Press, 2002.

Hayes, Geoffrey, Andrew Iarocci, and Mike Bechthold, eds. *Vimy Ridge: A Canadian Reassessment.* Waterloo: Wilfrid Laurier University Press, 2007.

Iarocci, Andrew. *Shoestring Soldiers: The 1st Canadian Division at War, 1914–1915.* Toronto: University of Toronto Press, 2008.

Isitt, Benjamin. *From Victoria to Vladivostok: Canada's Siberian Expedition, 1917–19.* Vancouver: UBC Press, 2010.

Morton, Desmond. *When Your Number's Up: The Canadian Soldier in the First World War.* Toronto: Random House of Canada, 1993.

Nicholson, G.W.L. *Canadian Expeditionary Force, 1914–1919: Official History of the Canadian Army in the First World War.* Ottawa: Queen's Printer, 1962.

– *Official History of the Canadian Army in the Second World War,* vol 2: *The Canadians in Italy, 1943–1945.* Ottawa: Queen's Printer, 1956.

Rawling, Bill. *Surviving Trench Warfare: Technology and the Canadian Corps, 1914–1918.* Toronto: University of Toronto Press, 1992.

Schreiber, Shane B. *Shock Army of the British Empire: The Canadian Corps in the Last 100 Days of the Great War.* Westport: Praeger, 1997.

Stacey, Charles Perry. *Official History of the Canadian Army in the Second World War.* 3 vols. Ottawa: Department of National Defence, 1955, 1960, 1966.

Villa, Brian Loring. *Unauthorized Action: Mountbatten and the Dieppe Raid.* Toronto: Oxford University Press, 1994.

Navy and Air Force

Douglas, W.A.B. *Official History of the Royal Canadian Air Force,* vol. 2. Toronto: University of Toronto Press, 1985.

Greenhous, Brereton. *The Making of Billy Bishop: The First World War Exploits of Billy Bishop, VC.* Toronto: Dundurn, 2002.

Greenhous, Brereton, Stephen Harris, William Johnston, and William Rawling. *The Crucible of War: The Official History of the Royal Canadian Air Force,* vol. 3. Toronto: University of Toronto Press, 1994.

Hadley, Michael L. *U-Boats against Canada: German Submarines in Canadian Waters.* Montreal and Kingston: McGill–Queen's University Press, 1985.

Hadley, Michael L., and Roger Sarty. *Tin-Pots and Pirate Ships: Canadian Naval Forces and German Sea Raiders, 1880–1918.* Montreal and Kingston: McGill–Queen's University Press, 1991.

Halford, Robert G. *The Unknown Navy: Canada's World War II Merchant Navy.* St Catharines: Vanwell Publishing, 1995.

Milner, Marc. *Canada's Navy: The First Century.* Toronto: University of Toronto Press, 1999.

– *North Atlantic Run: The Royal Canadian Navy and the Battle for the Convoys.* Toronto: University of Toronto Press, 1985.

Sarty, Roger. *Canada and the Battle of the Atlantic.* Montreal: Art Global, 1998.

Wise, S.F. *Canadian Airmen and the First World War.* Toronto: University of Toronto Press, 1980.

Prisoners of War

Auger, Martin F. *Prisoners of the Home Front: German POWs in Southern Quebec, 1940–1946.* Vancouver: UBC Press, 2005.

Dancocks, Daniel. *In Enemy Hands: Canadian Prisoners of War, 1939–1945.* Edmonton: Hurtig Publishers, 1983.

Margolian, Howard. *Conduct Unbecoming: The Story of the Murder of Canadian Prisoners of War in Normandy.* Toronto: University of Toronto Press, 1998.

Morton, Desmond. *Silent Battle: Canadian Prisoners of War in Germany, 1914–1919.* Toronto: Lester Publishing, 1992.

Vance, Jonathan F. *Objects of Concern: Canadian Prisoners of War through the Twentieth Century.* Vancouver: UBC Press, 1994.

Waiser, Bill. *Park Prisoners: The Untold Story of Western Canada's National Parks, 1915–1946.* Saskatoon: Fifth House, 1995.

Index

Themes In Canadian History

Editors:
Colin Coates 2003–
Craig Heron 1997–2010
Franca Iacovetta 1997–1999